Employment in the Lean Years

Employment in the Lean Years

Policy and Prospects for the Next Decade

Edited by

David Marsden

OXFORD
UNIVERSITY PRESS

OXFORD
UNIVERSITY PRESS

Great Clarendon Street, Oxford OX2 6DP

Oxford University Press is a department of the University of Oxford.
It furthers the University's objective of excellence in research, scholarship,
and education by publishing worldwide in

Oxford New York

Auckland Cape Town Dar es Salaam Hong Kong Karachi
Kuala Lumpur Madrid Melbourne Mexico City Nairobi
New Delhi Shanghai Taipei Toronto

With offices in

Argentina Austria Brazil Chile Czech Republic France Greece
Guatemala Hungary Italy Japan Poland Portugal Singapore
South Korea Switzerland Thailand Turkey Ukraine Vietnam

Oxford is a registered trade mark of Oxford University Press
in the UK and in certain other countries

Published in the United States
by Oxford University Press Inc., New York

British Library Cataloguing in Publication Data

Data available

Library of Congress Cataloging in Publication Data

Data available

Typeset by SPI Publisher Services, Pondicherry, India
Printed in Great Britain
on acid-free paper by
MPG Books Group, Bodmin and King's Lynn

ISBN 978–0–19–960543–9 (Hbk)
       978–0–19–960544–6 (Pbk)

1 3 5 7 9 10 8 6 4 2

☐ PREFACE

It is an enormous pleasure to reflect on David Metcalf's life as an economist, public figure, colleague, and friend. His influence has been enormous. David, more than anyone in Britain, brought economics into the study of the workplace. He wanted to know how laws, unions, and payment systems actually affect outcomes—how they influence productivity, pay, and morale. Before his research, it was the conventional wisdom that trade union legislation could have no effect on what actually happened. David proved that the opposite was true. Using the first Workplace Industrial Relations Survey, he had shown that in 1980 unions reduced both productivity and profit; but as the Thatcher reforms began to bite, those effects disappeared.[1] David showed this statistically, but he also checked how the closed shop worked in practice, getting up early day after day to study the Smithfield meat market.[2]

He also forecast the decline of unions long before most other people.[3] This came from applying multivariate methods, rather than univariate methods as was normal practice before then. From looking at the impact of legislation, industrial composition, and the birth and death of firms, David's analysis made clear that for private sector unions the writing was on the wall.

In recent decades, incentive pay has become increasingly common. David showed how well-designed incentive pay can have powerful effects on performance. If each worker's output can be measured, as with jockeys, this is not surprising.[4] Equally, incentives can work wonders when they are based on team performance, as in the call centres he studied.[5] But inappropriate pay systems have more ambiguous results. David did, however, show that worker participation in planning work organization has good effects on worker morale even if its effects on productivity are often neutral.[6]

Looking to the labour market as a whole, David has made important contributions on pay—including one of the first studies of the rate of return to education.[7] His work on regional Phillips curves showed the powerful national effects of labour market tightness in the South East of England[8]— this greatly reinforced the case for active regional policy.

David also did significant work on unemployment. On local area unemployment rates, he showed the huge effects of individual factors and not just local labour market conditions.[9] He also showed the value of special employment measures, like Short Time Working Compensation Schemes,[10] similar to those successfully used in the current European recession. And he offered good cost–benefit arguments for slowing the rate of pit closures.

David has not been an ivory-tower economist. He has carried his economics into the media and into policymaking. From 1997 to 2007, he was a key member of the Low Pay Commission appointed by Labour in 1997 to set the National Minimum Wage. He argued successfully for a low enough minimum to prevent any negative effects on employment. The success of the Minimum Wage owes much to him.

Since 2007 he has been chairman of the Migration Advisory Committee, charged with setting the criteria for admitting non-EU workers into Britain, a difficult but crucial task. And he is a member of the horse-race Starting Price Regulatory Commission, which guarantees the integrity of the process used to settle most off-course bets.

Anyone who knows David knows his warm heart, his wonderful sense of humour, and his great qualities as a colleague. I first knew him through sharing the next-door office. The loud tapping on the dividing wall turned out to be him teaching Stephen Nickell labour economics. Soon after that he started teaching me too. In 1974 the three of us established the centre which has evolved from the Centre for Labour Economics into the Centre for Economic Performance. It has been a wonderful collaboration and from 1995 to 2000 David was an excellent Deputy Director of the Centre. From all of us who have benefited so much from his work and his spirit, a huge thank you.

Richard Layard

☐ REFERENCES

1. Metcalf, D. (1989) 'Water Notes Dry up: The Impact of the Donovan Reform Proposals and Thatcherism at Work on Labour Productivity in British Manufacturing Industry', *British Journal of Industrial Relations*, 27(1), March, 1–32.
   Metcalf, D. (1993) 'Industrial Relations and Economic Performance', *British Journal of Industrial Relations*, 31(2), June, 255–84.
2. Metcalf, D. (1991) 'The Smithfield Meat Market: The Ultimate Pre-Entry Closed Shop', *Work, Employment & Society*, 5(2), 159–79.
3. Metcalf, D. (1991) 'British Unions: Dissolution or Resurgence?', *Oxford Review of Economic Policy*, 7(1), Spring, 18–31.
4. Fernie, S. and Metcalf, D. (1999) 'It's Not What You Pay it's the Way that You Pay it and That's What Gets Results: Jockeys' Pay and Performance', *Labour*, 13(2), 385–411.
5. Fernie, S. and Metcalf, D. (1999) '(Not) Hanging on the Telephone: Payments Systems in the New Sweatshops', *Advances in Industrial and Labor Relations*, 9, 23–67.
6. Fernie, S. and Metcalf, D. (1995) 'Participation, Contingent Pay, Representation and Workplace Performance: Evidence from Great Britain', *British Journal of Industrial Relations*, 33(3), September, 379–415.
7. Metcalf, D. (1973) 'Pay Dispersion, Information and Returns to Search in a Professional Labour Market', *Review of Economic Studies*, 40(4), October, 491–505.

8. Cowling, K. and Metcalf, D. (1967) 'Wage–Unemployment Relationships: A Regional Analysis for the UK, 1960–1965', *Bulletin of Oxford Institute of Statistics*, 29(1), February, 31–9.
9. Metcalf, D. (1975) 'Urban Unemployment in England', *Economic Journal*, 85(339), September, 578–89.
10. Metcalf, D. (1982) *Alternatives to Unemployment: Special Employment Measures in Britain*, London: Policy Studies Institute.

⬜ CONTENTS

☐ LIST OF FIGURES

☐ LIST OF TABLES

☐ LIST OF CONTRIBUTORS

William Brown, CBE, is Montague Burton Professor of Industrial Relations and Master of Darwin College, University of Cambridge

Richard Disney is Professor of Labour Economics at the Faculty of Social Sciences, Nottingham University

Susan Fernie is Lecturer in Industrial Relations at the Department of Management, London School of Economics and Political Science

Paul Gregg is Professor of Economics at the Centre for Market and Public Organization, the University of Bristol

Amy Humphris is a researcher at the Centre for Economic Performance, London School of Economics and Political Science

Morris M. Kleiner, Professor, Humphrey School of Public Affairs, University of Minnesota, and a research associate at the National Bureau of Economic Research.

Maria Koumenta is Senior Lecturer at the Department of Management and Organizational Studies at the Business School, Oxford Brookes University

Richard Layard, Emeritus Professor of Economics and Founder of the Centre for Economic Performance, London School of Economics and Political Science

Stephen Machin is Professor of Economics, University College London; and Research Director at the Centre for Economic Performance, LSE

Alan Manning is Professor of Economics, London School of Economics and Political Science

David Marsden is Professor of Industrial Relations at the London School of Economics and Political Science

Stephen Nickell, CBE, is Professor of Economics and Warden of Nuffield College at the University of Oxford

John Roberts is the John H. Scully Professor of Economics, Strategic Management, and International Business in the Graduate School of Business at Stanford University

Mark B. Stewart is Professor of Economics at the University of Warwick

Anna Vignoles is Professor of the Economics of Education at the Institute of Education; and Deputy Director at the Centre for the Economics of Education at the London School of Economics and Political Science

Jonathan Wadsworth is Professor of Economics at Royal Holloway College, University of London; Senior research fellow at the LSE's centre for Economic Performance Deputy Director of the Centre for Research and Analysis of Migration at UCI.

Christine M.E. Whitehead is Professor in Housing, Department of Economics, London School of Economics.

1 Employment in the Lean Years: Introduction[1]

DAVID MARSDEN

1.1. Introduction

After the fat years: the lean years. Over the last fifteen years, Britain's more deregulated labour markets have helped to deliver strong economic growth, new economic opportunities for many, and, by attracting immigrant workers, have eased skill bottlenecks and created a more varied and diverse society. When jobs are plentiful, individual solutions are easy to find. However, for the foreseeable future, buoyant labour markets have given way to job cuts, rising unemployment, income insecurity, and increased social strains. What can and should governments and the key labour market actors do about these?

Many of the recipes of earlier decades face new conditions which make their effectiveness questionable. The institutions and social conventions that governed employment as recently as two decades ago have been greatly weakened. Employee representation has been transformed by the decline of trade unions and the dramatic shrinkage of collective bargaining in the private sector. Many employer organizations have also withered, and where they have continued to flourish, they have reoriented their activity towards the political arena. This would seem to rule out much of the social partnership to be found in continental Europe. Alongside deregulation, pay inequality has vastly increased, reversing the gradual erosion of the inequalities of the post-war decades and suggesting that former restraints on higher pay have weakened or gone. There is increasing concern about the viability of the 'pension promise' to which many low- and middle-income workers thought they could look forward.

New forms of regulation are harder to pin down, but many appear to be emerging, and these could alter the assumptions on which labour market policies are based. Occupational licensing has been growing. In the United States, it now covers a similar percentage of workers to collective bargaining in its heyday. A National Minimum Wage (NMW) now directly affects the lowest paid 5 per cent of employees, and there is evidence that it may boost the pay of lowest paid 10 per cent. Employment law has filled some of the gaps left by the receding tide of collective agreements, and managers' complaints about the burden of compliance have largely replaced those about union restrictions. In the workplace, management benefits from greater freedom to direct labour according to the needs of the business, and has fostered alternative forms of employee voice to union-based channels. There may also be increased use of the employee individual voice in which the threat to quit replaces the threat to strike. Skill formation is more firmly in the hands of employers and the state, so that in theory, new skills should be free to follow labour demand. There are signs that increased use of variable pay, such as profit-sharing and performance pay, has increased the flexibility of firms' pay bills when they hit a recession. If developed further, this could provide an alternative buffer to lay-offs, and make it easier for firms to avoid losing valued employees when business turns down. A multiplication of employment statuses and working-time arrangements has facilitated the big advances in women's employment, although these can often leave them vulnerable in times of recession. Arguably, this has also facilitated the expansion of the immigrant workforce which has helped prevent the boom of recent years from being stifled by skill shortages. Thus on many counts, Britain's labour markets today differ radically from those of even twenty years ago at the time of the last major recession.

Another major change, albeit hard to pin down in detail, is that the norms of fairness in labour markets have been reconfigured. In the 1970s, fair pay differentials between different groups of workers were a major concern, and in Hugh Clegg's famous pamphlet, *How to Run an Incomes Policy*, they were the rocks into which incomes policies regularly crashed (Clegg 1971). Incomes policies of the 1970s repeatedly accepted the premise that higher paid workers should receive smaller percentage increases than the low paid. Yet, on the evidence of the interviews with high earners reported in Polly Toynbee and David Walker's book, *Unjust Rewards*, many high earners today feel little solidarity with those on average incomes, and have no idea how little they earn. The same interviews also revealed that most of the high paid believed their rewards were justified. A possible consequence is that so few British employees now trust their senior managers. With high rates of union membership, many of the less-skilled and lower paid, and particularly men, had a collective voice to argue for justice on their behalf. Today, many of the disadvantaged in the labour market have little or no collective voice, and are visible mostly in the statistics on exclusion and in reports by investigative journalists and researchers, and occasionally in campaigns by unions and advocacy groups.

In the past, many of the victims of recessions had advocates who could publicize their need and argue the case for solidarity, such as the need to protect the low paid from the ravages of inflation. Likewise, the arguments for sharing misery at the time of the oil shocks by means of work sharing and employment subsidies. Such broad-brush policies can be very expensive, putting great strain on budgets and on solidarity. Britain entered the current recession with very tight public finances and ill-defined contours of solidarity. This effectively rules out grand policies of public spending to improve labour market operations, and argues for policies that are much more carefully targeted. The authors in this book therefore focus primarily on labour market policies that address the issues of efficiency and fairness in a more focused way than either the incomes policies or job subsidies of the past. Grand policies are good for mobilizing public opinion, but the devil is usually in the detail. In Britain, the benefits of incomes policy were mostly short-term, and the evidence on job subsidy programmes reveals a large deadweight effect as many employers took them for people they would have hired or retained anyway. Given the current state of public finances, such poorly targeted and inefficient policies are not really an option.

This collection of short chapters takes up this challenge. It has been specially written by some of the most eminent experts and researchers on labour market issues. Each chapter seeks to map out the challenges, based on the latest theory and evidence, and then identify the areas of labour market policy that are needed. These chapters were first discussed at a one-day seminar held at LSE's Centre for Economic Performance in December 2009, in honour of David Metcalf's contribution to British labour market policy over the past forty years. The chapters are organized around four major challenges facing labour market policy in the coming years. It starts with unemployment, immigration, housing, and job subsidies. How should governments tackle the impact of the recession on jobs? Has the arrival of immigrant workers benefited the economy or displaced native-born workers from jobs and housing? It then turns to some of the key institutional changes, the decline of collective regulation, the rise of occupational licensing, and the first years of the NMW. It asks how far management authority has been reinforced in the workplace and who among employees are the winners and losers in the greater flexibility that has resulted. Is occupational licensing something that should be encouraged further, and what can be learned from the experience of ten years of the NMW. It then turns to pay inequality, skill-biased technical change, and policies on education and training. What does the growth of pay inequality tell us about education and training needs, and about the types of jobs that are in most demand in the economy? Finally, it considers public policy on pay setting, the size of pay bonuses, non-pay incentives in public services, whether employees are better paid in the public than in the private sectors, and how effectively has the national interest been served by the public sector pay review bodies. No doubt the list of policy areas and questions could be extended. These have been selected to give a broad cross section of important issues on which public policy will have to decide. The next part of the chapter presents each of these in a bit more detail.

1.2. **Labour market problems**

The origin of the current recession lies in a dramatic fall in demand owing to the credit crunch, and as Stephen Nickell observes in Chapter 2, macroeconomic policy holds the key to recovery in the short-term, whereas labour market policy provides one of the keys to a sustained recovery over the longer term. Financial reforms are also essential to longer term sustainability, and one aspect of these, reform of the bonus system, is tackled later by John Roberts in Chapter 13. Nickell observes that employment has responded in various ways in different countries reflecting the financial crisis directly in some cases, as in that of construction activity fuelled by speculative bubbles, such as in Spain, and in others, indirectly, as the demand for engineering goods fell as firms cut investment. Nickell therefore cautions against across-the-board job subsidies. He also counsels against use of early retirement. Although this eases the pain of adjustment in the short-term, in the longer term it reduces the available labour supply in the recovery, and it adds to the burden on pension systems. Given the tight budget constraints, the most important goal is to focus on labour force attachment: to avoid those laid off becoming long-term unemployed, and to facilitate the establishment of young workers. To achieve this, he argues for a mix of incentives and support. Incentives take the form of training and recruitment subsidies, and support, that of advice and counselling to unemployed workers with active job search linked to benefits. Over the longer run, he argues for greater use of apprenticeship-type schemes which combine training and work experience to ease the transition between education and work.

Across the OECD countries, immigration has risen in line with a growing international market for labour. By 2009, about one person in eight of Britain's working population had been born abroad. As Jonathan Wadsworth observes in Chapter 3, despite the high profile of immigration in the 2010 general election, the British figure was slightly below the OECD average. Immigration can bring important economic and cultural benefits to a society, increasing labour supply and easing the skill bottlenecks that in the past have given an inflationary bias to Britain's labour market. The work permit and points-based systems have sought to ensure that employers do not have to shelve expansion plans because they cannot recruit suitably skilled labour. However, these systems account for only 10–20 per cent of immigrants. The fear worrying many voters in the election was that increased immigrant numbers were crowding native-born workers out of jobs and depressing their wages. Wadsworth reviews economists' statistical research on the question, and as he shows, it is very difficult to estimate what pay and employment would have been in the absence of immigration. Thus one might compare regions or occupations with many and few immigrant workers. However, immigrants quite naturally tend to go where employment is growing, and they often take jobs that native-born workers do not want. He concludes that recent research shows that competition between immigrants and native-born workers is greatest among low-skilled occupations despite the former often having higher qualifications, but that fears of cheap substitute labour have been greatly exaggerated.

The impact of immigration on housing is somewhat different from that on jobs because the supply of housing in a particular locality is very inelastic. Wadsworth's chapter showed that immigrant workers tend to concentrate in areas where labour demand is strong. Even though immigrants may not be competing strongly with native-born workers in the jobs market, given the fixed supply of housing, it is much more likely that they will be competitors there. In Chapter 4 Christine Whitehead looks in detail at the impact of immigration on the housing market, and draws on the latest research. She examines the impact of housing costs on the net economic benefit of immigration as well as the effect on public resources and social cohesion. She argues that the estimates of immigration and its impact on housing demand have been significantly overestimated. The critical assumption relates to the rate at which immigrants form households, and hence require family accommodation of different types. According to Whitehead, as many as 40 per cent of immigrants return home within ten years, and many young immigrants return home before forming a household. Projections of immigrant housing needs that fail to take the effects of such turnover into account can produce misleading overestimates. Housing-use patterns of the immigrant population also differ from those of the native population with many lower income immigrants sharing accommodation. As Wadsworth's chapter showed, immigration is often concentrated in certain areas, such as London, where pressure on housing is already intense because of the strength of labour demand in the capital. Whitehead argues that rather than restricting immigration because of housing pressures, it would be better to improve the effectiveness of the housing market as this would also ease adverse pressures on housing-related welfare expenditure and social cohesion.

The impact of the current recession on unemployment, as Nickell pointed out, has been more delayed and possibly more benign in Britain than in previous recessions. The big exception has been young people leaving education who find the door to employment is shut as firms have cut recruitment. Paul Gregg asks, in Chapter 5 how can we prevent today's young entrants from becoming tomorrow's long-term unemployed, and what can be learned from the policies of the past two decades. He cites the extensive evidence that early unemployment has a scarring effect which disadvantages people throughout their careers as they miss out on the career and training tracks that lead to good jobs later on. It also undermines young workers' self-confidence and social skills which reduces their ability to perform well in job interviews and in the early stages of employment if they get a job. The problem of some past programmes, such as job guarantee and public sector job programmes, is that they have removed the incentive for continued job search which people delay until the end of their placement. He underscores the benefit of some recent programmes such as Work Trials, and the New Deal for Young People, which have encouraged young people to search for a job while on that the programme so that the transition into employment is seamless. Two important features of these programmes are of note. First, it is important that the placements provide limited income or hours so that there remains a strong incentive to seek permanent work. Second, that support is given by local intermediaries who act as providers seeking out links into mainstream employment activities for these young people. Similar policies can also be applied to help the long-term unemployed back into work. Although costly in the short run, such measures reduce the need for long-term benefits, and for the health-related expenditures that arise from long-term unemployment.

Employment relations in Britain have undergone profound change since the previous deep recession in the early 1990s. In the private sector, unionized workplaces and the number of workers covered by collective agreements are now but a small minority. This has been part of a long-term change over the past thirty years in which procedural collectivism in the private sector has collapsed and management has increased control over day-to-day work assignments. In Chapter 6 William Brown and David Marsden ask to what extent this sea change in employment relations has contributed to the robustness of employment levels at the onset of the recession. One notable change has been the gradual but steady growth in the use of variable pay which enables firms' pay bills to absorb a bigger proportion of a drop in demand without having to lay people off immediately. In view of the evidence cited by Nickell and Gregg about the importance of maintaining attachment to employment, this could represent an important benefit for the economy and the wider society. Brown and Marsden show how the first impact of the recession was absorbed by a dramatic fall in bonuses, large enough to cause the average earnings index for the whole economy to drop by more than 5 per cent on an annual basis. Changes within workplaces also show that employers now have much greater freedom to deploy labour without extensive renegotiation of employment contracts, and they have greater freedom to use a variety of different employment statuses according to their business needs. Nevertheless, this new-found flexibility has come at a price for many groups of employees, and in conclusion, Brown and Marsden look at the winners, mostly higher paid and more educated workers, and losers, mostly lower paid and less skilled. Thus this newly flexible labour market poses questions of social cohesion and sustainability over the longer run, especially in view of evidence on the transmission of disadvantage over time and across generations considered in chapters 5 and 12 by Gregg and Vignoles.

In the United States, occupational licensing now covers almost as many employees as did unionization in its heyday. In Chapter 7 Amy Humphris, Morris Kleiner, and Maria Koumenta observe similar developments in the United Kingdom. Given the reputation of the US economy for its flexible, deregulated labour markets, it is natural to ask whether licensing contributes to their efficiency, and therefore whether its development should be encouraged in Britain. According to Humphris and her co-authors, US research shows that although licensing provides some important public benefits such as quality assurance, these tend to be weaker than the private benefits for occupation members of restricting entry and raising their pay. Its net effect resembles that of craft unionism and the pre-entry closed shop, which in their heyday also provided a mix of public and private benefits, as shown in Zweig's famous study (1951) of restrictive practices in British industry. The difference between Zweig's field-based research and that of modern-day labour economists is that it is now possible to measure the balance of public and private benefits more precisely, hence the finding of a number of US studies that increased costs outweigh quality benefits. To illustrate the cost of licensing for public budgets, the authors take the example of US health care. The sums are large in absolute terms, but modest in relation to total health care expenditure. They argue that there are other methods for providing quality assurance to consumers, such as certification, that avoid entry restrictions and they urge governments to consider the full range of options before agreeing to licensing. They also observe that licensing in the United States has tended to benefit higher paid occupations.

Although more advanced in the United States, the same overall trends of a decline of unionism and an increase in registration and licensing can be observed in Britain according to the data assembled by Humphris and her co-authors. Sue Fernie extends this work in chapter 8, reporting the results of a case study of licensing in the British private security industry, focusing on security guards and door supervisors. This industry had posed major problems of quality assurance owing to the infiltration by criminal gangs into security provision. Many reputable firms felt that they were being undercut by disreputable ones and that the poor reputation of the industry as a whole was depressing demand for its services. This was bad also for many employees who suffered from low pay and a lack of training. The Private Security Industry Act (2001) sought to address many of these issues. Licensing workers proved difficult to implement properly in the short time scale allowed, and led to inadequate training. Nevertheless, many of the door supervisors interviewed after implementation thought that their new status and training had improved their ability to do their jobs and their relations with the public and the police. There had also been changes in management practices by the higher quality firms as a means of reassuring customers, such as greater use of CCTV, improved monitoring and support, and investments in human resources.

Fernie also reports that the Act had helped to force some of the long tail of disreputable firms out of the market. Unlike many of the studies reviewed in Chapter 7, which focused disproportionately on the effects of licensing on skilled and professional occupations, Fernie's study focuses on a predominantly low-skilled occupation. It shows the difficulty of introducing licensing quickly and on a large scale, and the reputational risk for the licensing body if this does not go smoothly. In conclusion, she argues that instead of licensing workers it would be often more effective to focus on licensing the firms providing security.

The NMW celebrated the tenth anniversary of its implementation in 2009. It had long been a piece of received wisdom among many economists that minimum wages, if effective, raise pay at the expense of jobs. In more recent years, this wisdom has been challenged by a number of studies which argue that employer bargaining power in low wage labour markets is more pervasive than previously thought (see Card and Krueger 1995; Manning 2003). Nevertheless, dire employment consequences had been predicted during the election preceding its introduction. In Chapter 9 Mark Stewart examines the evidence on possible employment effects of the NMW since its introduction. As he points out, the United Kingdom has come to be regarded as a laboratory internationally. Overall, the studies suggest that the NMW has not damaged the employment of workers whose pay was directly affected. He observes that a number of different methods have been used to assess its impact on pay and employment. In such an exercise, one needs always to compare the experience of those affected with a control group identical except for coverage by the NMW initially or at its subsequent upratings. This has not been easy, so it is important that a number of different estimation methods have led to the same conclusion. Stewart argues that there are many reasons why minimum wages should not cost jobs in practice because labour markets are not perfectly competitive. By proceeding cautiously, and giving careful attention to these, the Low Pay Commission (LPC) managed to set a minimum, and its subsequent upratings, that avoided harming jobs. Too high a level, affecting too many workers, could easily have had a negative effect on employment, and too low a level would have disappointed the expectations of low-paid workers and their unions. The work of the LPC has been conducted with a close eye on the British and international evidence on minimum wages and employment, and provides a good example of evidence-based policy choices.

In Chapter 10 Alan Manning considers the indirect effects of minimum wages on the pay of other low-paid workers whose pay is above the minimum, and their implications for the work of the LPC. Manning reports evidence from the United States and Britain. Although directly affecting only the lowest-paid 5 per cent of employees in Britain, the NMW may have a spillover effect benefiting all those among the bottom-paid 10 per cent, and possibly more. This is reflected in correlations between minimum wage increases and improvements in the lowest decile compared to median hourly pay. Although the full extent of such spillovers is hard to estimate statistically, it raises some very important questions for the work of the LPC. The benefit for low-paid workers may extend further than previously thought (see Stewart in Chapter 9 of this volume), but it also means that the LPC may also need to consider the potential effect this greater reach has on employment. The LPC needs to consider the likely causes. The traditional reason for expecting spillover effects was that union bargainers would seek to restore pay relativities, but the evidence presented by Brown and Marsden in Chapter 6 of this volume makes this seem unlikely today. Alternatively, Manning suggests the impact on labour supply. Once the lowest paying firms raise their pay to the minimum wage, those that used to pay just above that level find they have to compete harder to attract good quality employees, so they raise their pay. Such spillovers are likely to become progressively weaker at higher levels of pay, so it is not clear whether they extend much higher up the pay distribution. They could diminish faster the fewer bottlenecks there are in the labour supply, hence the importance of immigration, training, and housing.

Pay inequality has grown steadily in Britain and a number of other countries over the past three decades, reversing the long-term trend towards greater equality that characterized the mid-twentieth century. Whereas it was common in the late 1970s for employers to complain about a lack of incentives for their skilled workers and their managers, particularly in reference to incomes policy, such complaints are far less common now. In Chapter 11 Stephen Machin charts the growing wage inequality in Britain over the past four decades: a rapid widening at both ends of the distribution in the 1980s; a more muted increase during the 1990s; and then in the 2000s, some improvement for the lowest paid, especially for women, and a renewed surge at the top. He observes that the decline of unions facilitated rising pay inequality, although estimates for the 1980s put it at only 20 per cent of total change. Likewise, he argues that international trade has so far had a relatively small impact. More important factors have been changes in demand and supply. Machin observes that over the whole period, the pay premium received by university graduates over non-graduates has increased, together with a 'hollowing out' of jobs at the middle-pay levels. He attributes the prime cause of increased pay inequality to skill-biased technical change, which has shifted labour demand in favour of more-skilled and more-educated workers, and at a rate that has outstripped supply—hence the continued rise in graduate/non-graduate earnings. Computers have also contributed to these changes. In what has been referred to as 'task-biased' technical change, they have substituted for middle-ranking routine-type jobs, and increased demand at the bottom for low-skill personal-service jobs, and at the top, for problem-solving jobs that require analytical skills.

The apparent inability of the education and training system to supply the quantity and types of skills required by employers and the persistent under-achievement of pupils from poorer socio-economic backgrounds have been enduring problems in Britain. Limitations of the educational system are likely to have contributed to the rise in graduate relative to non-graduate pay as demand has outstripped supply, as observed in Machin's Chapter 11 on pay inequality. In Chapter 12 Anna Vignoles observes that these problems are likely to be intensified in the current labour market climate as young workers are shut out of employment by freezes on recruitment. Despite improvements in school achievement during the past fifteen years, Britain has narrowed the gap, but not caught up, with other major OECD countries because they too have advanced. It faces a moving target. A telling piece of evidence is that the wage differential between qualified and unqualified adults, even for basic literacy and numeracy, is larger in Britain than in many other industrial countries, implying a bigger gap between supply and demand than elsewhere. Britain does relatively well in PISA international tests when students are aged 15 and yet poorly when we compare adult skill levels. This is because, compared with other countries, fewer UK students remain in education and so miss out on the skills that are acquired after the age of 15. Social divisions in the United Kingdom are partly to blame, and especially the factors that hold back pupils from poorer backgrounds causing them to underachieve in school. Underachievement limits the supply of skills and intensifies the problems of long-term unemployment. Vignoles argues that it is important to invest early. She observes that policies directed at the final stages of secondary schooling have had disappointing results compared with those directed at primary school students. Investing in primary schools and in family support, before students become disillusioned with education, yields better results. Finally, she argues that education has been an area in which there has been a persistent overload of new policies. Governments should evaluate their interventions more rigorously, and be prepared to cut those that show no clear return.

Over the past quarter of a century, there has been a growing use of incentive pay of various kinds to improve motivation and to help managers clarify the work objectives of public employees. Much of the original impetus for this came from a belief that private sector ideas on rewards had much to offer. The banking crisis, and the view that excessive use of bonuses was partly responsi-ble, has forced governments across the world to look more closely at their operation. In Britain, as the state intervened to prevent the collapse of two of its largest banks, the question of top pay and incentives took a new twist: the private sector lost its aura as the exemplar for effective reward policies, and the government had to decide what to do about pay in the banks it now owned. In Chapter 13, John Roberts takes a hard look at the theory and evidence on incentive pay, asking how this guides us as to when to use different kinds of incentive pay and how large the incentive element should be. The problem with strong incentives, he argues, is that when applied to inappropriate circumstances, or focused on the wrong performance measures, they reward the wrong kind of performance, which in the banking case, had disastrous consequences. The familiar problems include when employees have to multi-task, but the reward focuses on only one indicator, often quantity rather than quality. They also include when measures are biased or can be manipulated, an issue raised in connection with public service targets, and in the financial sector, with 'subprime mortgages'. In such cases, lesser reliance on strong incentives geared to bad performance measures would have been less harmful. Roberts also raises some recent advances, notably in relation to the use of weak incentives to encourage cooperation and experimentation, and where beliefs about the best methods differ between those setting objectives and those carrying them out, a problem not unknown when governments contract out services. Finally, Roberts has a serious warning about the mechanics of setting top pay and deciding on the design of incentive systems: often the body setting pay is not the true principal. Instead, it operates at one remove from the true principals who are shareholders and citizens, and its members may not bear the risks when things go wrong.

Despite the current budget cuts and public service reform, for the foreseeable future, the state will remain a major provider of public services whether as a direct employer or a purchaser from profit and non-profit organizations. As such, the motivation of those engaged in these activities is a major public policy concern. Maria Koumenta in Chapter 14 asks whether there is a public service 'ethos' that contributes to the quality of public services, and looks at recent attempts to change its orientation to become more customer-focused. Koumenta brings recent research on public service motivation to bear on whether such an ethos is worth cultivating and its implications for policymakers and public sector human resource managers. She argues that the public service ethos has the potential to create 'principled agents', and thus compensate for 'noisy' performance measures, costly monitoring procedures, and reliance on employee discretion commonly found in public service contexts. She also asks whether the public service ethos stems from the relationship between employees and their employer, public or private, or between them and the activity in which they are engaged. Recent economic theories of 'donated' labour, that is, employee willingness to provide extra effort or time regardless of whether or not it is paid, indicate that public service provision through private means is restricted in its ability to elicit such labour donations. Her own research on prison staff working under public and private sector arrangements confirms that the nature of the employer is important: people are more willing to donate their effort for the public good than for private profit. Although there has been a long debate about the existence and nature of a public service ethos— are public servants pro-social knights, self-serving knaves, or just pawns

(Le Grand 1997)—governments also need to consider reorienting such norms from time to time in order to meet citizens' changing expectations. Koumenta concludes by considering the circumstances under which public motives should be an integral part of service delivery, such as in the case of front-line services, and ways in which this can be achieved.

Public sector employers have to compete with their private sector counterparts to recruit, retain, and motivate their employees. At a time of financial stringency, governments need to know how far they can squeeze public sector pay before morale, recruitment, and retention difficulties begin to erode their ability to carry out their programmes. Likewise, when private employees see their own pay and jobs at risk, they quite naturally want to know whether the pain is being shared equally among all citizens. Thus whether public employees are better paid than those doing the similar jobs in the private sector is a question with wide ramifications. In Chapter 15 Richard Disney shows that there is no simple answer to this question because their pay advantage varies cyclically: when the economy is booming, the pay gap benefits private sector employees, and when it is in recession, those in the public sector do better. Overall comparisons of levels and trends in the two sectors are heavily influenced by the time period used. Pay patterns in the two sectors also differ over the life cycle as the public sector offers more career pay which tends to peak at higher ages. Disney also shows that it is in practice very difficult to identify 'similar' employees in the two sectors: even if one can isolate similar occupations, it is not easy to control for differences in ability and drive that are very hard to measure in large-scale surveys. He describes how economists have attempted to overcome these measurement problems, for example, by panel data methods which follow the same employees over time, and by following groups of employees when their employer changes sector, for example, with contracting out and privatization. He concludes that over the long run, there is not a great deal of difference between public and private sector pay once account is taken of differences in occupations and ability. This is what one would expect when both types of employers compete in the same labour markets. These labour market pressures mean that measures to restrict public employees' pay may be beneficial to the public purse in the short run, but the longer run price will be pressure on recruitment, retention, quality of job applicants, and in past decades, pay explosions. Governments have managed these in the past, but major reforms, such as those proposed by the Coalition, have often been easier to achieve during the 'catch-up' phase, when it is possible to 'give something for something' than in the austerity phase.

Whereas Disney's chapter addresses levels of public service pay, Chapter 16 examines evidence on how it has been set in recent years, and in particular, the outcomes of the pay review process for a number of key public service occupations such as teachering and the health professions. Pay review is a form of public service pay setting that is unique to Britain and covers a quarter of public sector employees. The pay review bodies (PRBs) are set up on a statutory basis, and collect evidence from employee organizations, employer bodies, and the government relating to the employees in their remit. They then make a recommendation, which the government then decides whether and how to implement. At various times over the past quarter of a century, it has been alleged that public employees covered by pay review do better than those who are not. A. N. Other looks at the statistical evidence over the period for each of the major PRBs, examining the factors that influence their recommendations and the resulting pay levels. In recent years, he finds that the recommendations have been sensitive to the factors weighing on government economic policy, such as budgets and whether or not inflation is accelerating, as well as to the concerns of employees, as reflected by forecast inflation (eroding living standards), labour militancy, and unemployment. The actual pay awards were similarly affected. A. N. Other concludes that this evidence shows that the PRB system has been quite successful in ensuring that government budgetary and economic concerns are reflected in both PRB recommendations and the actual pay awards, and the employee concerns about inflation are represented. Thus the PRBs can be deemed a success as they have identified a compromise that satisfies the national interest and have avoided the disruption caused by industrial disputes.

1.3. Conclusion

All in all, the challenges facing labour market policy for the coming years are considerable. The chapters in this volume identify more than a dozen key areas. Flexible markets are best sustained if there is a social consensus supporting them. This is truer of labour than most other markets because it is through them that the great majority of citizens engage in economic activity. For the foreseeable future, British public finances will be extremely tight so that even if the branding of policies sounds grandiose, their substance will have to be carefully targeted. In the previous government, Tony Blair was strong on branding, and Gordon Brown strong on substance. As yet, it is too early to judge where the balance will lie with the Coalition government. Big pictures are needed in politics to mobilize consent, but detail is needed for successful delivery of policies. As the chapters in this volume show, a great deal has been learned in recent decades about where to aim labour market policies, and the research and policy communities have developed growing skills in the evaluation and analysis of policies, why some succeed where others fail, and what can be learned. The drama of the clash of ideas inherent in the big pictures often obscures the contribution of what Henry Phelps Brown, one of David Metcalf's predecessors in both academia and public service, described as the 'hewers and grinders of facts'.

☐ NOTE

1. *Acknowledgements*: The editor would like to acknowledge the financial support given to the organization of the seminar by the Centre for Economic Performance and the Department of Management's Employment Relations and Organisational Behaviour Group, and would like to thank Jo Cantlay, Nigel Rogers, and Giulia Faggio for their invaluable help and advice, and Francesco d'Amico for assistance in preparing the charts.

☐ REFERENCES

Card, D. and Krueger, A. (1995) *Myth and Measurement: The New Economics of the Minimum Wage.* Princeton, NJ: Princeton University Press.

Clegg, H.A. (1971) *How to Run an Incomes Policy: And Why we Made such a Mess of the Last One.* London: Heinemann.

Le Grand, J. (1997) 'Knights, Knaves or Pawns? Human Behaviour and Social Policy', *Journal of Social Policy*, 26(2), 149–69.

Manning, A. (2003) *Monopsony in Motion: Imperfect Competition in Labor Markets.* Princeton, NJ: Princeton University Press.

Toynbee, P. and Walker, D. (2009) *Unjust Rewards: Exposing Greed and Inequality in Britain Today.* London: Granta.

Zweig, F. (1951) *Productivity and Trade Unions.* Oxford: Blackwell.

Part I

Employment, Immigration, and Housing

2 The European Unemployment Challenge

STEPHEN NICKELL

2.1. Introduction: where are we now?[1]

Europe, like much of the world economy, is in the middle of a serious recession with GDP in many countries having fallen significantly. Interestingly enough, looking across the OECD countries, there has not been a very strong correlation between the rise in unemployment and the fall in GDP. For example, in year up to mid-2009 (Q2), GDP in the US fell by 3.8 per cent and unemployment rose by four percentage points. By contrast, German GDP fell by 5.9 per cent but unemployment rose by less than one percentage point. On the other hand, Spanish GDP fell by 4.2 per cent whereas unemployment rose by over seven percentage points over the same period. These variations will be analysed in the next Section.

The overall prospects for the world economy indicate a recovery but its strength is the subject of much uncertainty. The balance of recent data is on the upside and there is some evidence of a slowdown in the rate of increase in unemployment. However, unless GDP growth in Europe rises above trend after 2010, it is hard to see how unemployment can fall to any significant degree. So, in Section 3, we discuss the role of labour market policies in the context of a sharp fall in GDP followed by a gradual recovery. Then, in Section 4, we consider how we might tackle the problems of vulnerable groups both in the short run and the longer term. We conclude with a summary and some conclusions.

2.2. The rise in unemployment

2.2.1. MACROECONOMIC POLICY

It goes without saying that the recent rise in unemployment has not been generated within European labour markets but is a consequence of the worldwide credit crunch and the collapse in aggregate demand. So the immediate macroeconomic policy response is the major factor in determining the subsequent path of GDP. Across the world, we have seen expansionary fiscal policy accompanied by a dramatic loosening of the stance of monetary policy. This is a sensible response to a situation where aggregate demand has fallen and there was little in the way of core inflationary pressure even before this fall. More recently, there has been some tightening of fiscal policy across Europe in response to market anxiety about excessive sovereign debt. Whether this tightening has started too early remains to be seen. Nevertheless, in our discussion of unemployment and labour market policies, we shall take the path of GDP as more or less a given and focus on the consequent impact on unemployment. Labour market policies per se are not going to be important determinants of GDP growth in the short run.

2.2.2. LABOUR MARKET POLICIES AND UNEMPLOYMENT IN THE CONTEXT OF THE RECESSION

As we can see from Table 2.1, there are large cross-country variations in the rise in unemployment relative to the fall in GDP in the recent downturn. To some extent these differences reflect the productivity levels in the hardest hit industries. For example, in Spain, there has been a huge contraction in the relatively low productivity construction sector generating large falls in employment relative to GDP. This was an almost inevitable consequence of the enormous build-up of the construction sector during the house building boom of the mid-2000s. In Germany, on the other hand, it is the high productivity capital goods sector that has been badly hit, leading to much smaller falls in employment relative to GDP.

A second important factor explaining the differences in unemployment rises relative to GDP falls is the strictness of employment protection legislation. The stricter the rules governing redundancy, the slower will be the rise in unemployment for any given fall in output (for a summary of these issues, see Nickell and Layard 1999: sect. 7). Strict rules can, however, be avoided if a high proportion of employees are on short-term contracts, for when these contracts come to an end, employment can be costlessly adjusted downwards. Thus, while Spain has relatively strict employment protection rules, the fact that nearly a third of employees are on short-term contracts means that there can be very sharp downward adjustments in employment. Italy, on the other hand, also has among the strictest employment protection laws in the OECD but a smaller number of short-term contract employees. As a consequence, downward employment adjustments are likely to be very sluggish in response to falls in output. By contrast, the United States has very low levels of employment protection which helps to explain why there is a very large rise in unemployment relative to the fall in output. Another factor here was the

Table 2.1. Changes in Unemployment and GDP

	% change in GDP (2008 Q2–2009 Q2)	% point change in unemployment (May 2008–May 09)	Employment protection laws index (2003)	Employment protection laws index (2008)	% Share of short-term contracts (2004)	% Share of short-term contracts (2008)
Belgium	−3.7	1.5	2.7	2.5	8.7	7.6
Canada	−3.2	2.3	1.2	1.1	12.8	12.3
Denmark	−7.2	2.8	1.6	1.8	9.8	8.6
Finland	−9.0	2.0	2.3	2.0	16.2	15.1
France	−2.8	1.6	3.0	2.9	13.0	14.2
Germany	−5.9	0.3	2.1	2.4	12.4	14.6
Ireland	−7.3	6.7	1.4	1.3	3.4	8.1
Italy	−6.0	0.6	3.4	2.4	11.9	14.0
The Netherlands	−5.4	0.4	2.4	2.1	14.6	18.3
Spain	−4.2	7.4	2.3	3.0	32.1	29.4
Sweden	−6.0	3.2	2.7	2.2	15.1	16.1
The United Kingdom	−5.5	2.3	1.4	1.1	5.7	5.3
The United States	−3.8	4.0	0.6	0.7	4.2	4.2*

Sources: OECD, Allard (2005), OECD (Employment Statistics) 2008 Online OECD Employment Database. Employment Protection index EP-V2 is used. *US figure is for 2005.
Allard's employment protection series is based on OECD methodology.

great severity of the credit crunch in the United States which undermined firms' working capital and forced an extensive shakeout of labour.

The final important factor in this context is the extent to which subsidies are provided to firms whose employees are placed on short-time working in response to falls in demand. Of course, even without subsidies, firms who wish to retain valuable workers in the face of a downturn will negotiate a shorter work week, extra unpaid holidays, and the like. But when the government subsidizes this type of response directly, obviously such responses will be much more widespread. Extensive subsidy policies of this type have been introduced in Belgium, Denmark, France, Germany, Italy, and the Netherlands (see European Commission, 2009). These policies are often accompanied by incentives to use some of the workers' 'spare-time' for extra training. The advantage of short-time working subsidies is that they maintain the attachment of workers to the labour market over the period of the recession. Subsidies of this kind have been particularly successful in maintaining employment in Germany, with well over one million workers involved in subsidy schemes (see IMF 2009: 13–17 for a useful summary of these issues). Two problems arise with schemes of this type. First, they are generally time-limited because they are not cheap. So, if they finish before the economic recovery is complete, this may impede the recovery process. Second, they may inter-rupt the movement of workers to more productive activities and prevent the contraction of less-productive industries or industries where there is general overcapacity. For example, competitive protection of automobile manufacturing across the world may ensure that overcapacity is sustained even as the world emerges from the recession. Of course, there is a collective action problem here since no one country wishes to contract its domestic car industry to the long-run benefit of the rest of the world. This kind of problem means that short-time working subsidies should generally be used for firms whose long-term prospects are strong, such as the capital goods producers typical of Germany. They cannot possibly be used for construction firms which have grown significantly in the sort of construction booms seen in Spain and Ireland, because after the recession they are bound to employ far fewer people.

Overall, therefore, the industrial pattern of the recession, the structure of labour market institutions, and the use of specific subsidy policies to sustain employment interact to generate the large observed cross-country differences in the increases in unemployment relative to the falls in output.

2.3. **Labour market policies and the recovery**

2.3.1. POLICY IN THE SHORT RUN

The speed of the recovery in GDP in different countries will, of course, depend crucially on how macroeconomic policy develops, how credit markets recover, and how the manifest problems facing the world economy are resolved. In particular, it is important not to tighten policy too early because of anxieties about the sharp rise in public debt. Indeed, there is a risk that this is precisely what is happening in many European countries. Generally speaking, those economies which have seen faster falls in employment relative to GDP in the downturn will probably see faster rises in employment relative to GDP in the recovery (see, again, IMF 2009: 13–17). Indeed, the existence of flexible short-term contracts and, particularly, widespread temporary employment agencies may allow faster expansion of GDP without excessive inflationary pressure.

2.3.2. WHAT MEASURES ARE TO BE AVOIDED?

In order to prevent unemployment persistence and, indeed, to sustain labour supply more generally, it is crucial to continue the labour market attachment of those who lose their jobs. Historically, we have not been good at this. Under the pressure of rising unemployment, the force of the 'something must be done' argument tended to grow and it was easy to succumb by removing people from the labour force via early retirement, disability, and so on. While this reduced the number of the non-employed who were actually looking for work (the unemployed) in the short run, in the long run the inactive population became larger while the unemployment rate was unaffected. The growth potential of the economy was reduced and the fiscal position was worsened (see Faggio and Nickell 2007 for an extensive discussion of these issues).

There is a long and unfortunate history of this policy response, so, as we can see in Table 2.2, by 2007, in the vast majority of OECD countries there were more inactive men aged 25–54 than unemployed men in the same age group, mostly long-term sick or disabled. Furthermore, in many countries, inactivity rates among men aged 55–64 had risen to very high levels in the three decades up to the mid-1990s, despite male life expectancy having risen steadily throughout. The consequences for pension systems were plainly adverse. Indeed, it is these consequences which have led many countries to stop providing incentives to encourage early retirement. Thus, after 1995, we see falling rates of inactivity for older men. Overall, therefore, one thing to avoid above all others is to be tempted into providing individuals with

Table 2.2. Inactivity Rates among Prime Age and Older Men

| | Men aged 25–54 (%) | | | Men aged 55–64 (%) | | |
	1971	2007 (unemployment rate in brackets)	2008 (unemployment rate in brackets)	1971	1995	2008
Finland	7.2	9.7 (4.8)	8.8 (4.3)	26.8	58.4	39.5
France	3.2	6.0 (6.3)	5.5 (5.6)	25.4	58.8	57.4
Germany	3.7	6.2 (7.5)	6.5 (6.9)	21.5	47.3	32.8
Ireland	2.8	8.2 (4.3)	8.4 (5.5)	9.0	36.1	31.6
Italy	5.9	9.0 (4.0)	9.0 (4.7)	40.7	55.9	53.0
The Netherlands	5.1	8.3 (2.2)	6.2 (1.9)	19.4	58.6	37.3
Spain	3.5	7.4 (5.4)	7.4 (8.9)	15.4	45.1	34.9
Sweden	5.3	7.1 (4.1)	6.9 (4.0)	15.3	29.6	23.3
The United Kingdom	1.6	8.4 (3.7)	8.3 (4.1)	11.6	37.6	29.9
The United States	4.5	9.1 (3.7)	9.5 (5.0)	17.9	34.0	29.6

Notes: Individuals in institutions are not included. The numbers are generally small except that close to 2 per cent of the prime age male population in the United States is incarcerated.

Sources: *OECD Labour Market Statistics* and *OECD Employment Outlook*, Table C, various issues. For the United Kingdom in 1971, we use the *UK General Household Survey* (1972). For 2008, Online OECD Employment Database.

incentives to retire early or to enter long-term sickness or disability. Sustaining and enhancing long-run labour supply is the direction in which to move.

2.3.3. HOW DO WE MAINTAIN LABOUR FORCE ATTACHMENT?

As we have already noted, the key to maintaining the long-term growth potential of the economy is to prevent those who lose their jobs from getting into a situation where it is very hard to get back into work. So they must avoid going into long-term unemployment, early retirement, or the disability benefit system. In normal times, it is sensible to devote significant resources to assisting those who are already in one or other of these states back into the labour market. In a recession, given limited resources, the main focus has to be on those entering unemployment. There will, of course, be much larger numbers of these than in normal times.

The standard policy shortly after entry into unemployment is mandatory participation in an activation programme, monitoring of job search, counselling, and job-search assistance in return for receipt of benefits. For those lacking skills, policies to enhance employability may be in order although such evidence as we have suggests that training for the unemployed is not a very successful policy. Targeted recruitment subsidies can be more effective. EU countries vary greatly in the rigour and effectiveness of their activation policies. For an excellent discussion of activation policy, see chapter 5 of the 2009 report of the Swedish Fiscal Policy Council (see also Martin and Grubb 2001; Eichhorst and Konle-Seidl 2008).

When unemployment duration reaches a given point, six months or twelve months say, then to sustain labour market attachment it is worth introducing a job/training guarantee in return for continuing receipt of benefits. For adults, the emphasis should be on work rather than training (see Bloom et al. 2001). The work would be temporary (6–12 months) and part-time with the individual continuing to search for a regular job at the same time. The work would be socially useful, requiring minimal training, organized at public expense by local authorities or voluntary groups. Only a small minority of EU countries have mandatory schemes for all those who reach a certain duration of unemployment, although in most EU countries unemployed individuals can be referred to such schemes by the employment service.

There are two problems with all these kinds of policies. First, they are expensive. However, in a serious recession, fiscal policy is going to be expansionary and some of the extra expenditure should be diverted in this direction. Second, a highly professional and well-organized employment service is required. Furthermore, its capacity must be increased rapidly as the inflow into unemployment rises, otherwise activation and related policies may be overwhelmed.

2.3.4. EUROPEAN ECONOMIC RECOVERY PLAN

It is worth briefly commenting on the labour market aspects of the European Economic Recovery Plan in this context. The plan is set out in European Commission (2008) and was produced in order to assist member states with their policy responses to the recession. It covers a number of the points considered here. In particular, it focuses on using flexible working time to avoid 'wasteful' labour shedding due to temporary demand disturbances. The problem is, of course, knowing what demand disturbances are going to be temporary. We can be fairly certain that the demand for sophisticated capital goods will recover with the world economy and that the demand for new housing will not recover rapidly in countries which have seen huge house building booms. But, in many industries, the longer term prospects are less certain.

The plan rightly concentrates on activation measures for the unemployed and the necessity of avoiding long-term unemployment, recommending the use of temporary hiring subsidies. It also recommends reducing social charges on lower incomes to support the low skilled. As a temporary measure as part of a recovery plan this is, perhaps, not a well-targeted policy. It is expensive, has little impact on poverty since most low paid individuals are not in poor households, and will probably have little impact on employment.

2.4. **Tackling vulnerable groups in the short and long run**

2.4.1. THE SHORT RUN

The vulnerable groups are the young, the unskilled, and those potentially suffering from long-term sickness or disability. As we have already noted, for the first two groups, the focus has to be on assistance in obtaining work and enhancing employability which should start immediately upon entry into unemployment. For the third group, if individuals lose their jobs because of sickness or ill health, it is vital to mobilize support before they enter long-term disability. This plainly involves medical support, a focus on the sort of work which the individual can manage, and immediate access to effective psychological therapies for those affected by depression and anxiety disorders which may indeed be worsened by unemployment. The worst strategy is simply to allow general practitioners to sign people off work with no further intervention. For example, the Work Capability Assessment, introduced by the UK Department of Work and Pensions in October 2008, is a comprehensive attempt to maintain attachment to the labour force for those starting to claim income support on grounds of incapacity. There is evidence that it has had some success in slowing the rate at which people enter long-term disability.

2.4.2. THE LONG RUN

For the young, the evidence suggests that countries which have the so-called dual systems have lower levels of relative youth unemployment and smoother and more rapid transitions from education into work (see OECD 2008: ch. 1). A dual system is simply one where a national apprenticeship is the way into skilled work for those outside university. The essence of these schemes is that they are national, there is a contractual relationship between employers and workers, the training is of high quality, and there are standards which are imposed at a national level, like a driving test. These schemes have been around for a very long time in Austria, Denmark, Germany, and Switzerland, and are hard to start up from scratch. However, some countries feel that it is worthwhile trying to move in that direction, notably Norway, Australia, and the United Kingdom, because the benefits for the young are so great.

For the unskilled and those without qualifications, it is plain that the quality of schooling at the lower end of the ability range is a key factor. Evidence from the International Adult Literacy Survey indicates that there are huge cross-country variations in the proportion of the population of working age who have minimal skills (see OECD 2000). It is clear that the labour market will work much better and poverty will tend to be much lower if there is only a small group of individuals with very low literacy and numeracy skills. Those at the bottom of the ability range require additional resources for them to receive effective education. If they can develop marketable skills when young, their entry into the labour market is much easier to organize effectively.

In many, if not most, countries of the developed world, there are more prime age men (aged 25–54) on disability benefit than there are on unemployment benefit. This was not the case in the 1970s. The key factors are the structure of the disability benefit system and the way in which individuals are moved into this system from employment or unemployment. In order to reduce the numbers on disability benefit, two things are required. The first is to control the inflow using policies described above. The second is to apply the standard activation mechanisms allied to medical support to individuals who are already on disability benefit. A good example is the Pathways to Work scheme introduced recently in the United Kingdom which has already had some success. In 2010, the Work Capability Assessment was introduced for those currently on disability benefits to reinforce this scheme.

Overall, policies should be work friendly and always aim at enhancing labour supply over the longer term.

2.5. **Summary and Conclusions**

The key in a recession is to sustain the attachment of workers to the labour force and to protect those who lose their jobs.

1. It is worth subsidizing worker retention in those sectors where demand is likely to return to pre-recession levels. This can be a very effective policy for sustaining attachment to the labour force.
2. At all costs, countries should avoid providing individuals with incentives to retire early or to enter long-term sickness or disability.
3. Those entering unemployment should participate in an activation programme including monitoring of job search, counselling, job-search assistance, and medical/psychological support for those suffering from ill health. Policies to enhance employability and targeted recruitment subsidies may be worthwhile. It is important to expand the capacity of the system to cope with the increased inflow into unemployment.
4. Beyond a certain level of unemployment duration, it is worth introducing a job/training guarantee in return for continuing receipt of benefits.
5. National apprenticeship systems generate smoother and more rapid transitions from education to work and lower youth unemployment than average. Things are even better if those towards the lower end of the ability range have achieved high levels of literacy and numeracy by the end of compulsory school.
6. Strict controls over entry into long-term disability and activation mechanisms plus medical support for those already in long-term disability help to control the number of inactive individuals in the working-age population.

☐ NOTE

1. This is an extended version of a note presented to EU Finance Ministers at the Informal Ecofin Meeting, Gothenburg, 2 October 2009. I am grateful for the helpful comments on an earlier draft from David Marsden.

☐ REFERENCES

Allard, G. (2005) 'Measuring Job Security Over Time: In Search of a Historical Indicator', 'Instituto de Empressa', *Working Paper* WP-05 (http://www.ie.edu/eng/claustro/claustro_working_papers.asp).

Bloom, H.S., Hill, C.J., and Riccio, J. (2001) 'Modeling the Performance of Welfare-to-Work Programs: The Effects of Program Management and Services, Economic Environment, and Client Characteristics', New York: Manpower Demonstration Research Corporation.

Eichhorst, W. and Konle-Seidl, R. (2008) 'Contingent Convergence: A Comparative Analysis of Activation Policies', *IZA Discussion Paper* No. 3905, December.

European Commission (2008) 'A European Economic Recovery Plan', COM (2008) 800, 26/11/2008.

—— (2009) 'The EU's Response to Support the Real Economy during the Economic Crisis: An Overview of Member States' Recovery Measures', Directorate-General for Economic and Financial Affairs, *Occasional Papers*, 51, July.

Faggio, G. and Nickell, S. (2007) 'Patterns of Work Across the OECD', *Economic Journal*, 117, June, F416–40.

IMF (2009) *World Economic Outlook*, October, Washington, DC: IMF.

Martin, J.P. and Grubb, D. (2001) 'What Works and for Whom: A Review of OECD Countries' Experiences with Active Labour Market Policies', *Swedish Economic Policy Review*, 8, 9–56.

Nickell, S. and Layard, R. (1999) 'Labor Market Institutions and Economic Performance', in O. Ashenfelter and D. Card (eds.) *Handbook of Labor Economics*, Amsterdam: Elsevier.

OECD (2000) *Literacy in the Information Age*, Paris: OECD.

—— (2008) *Employment Outlook*, Paris: OECD.

Swedish Fiscal Policy Council (2009) Annual Report, May (www.finanspolitiskaradet.ses).

3 Immigration and the UK Labour Market

JONATHAN WADSWORTH

3.1. Introduction

Rising immigration has been one of the most significant labour market developments in the United Kingdom over the past fifteen years. At the beginning of 2009, around 13.2 per cent of the working-age population had been born abroad, up from around 8 per cent at the end of the 1990–3 recession (Figure 3.1). As a result, the stock of working-age immigrants rose from 2.3 to 5.3 million over this period. Since then, the immigrant population has fallen back slightly, in part the result of the latest recession. Recessions reduce the opportunities for work and immigration typically falls in a downturn. The latest recession was no exception. The United Kingdom is not alone in having experienced increased inflows from abroad. Immigration has risen in almost all industrialized countries over the past decade. The average share of migrants in the OECD increased from 10.7 per cent of the population to

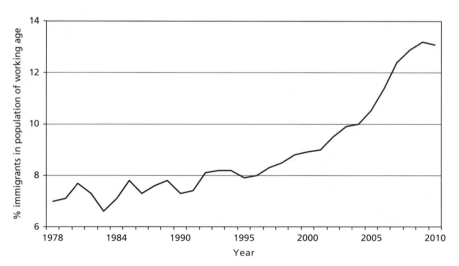

Figure 3.1. Share of Immigrants in the UK's Working-Age Population
Source: Labour Force Survey (LFS).

13.8 per cent between 1998 and 2007 (OECD 2009). Nor is such an increase in the UK's population over a similar time period unprecedented. Between 1977 and 1994 the UK-born population of working age grew by 2.2 million, from 29.5 to 32.7 million, the result of the baby boom generation reaching maturity.

In the face of a rapid increase in the number of immigrants, interest in the issue among academics, policymakers, and commentators has risen appreciably. Rising immigration means rising labour supply, unless offset by increased emigration. Since the mid-1990s immigration to the United Kingdom has exceeded emigration from the United Kingdom in every year.[1] One starting point is to ask why a rise in labour supply caused by immigration need be any different to that caused by changing fertility patterns. Certainly, differences in age, skill, and the timing of any rise in population could potentially differentiate between these two labour supply stimuli and we return to these issues below. Whenever immigration is discussed with regard to labour market performance, the issues of growth, productivity, and displacement are usually central to any debate. While it is relatively trivial to achieve higher levels of GDP by expanding the labour force, it is less obvious that GDP per head or productivity need increase as a result of rising labour supply, whether caused by immigration or by other factors. The existence of skill shortages and hence productivity can be addressed by targeted immigration with few concerns about displacement of existing workers. However, targeting, or any form of planning for skills, is not easy, nor is this principle applied to the majority of immigrants entering the United Kingdom in any year, since the work permit system and its points-based successor impose skill requirements on, currently, some 10–20 per cent of the annual inflow of immigrants.[2] Hence the issue of whether immigration puts downward pressure on the wages of incumbents or reduces job prospects becomes central to the debate on labour market efficacy.

The attempt to replace anecdotes about the labour market effects of immigration with hard evidence has bedevilled the Economics profession for some time now. While establishing correlations between immigration patterns and labour market trends is straightforward, it is much harder to establish whether changes in immigration *cause* changes in wages and employment and if so by how much. Yet policy needs to be built around evidence of causal effects. In Section 2 we discuss the theoretical search for identification of any causal effect of immigration on wages and unemployment. In Section 3 we examine trends in immigration, and the accumulated evidence on immigration and labour market performance for the United Kingdom is discussed in Section 4. Section 5 concludes.

3.2. **Drivers of immigration**

Immigration will rise if relative opportunities in the United Kingdom are better than in the source countries or in other potential destination countries. Indeed, one of the reasons why the United Kingdom was able to attract so many migrants over the previous decade was undoubtedly because the economy was growing much faster than many other major economies over this period. Each country's migrant stock is also directly affected by its national immigration policy and there are barriers to entry of varying stringency that differ over time and across countries. Indeed, many regulations in the industrialized countries are explicitly designed to favour the entry of skilled over unskilled migrants. A focus on skilled immigration in particular is built in to the migration rules common to many EU countries and countries such as Canada and Australia.

UK policy has, at times, sought to encourage immigrants from both ends of the skill distribution, with the supply of immigrants greatly influenced by its links with former colonies. Before 1962, any commonwealth or Irish citizen had the right of entry into the United Kingdom. A system of work permits was introduced after that point and the principle of right of entry to commonwealth citizens was abolished in 1973. It was replaced by a system of work permits that favoured skilled workers in short supply along with entry rights for dependants that has continued, subject to periodic modifications, to this day. The United Kingdom was one of only three member countries that allowed access to migrants from the new European Union (EU) accession states in 2004 and this has been a significant, though by no means exclusive, driver behind the recent increase in migration.

The present points-based migration system, overseen by the UK Home Office and advised by the Migration Advisory Committee, continues to restrict entry of less-skilled migrants from outside the EU, while promoting controlled entry of more highly skilled migrants. However, it is important to stress that the share of the inflow of immigrants accounted for by the points-based system is quite small (MAC 2008).

Faced with an increase in labour supply and hence potentially increased competition for jobs, concerns have been raised over whether immigration has been associated with a rise in unemployment or falling wages. To a certain extent the relative level of demand matters here. If labour demand exceeds labour supply in the receiving country, the impact of immigration will be different from that in a country already at full employment. Rising demand for labour will more readily absorb increases in labour supply. The strength of Britain's economic growth over the previous decade, compared with other major economies, was a significant contributor to its attractiveness to migrant labour. The relative strength of the pound also makes UK salaries more attractive when viewed from abroad. Just as with reintegrating the long-term unemployed or the inactive, or increasing the retirement age, migration is one way of dealing with potential obstacles to non-inflationary growth caused by labour supply shortages. However, concerns about substitution of the standing workforce with an alternative labour supply potentially willing to work for lower wages or displacement of high-wage firms with low-wage firms become more prevalent when output is more constrained by lack of demand than lack of supply, as in a recession.

The distribution of skills and demand within a country also matters. Any effects of immigration are likely to be most profound among those groups that are the closest substitutes for immigrant labour. The skill composition of immigrants also matters. If this differs from that of the receiving country there will be differential pressures across skill groups. If not then the economy effectively grows by replicating itself. Similarly the output mix, the level of technological intensity, and prices are other additional adjustment mechanisms that need not mean that wages are the only source of adjustment to an increase in supply.

3.3. **UK immigration trends**

Rising immigration to the United Kingdom has been associated with a change in the country of origin mix (Figure 3.2). The immigrant population disaggregated by country of origin is becoming much more diverse. Twenty years ago, one-third of all immigrants came from just two countries, Ireland and India. Now these two countries account for just 12 per cent of all immigrants. The top three sender countries for the new arrivals to the United Kingdom in 2009 were India, Poland, and Pakistan. While the share of immigrants from EU Europe has remained broadly constant over this period, the share of immigrants from Africa and Asia has risen (Table 3.1).

Immigrants are, on average, more educated than their UK-born counterparts, and the educational attainment gap has been rising over time, since more recent immigrants are more educated, on average, than other immigrants (see Table 3.2). While more than half of the UK-born workforce left school at 16 or earlier, fewer than one-sixth of new immigrants finished their education by the age of 16. Just under one in five UK-born members of the workforce finished education at 21 or after compared with more than one in three immigrants and more than 50 per cent of all new immigrants. Other things being equal, this might be expected to put more supply pressure on the skilled end of the labour market.

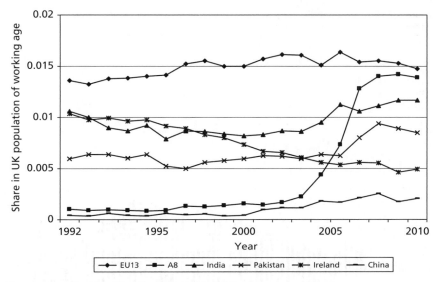

Figure 3.2. The Changing Country of Origin Mix

Source: LFS. A8 refers to the eight EU accession countries.

Table 3.1. Immigrant Shares and Area of Origin, 1979–2009

	1979	1989	1999	2009
Immigrant share	7.6	8.3	9.7	12.7
Of which % from:				
Europe	41.6	35.9	32.2	31.1
Asia	28.0	32.9	32.4	35.1
Africa	11.8	15.0	19.7	21.2
Americas	16.3	13.2	11.8	9.4
Oceania	2.3	3.0	3.9	3.3
Largest senders (% of all immigrants)				
1	Ireland (19.3)	Ireland (15.8)	India (9.6)	India (9.8)
2	India (13.3)	India (12.3)	Ireland (8.9)	Poland (8.6)
3	Jamaica (6.2)	Pakistan (7.3)	Pakistan (6.8)	Pakistan (7.6)
4	Pakistan (5.8)	Germany (4.4)	Germany (5.3)	Germany (5.1)
5	Italy (4.3)	Jamaica (4.0)	Bangladesh (4.4)	South Africa (3.5)

Source: LFS. Percentage share of all immigrants in brackets.

Some, but by no means all, of the education differences are because immigrants are younger, on average by around 5 years, and so belong to cohorts more likely to have benefited from expanded tertiary education opportunities.[3] Figure 3.3 compares the numbers of immigrants in each age group

Table 3.2. Education and Immigrant Status (Working-Age Population), 2009

	Percentage of group with each level of education		
	UK-born	All immigrants	New immigrants
Age finished education (year)			
≤16	53.1	24.8	15.4
17–20	28.2	36.5	34.0
21+	18.7	38.7	50.6

Source: LFS (excluding students).

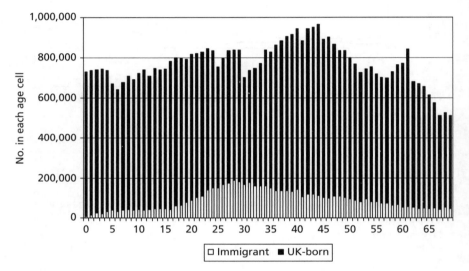

Figure 3.3. The Distribution of Immigrants by Age
Source: LFS.

with the numbers of UK-born in the same age group. Since most immigrants to the United Kingdom arrive as young adults, there are few children among the stock of immigrants. With regard to the adult population there is clearly most supply pressure among adults in their late twenties, particularly as this coincides with a fall in the size of the cohort among UK-born individuals. Whether immigrants are substitutes within or across age groups is an issue we return to below.

While the stock of immigrants has risen in all regions over time, it has risen most in London. While anecdotal commentary has hinted that new immigrants are more regionally dispersed than in the past, the overall population of immigrants has become more concentrated in London and the south-east of England over time.[4] Some 32 per cent of immigrants still live in London and,

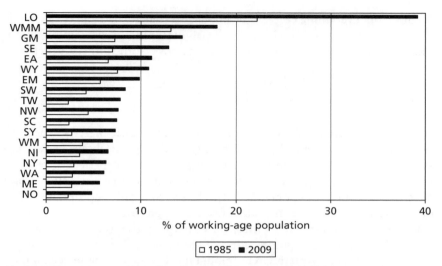

Figure 3.4. Immigrant Share of Regions' Working-Age Populations

Source: LFS.

Note: LO = London, WMM = West Midlands Met., GM = Greater Manchester, SE = South East, EA = East Anglia, WY = West Yorkshire, EM = East Midlands, SW = South West, TW = Tyne & Wear, NW = North West, SC = Scotland, SY = South Yorkshire, WM = Rest of West Midlands, NI = Northern Ireland, NY = North Yorkshire, WA = Wales, ME = Merseyside, NO = North of England.

in 2009, 39 per cent of London's population are immigrants (see Figure 3.4). The geographic dispersion of immigrant share across local areas is much larger. Some 60 per cent of the working-age populations of Brent and Westminster were born overseas compared to under 3 per cent of the populations of Knowsley or Redcar & Cleveland.

3.4. **Trying to estimate the labour market impact of immigration**

One way to try to assess the effect of immigration is to compare average wages or unemployment in the years before and after a change in labour supply. However, because other mechanisms such as the economic cycle or shifting sectoral demands will also have affected wages over the same period, this will not answer the question of whether immigration has an effect on the wages of resident workers.

Ideally, we want to compare the observed wage *change* with the 'counterfactual' wage change that would have taken place had immigration not occurred but everything else (e.g. technological change) had and to relate this difference to the size of the change in the labour force caused by immigration. The effect immigration has on the wages of native-born workers is then

$$\frac{(W_{\text{after}}^{\text{observed}} - W_{\text{before}}^{\text{observed}}) - (W_{\text{after}}^{\text{counterfactual}} - W_{\text{before}}^{\text{observed}})}{\Delta\text{immigration}}$$

However, such counterfactuals are not observed and so there is a need to circumvent this problem. Typically, researchers divide the labour market into subgroups in order to compare wages in groups that experienced a lot of immigration with wages for groups that did not (so that this latter group effectively becomes the counterfactual). The search for the appropriate choice of counterfactual—and hence identification of an immigration effect—has led to the development of a variety of techniques. The 'spatial correlations' approach identifies immigration effects by comparing changes in wages across local labour markets with different immigrant shares. Dustmann et al. (2005) use regional-level data disaggregated by skill over time for the United Kingdom and conclude that migration had no discernible effect on the level of native wages.

However, some people have objected to this approach because of worries about the endogeneity of both immigrant and native-born location choice. Immigrants may be attracted to the best-performing local labour markets (so wages determine immigrant location rather than immigrant location determines wages). Certainly, the concentration of immigrants in London suggests that there is a positive correlation between location and local economic opportunities (though there may also be 'network effects', informational flows stemming from the presence of earlier immigrant cohorts living in the same area). However, correlations do not prove causality from one direction to the other. Similar concerns over the efficacy of this strategy have been raised because native-born workers may move in response to an inflow of immigrants. This may in turn affect local labour supplies in both source and destination areas of these secondary internal migrants and hence any impact of immigration is not confined to the local area of arrival. Recent evidence for the United Kingdom suggests that the correlation between UK-born mobility and immigrant inflows is very weak, so that this particular issue may not be of too much concern. However, the fact that immigrant inflows do appear to be correlated with local area performance does tend to reduce the usefulness of these exercises (Wadsworth 2010).

One way to deal with the endogeneity of location choice is to look at the consequence of policy-driven (exogenous) residential location of immigrants caused, for example, by allocations of refugees across areas. However, such interventions are rare. One alternative is to proxy current immigration levels using the pattern of previous settlements (instrumentation). The idea is that past immigration is correlated with current immigration location decisions and, hopefully, uncorrelated with current local area performance. While this is possible, concerns remain over this strategy since previous residential choice may have been correlated with economic performance in the past and local area economic performance appears to be quite persistent over time.

Consequently, recent attention has shifted towards a more aggregated economy approach. This involves dividing the working population into subgroups, disaggregated according to a combination of age, skill, and year of observation rather than disaggregated by region. The idea is that it is hard to choose age and gender and, more contentiously, skill than it is to choose location. Given this, researchers look to see if differences in the shares of immigrants across cells are associated with differences in wages. This reduces any local labour market endogeneity concerns but has, in the past, assumed that immigrants are perfect substitutes for natives within a cell (so that everyone does much the same job within a given age/skill cell). Borjas (2003) adopts this approach for the United States and finds small, negative effects of immigration on wages and employment.

However, just as skilled and unskilled labour may not be able to do the same tasks, there are reasons to think that because of factors like barriers to immigrants with overseas qualifications practising in certain occupations, barriers caused by lack of fluency in English, or the time needed to adapt existing skills in a new country—immigrants may not always be able to do the same job that they held in the source country on arrival and this reduces the labour supply pressure on native-born individuals. This means that, if true, then any supply pressures on wages and employment of the UK-born will be reduced if any newcomers are imperfect substitutes.

Work by Manacorda et al. (2010) does suggest that, on average, immigrants and UK-born workers may well be imperfect substitutes in the United Kingdom.[5] If so then the effects of rising labour supply caused by immigration may be felt by groups considered the closer substitutes for migrants, namely earlier cohorts of migrants rather than by UK-born workers. There may well be some differences around this average, so that the degree of substitution may be greater among the less skilled than among the skilled. This is consistent with recent work by Dustmann et al. (2008) and Nickell and Salaheen (2008) who also find that competition for jobs may be greater among the less skilled. Some evidence supportive of this is given in Table 3.3, which outlines the percentage shares of immigrants and UK-born workers in different occupations conditional on the level of education.

The majority of certain immigrant groups are concentrated in certain unskilled jobs, despite being more highly qualified, on average, than UK-born workers. This is particularly noticeable for immigrants educated to degree level. So this may help explain why there could be more pressure in less skilled jobs.

Table 3.3. Occupation, Immigrant Status, and Education

	% in each occupation						
	Manager/ professional	Associate professional	Administrator	Skilled manual	Personal services	Sales	Elementary
Secondary							
UK-born	20.9	13.2	13.1	13.6	10.1	7.6	21.5
A8 EU accession	3.4	2.7	4.4	17.7	5.8	3.1	63.0
Other immigrants	20.0	13.5	10.3	10.5	10.4	7.7	27.6
University UK-born	60.6	21.1	7.2	2.9	3.0	2.5	2.8
A8 EU accession	13.2	6.9	6.4	10.7	8.8	4.0	49.9
Other immigrants	49.8	19.6	7.6	3.3	5.8	4.2	9.6

Source: LFS.

3.5. **Conclusion**

On balance the evidence for the UK labour market, suggests that, as with the minimum wage, fears over the consequences of rising immigration have been greatly exaggerated. It is hard to find evidence of much displacement of incumbent workers or lower wages, on average. The labour market appears to have absorbed the increase in population, much as it absorbed earlier similar-sized increases caused by the baby boom. This is however, only an average effect, averaged over different groups and different time periods and there do seem to be variations around this average. As ever, the less skilled may have experienced greater downward pressure on wages and greater competition for jobs than others, but these effects still appear to have been relatively modest. Since these effects are averaged across good and bad times we know less about the effects in downturns and there is a need to look at these effects in more detail. We also need to understand more about how both capital supply and sectoral shifts in demand respond to immigration over the medium and longer term. Future migration trends will, as ever, depend on relative economic performance and opportunity but we still need to know more about the effects of rising immigration beyond the labour market in areas like prices, consumption, housing, health, crime, and welfare. The list of unknowns and undones is still large, but increasingly we have the analytical tools and data to allow us to investigate this.

☐ NOTES

1. See for example ONS (2010), http://www.statistics.gov.uk/pdfdir/mig0510.pdf
2. Students, migrants from the EU, and migrants arriving for reasons of family reunion are the principal migrant blocks, the shares of which in the annual inflow are broadly equal; see for example Home Office Control of Immigrations Statistics, http://rds.homeoffice.gov.uk/rds/pdfs10/immiq110.pdf
3. The median age of the UK-born population of working age is 41, the median age of UK immigrants is 36; source: Labour Force Survey (2010). Among the population under 40, 41 per cent of UK-born and 18 per cent of immigrants left school at 16.
4. The coefficient of variation in the immigrant share of the population across eighteen regions fell from 0.86 in 1985 to 0.75 in 2009 (according to the LFS).
5. Work by Ottaviano and Peri (2006) suggests a similar effect is present in the United States.

☐ REFERENCES

Borjas, G. (2003) 'The Labour Demand Curve is Downward Sloping: Re-examining the Impact of Immigration on the Labour Market', *Quarterly Journal of Economics*, 118, 1335–74.

Dustmann, C., Fabbri, F., and Preston, I. (2005) 'The Impact of Immigration on the UK Labour Market', *Economic Journal*, 115, F324–41.

—— Frattini, T., and Preston, I. (2008) 'The Effect of Immigration Along the Distribution of Wages', *CREAM Discussion Paper*, No. 03/08.

MAC (2008) *Skilled Shortage, Sensible*, Migration Advisory Committee, London: Home Office.

Manacorda, M., Manning, A., and Wadsworth, J. (2011) 'The Impact of Immigration on the Structure of Wages in Britain', *Journal of the European Economic Association* (forthcoming).

Nickell, S. and Salaheen, J. (2008) 'The Impact of Immigration on Occupational Wages: British Evidence', *Working Paper*, Oxford: Nuffield College.

OECD (2009) *International Migration Outlook*, Paris: OECD.

ONS (2010) *Migration Statistics Quarterly Report*, No. 5, May.

Ottaviano, G. and Peri, G. (2006) 'Rethinking the Effects of Immigration on Wages', *NBER Working Paper* No. 12497.

Wadsworth, J. (2010) 'The UK Labour Market and Immigration', *National Institute of Economic Review*, July 2010, R35–51.

4 Migration and its Impact on Housing Costs

CHRISTINE M.E. WHITEHEAD[1]

4.1. The problem

The high levels of net immigration into the United Kingdom have been a matter of political concern over the last few years. At their peak in 2004, net immigration numbers were running at almost a quarter of a million each year and even in 2009 they were not far short of 150,000 (ONS 2010). In the election campaign of 2010, the major parties took very different positions: the Labour Party argued that their current policy had brought the numbers under control through the points system, which limits immigration from outside Europe to those with skills that are in short supply; the Conservatives on the other hand stated that current levels of net immigration were unsustainable and that non-European migration should be capped; while the Liberal Democrats, taking a very different line, called for an amnesty for illegal migrants already established in the country.

Much of the debate has been simply about the impact that continuing immigration will have on population numbers, with the latest government estimates suggesting that the UK population could reach 70 million by 2031 significantly as a result of immigration and the age structure of new entrants (ONS 2009). A second strand of the debate has concentrated on the potential cost of further immigration in terms of welfare support, while a third has been around social integration and cohesion. Throughout, the core of the argument has been on the need for constraint, based on the implicit assumption that net immigration will generate more costs than benefits to the economy, society, and the public purse.

Housing has been a central part of all three arguments: increased population and household growth means more housing is required, resulting in higher house prices, overcrowding, and the loss of green space. The provision of social housing and income-related housing allowances are large elements in welfare costs. And a major tension in the context of social integration is competition for scarce housing, especially social housing. This aspect was particularly stressed in the pre-election debates, for instance in the British National Party manifesto.

The rapid rise in net immigration, especially in the early part of the decade, has undoubtedly added to the pressures on the housing system in a number of distinct ways:

- any net increase in the number of households as a result of immigration involves more demand for housing and helps raise prices, particularly because of the inelastic supply of new housing in the United Kingdom (Barker 2003);
- refugees have immediate access to government housing support and therefore increase public expenditure and the need for social housing;
- even though initially most non-European migrant households have no right to housing assistance, over time they may become eligible, depending upon their immigration status, incomes, and household circumstances;
- migrants tend to settle in areas where housing is particularly constrained, so their demands impact directly and negatively on the housing available to the local population. This in turn can adversely affect social cohesion and integration.

Estimates of the net economic benefits of immigration suggest that housing costs are a significant element in determining the extent to which immigration has a positive effect on government finances, as well as on gross domestic product (GDP), the most usual measure of welfare. An important example of this concern is the report of a Select Committee of the House of Lords on 'The Economic Impact of Immigration', which argued that the positive GDP per capita impacts were at best small (House of Lords 2008a: ch. 6, para. 171). Moreover, according to the evidence presented to the committee by the National Housing and Planning Advisory Unit (NHPAU), maintaining net rates at 2008 levels for twenty years would increase real house prices by 13 per cent as compared to a zero net migration scenario. This in turn would impact negatively on wage rates and ultimately on UK competitiveness.

The Committee noted particular concerns about the potential effect on social housing requirements; the increased pressure on the existing stock and on infrastructure; and wider welfare and environmental issues arising both from meeting migrant housing needs and the concentration of the migrant population in London and the South East. Their conclusions suggested that housing was the key issue in determining whether migration would continue to be a net gain to the economy.

This view that housing is the key issue is strongly supported by other commentators. For instance, Migration Watch stated 'We will have to build a home every six minutes, day and night, to house the new arrivals . . . two thirds of them will settle in London and the South East, which is already the most congested part of England . . . and there is also the question of who will pay for this' (Green 2009).

In order to assess the importance of housing in the debate on the value of immigration and its impacts on public resources and social cohesion, it is necessary

- to have a much clearer idea of the scale of the additional housing requirements that are specific to immigration;
- to clarify the extent to which these demands necessarily put an additional burden on government resources; and
- to understand how competition for housing impacts on local services and communities.

These issues are not straightforward, in part because of the deficiencies in the available data; in part because the behaviour of the unprecedented numbers of migrants from the turn of the century may well be somewhat different from earlier waves therefore impacting on housing differently; and in part because information about migrant housing circumstances in general (as opposed to particular problems such as street homelessness among migrants from the European accession (known as A8) countries) is relatively limited. More fundamentally, evidence on the impact of migration is often muddled with that relating to both race and ethnicity on which housing data are more readily available. To address these issues requires something of a jigsaw mentality—pulling together data from many different sources to build up an overall picture of the impact of migration on housing.

In this chapter we concentrate on four elements of the jigsaw—the numbers of migrant households; how much housing they consume; their eligibility for government support; and the potential effect on social cohesion. Section 2 examines the government's own figures on the extent to which the numbers of new homes required in England is affected by net immigration. We suggest that, even assuming the basic migration figures are correct, the numbers of additional households—and therefore the numbers of homes required—are significantly overestimated. Section 3 looks at some evidence on the relative consumption of housing by migrants and UK-born households, which suggests that, at least in the early years, migrants consume less housing than the equivalent UK-born population. In Section 4 the potential impact on social housing requirements and other forms of housing support is addressed. Here the important questions relate to when migrant households obtain similar welfare rights to those available to UK citizens, how much they can be expected to earn, and therefore whether and for how long they might receive housing assistance. In Section 5, we address the issue of social cohesion and integration and bring together indicative material on the extent to which competition for scarce housing resources impacts on local communities and local public sector costs. In the final section, we bring the jigsaw together to ask whether commentators are right to place housing at the centre of the debate about immigration; whether the potentially negative impacts might be alleviated; and how housing policy might be modified to improve conditions for migrant and UK-born households alike.

4.2. Migration, population, and housing formation

Much of the debate about the potential costs of migration on housing is based on government figures of population and households provided by the Office for National Statistics (ONS) and the Department of Communities and Local Government (DCLG). These are not forecasts but projections based on past trends and assumptions as indeed are the housing requirement figures which are developed from these estimates (NHPAU 2009).

In 2009, the new 2006-based household projections, and covering the period to 2031, suggested that the increase in the number of households in England would be of the order of 260,000 per annum (DCLG 2009b). Comparison with a household estimate derived from the ONS zero net migration population suggests that almost 40 per cent of this increase might be attributable to migration. These figures were very much higher than the earlier 2004-based projections which were for around 225,000 additional households per annum with net international migration accounting for around a third of that growth (House of Lords 2008b).

These projections suggest that (*a*) migration is an immensely important part of the expected growth in the number of households and (*b*) the figures are extremely sensitive to assumptions. Indeed, on a high migration variant of population growth, which is still well below the levels of immigration observed in the mid decade, the total number of additional households would be over 285,000 per annum (DCLG 2009b). In this context it should be stressed that these projections form the basis for government targets for both required new building overall and for affordable housing in particular (NHPAU 2009). They are therefore core to housing policy.[2]

How well-based are these figures? There are a number of reasons for doubting their accuracy, most of which suggest that the projected increases in population, in household numbers, and therefore the need for additional housing may each have been overestimated.

The three main reasons why population is projected to grow so fast are increasing longevity, higher fertility, and more immigration. The first is, as yet, very little affected by migration. The second arises in part from the growth in the number of females of child-bearing age which is directly related to migration. The third is based on past trends except that migration from accession countries is presumed to balance by 2014–15. This last is clearly the least easy to estimate, given variations in migration especially over the last decade. Indeed, the net flow from the A8 accession countries has already been reversed in 2008–9 (ONS 2010). Actual levels can be expected to vary in relation to relative economic conditions in the United Kingdom as compared to the migrants' home country, including prevailing exchange rates.

The second great uncertainty relates to non-European migration rates. Since the very large increases around the turn of the century, the policy with respect to refugees has been tightened and the points system for economic migrants has been introduced (Home Office 2008; Gordon et al. 2009). Both of these policy changes can be expected to reduce net immigration. So while population projections already include smoothing, the chances are that current estimates are too high because of structural changes in policy.

Population projections are then transposed into household numbers using existing trends in average headship rates by age, gender, and household composition.[3] Most importantly, a migrant with similar attributes is assumed to have the same probability of forming a separate household as the equivalent indigenous person. In particular, no account is taken of how long a migrant has been in the country.

The evidence suggests that these assumptions are over-simplistic. Analysis by Holmans and Whitehead (2008) shows that, on average, those born outside the United Kingdom form significantly fewer households than the equivalent indigenous population for at least the first ten years. Table 4.1 shows that, among the population born outside the United Kingdom, those in age groups between 25 and 44—the core migrant group—are around 7 per cent less likely to form a separate household in the first five years that they are in the country and this lower rate persists for at least a further five years. An analysis of the 2008 Labour Force Survey (LFS) by Ian Gordon also suggests that the observed lower headship rates are concentrated among migrants from poorer countries and that headship rates for this group appear initially to be

Table 4.1. Headship Rates by Age and Length of Time in England, 2002–5 (%)

	Age				
	16–24	25–29	30–44	45–64	65 and over
Born outside the United Kingdom					
Entered UK less than five years ago	23.8	37.9	49.1	57.8	29.4
Entered UK five but less than ten years ago	19.6	43.3	52.9	57.9	43.6
Entered UK ten but less than twenty years ago	10.5	45.9	55.6	60.5	50.5
Entered UK twenty years or more ago	23.5	41.4	58.1	60.0	69.8
Born in the United Kingdom	13.7	45.9	57.3	59.1	70.5
Whole private household population	13.7	43.5	56.3	59.0	70.1

Source: Holmans and Whitehead (2008).

as much as one-third lower than average and do not converge with those for the indigenous population for about twenty years.

The ONS assumption further implies that the household formation behaviour of migrants coming into the country is no different from that of those leaving the country. This generates a further upward bias to household estimates because the dynamics of household formation mean that new migrants in fact form fewer households than those leaving (Holmans and Whitehead 2008). Turnover therefore matters. Calculations using the ratios in Table 4.1 and the 2006-based population projections indicate that the upward bias from assuming immigrants have the same propensity to form households as the UK-born population is about 30,000 a year (Holmans and Whitehead 2008). More complex estimates would take greater account of exactly how long different population groups stay in the country. The greater the propensity to leave after a relatively short period, the greater the reduction in households formed from a given migrant population.

A big question here is how good is the information on who goes home? These data come from the International Passenger Survey, a very small survey with very little information on each migrant. The lack of robust data is a major source of uncertainty not only about the total number but also about the make-up and location of the migrant population. Analysis of the LFS suggests that in the past at least 40 per cent of migrants, and maybe more, have gone home within a decade. It also shows that the group that goes home is concentrated among economic migrants from richer countries. Those from poorer countries are more likely to stay longer but, as we have already noted, tend to have lower household formation rates.

Another statistical source from which to examine who leaves is the Census Longitudinal Survey (LS). Data for the period 1991–2001 suggest that some 60 per cent of people identified as migrants in the 1991 LS sample in London were not found anywhere in England and Wales in 2001, but that proportion not found was only around 40 per cent for those located in the rest of England and Wales (Holmans, forthcoming). Overall, therefore, some 50 per cent of those identified as migrants in 1991 were not present in 2001. These numbers are subject to error and it is impossible to say how many might not have been enumerated although still present as opposed to how many may have left the country. However, the numbers are not inconsistent with those from the LFS and point to very significant turnover, which directly affects the numbers of households that can be expected to form. They also suggest that, although there may be some differential enumeration, migrants to London are more likely to leave the country more quickly. This is particularly important because while for most regions, immigration is close to the national average, in London, net immigration accounts for over two-thirds of the projected increase in households over the next decade (Holmans et al. 2008).

Taken together, the evidence on population, on turnover among the migrant population, and on differential headship rates points to at least five important conclusions which impact on housing requirements:

1. The population projections currently being made reflect past trends which may not continue because of modifications in policy and economic circumstances;
2. On average, migrants do not make the same demands on the housing system in terms of household formation as equivalent individuals born in the United Kingdom for at least a decade;
3. The extent and make-up of outmigration is particularly important in determining what demands are actually made—the shorter the period that migrants stay, the lower the numbers of households from a given population;
4. Households from richer countries which can be expected to make larger demands on market housing tend to stay for shorter periods while those from poorer countries who take longer to form households tend to stay longer; and
5. Where migrants live also differentially affects demand. Here, the most important distinction is between London and the rest of the country. However, there are also important differential impacts with respect to other regions. For instance, in the West Midlands, although the proportions of migrants are far less, those that come tend to be from poorer countries and probably stay longer.

4.3. Migrants' housing consumption

The government's estimates of housing requirements have taken into account both the demographic projections and economic factors to assess the numbers of additional dwellings necessary to meet the projected demand and to ensure that, at the least, affordability does not worsen (NHPAU 2009). These estimates are based on average behaviour of different types of household in terms of their housing consumption and tenure. The analysis above has made it clear that the projected number of additional households arising from migration has almost certainly been overestimated. But housing demand is not just about the number of units required. It is about how the existing stock is used, whether dwellings are shared, or whether one household lives concealed within another. In this context there is mainly indirect, but persuasive, evidence that migrant households live at higher densities than equivalent UK-born households and therefore consume less housing per household.

To examine this question, we look at two important attributes which tend to differ between migrants and the UK-born: income distribution and tenure. We additionally make a distinction between migrants from rich countries who tend to be higher up the income scale and those from poorer countries (including in particular countries from which asylum seekers tend to be drawn—see Gordon et al. (2007) for more details).

First, Table 4.2 shows that the income distribution of migrants, especially relatively new migrants, is very different from that of UK-born workers. Those from richer countries tend to be better off than the indigenous population but those from poor countries are significantly worse off, even though other evidence shows that they are likely to be relatively better educated (Gordon et al. 2007). For instance, over 40 per cent of those from poorer countries who have been in the country for less than three years are among the bottom 20 per cent of earners in the United Kingdom.

In terms of housing consumption, the second part of the jigsaw is the tenure choice made by migrant households.

Table 4.3 shows that relatively new migrants are far more likely to find accommodation in the private rented sector, where dwellings are smaller and densities of occupation are far higher than average. So, for instance, 82 per cent of those from poorer countries who have been in the country for less than three years are private tenants. Moreover, a large proportion of longer stay migrants, as compared to UK-born, remain in the private rented sector. This is particularly true of those from richer countries, even though this group is relatively highly paid, perhaps because they also own housing in their country of origin.

Table 4.2. Income Distribution by Type of Household and Length of Time in the Country (%)

The United Kingdom	UK-born	Migrants from poor countries		Migrants from rich countries		Total	
Quintile		<3 years	3+ years	<3 years	3+ years	<3 years	3+ years
1	18.9	40.2	25.9	15.9	14.7	34.2	19.3
2	20.5	27.5	22.0	14.9	14.7	24.4	20.4
3	19.7	11.7	15.7	9.3	14.4	11.1	19.2
4	20.6	7.0	17.4	25.9	24.6	11.7	20.5
5	20.3	13.5	19.0	33.9	31.7	18.5	20.6

London		Migrants from poor countries		Migrants from rich countries		Total	
Quintile		<3 years	3+ years	<3 years	3+ years	<3 years	3+ years
1	11.3	40.5	23.9	13.5	14.5	29.3	14.5
2	16.0	19.7	21.3	11.6	17.1	16.3	17.1
3	17.4	9.0	17.7	10.2	16.8	9.5	16.8
4	24.0	9.1	17.3	24.3	22.2	15.4	22.2
5	31.3	21.7	19.8	40.5	29.3	29.5	29.3

Source: LFS (2009).

Table 4.3. Tenure by Type of Household and Length of Time in the Country (%)

The United Kingdom	UK-born	From poor countries		From rich countries		Total	
		<3 years	3+ years	<3 years	3+ years	<3 years	3+ years
Owner outright	18.9	2.1	11.9	2.1	12.4	2.1	18.0
Owned with mortgage	53.0	6.7	36.9	10.1	45.6	7.5	51.3
Social rented	15.1	9.0	20.6	3.5	10.6	7.7	15.5
Private rent	13.1	82.2	30.6	84.4	31.4	82.7	15.2

London		From poor countries		From rich countries		Total	
		<3 years	3+ years	<3 years	3+ years	<3 years	3+ years
Owner outright	17.1	1.7	8.5	0.4	10.2	1.3	14.0
Owned with mortgage	46.0	7.6	30.5	8.1	37.1	7.8	40.7
Social rented	20.5	11.9	29.6	4.1	11.4	9.1	22.5
Private rent	16.4	78.8	31.4	87.4	41.3	81.9	22.8

Source: LFS (2009).

Longitudinal evidence supports the continued importance of private renting. Over each ten-year period that can be analysed from 1971–81, 1981–91, and 1991–2001, although the majority of those who were in private renting had moved into owner-occupation, the proportions remaining in the private rented sector, or moving into it, were very much higher than for those born in the United Kingdom. This suggests very strongly that, although there is undoubtedly a proportion of richer migrants who consume as much or more housing than native-born households, on average, consumption of housing will be considerably less. As a result housing is used more effectively because densities of occupation are higher. This is particularly true in London, where densities have increased significantly over the last decade.

A further element in the jigsaw relates to sharing and concealed households and housing quality. Here there is only limited survey evidence available since the Census 2001, and much of this relates to ethnicity rather than to migration. Even so there is strong evidence that newly arriving migrants are far more likely than others to live within or share with another household, often a family member. Equally many students, who make up an important element in newly arriving migrants, share accommodation or live in hostels. In particular, there is evidence that migrants are disproportionately to be found in Houses in Multiple Occupation which are subject to specific regulation because of issues associated with poor standards and unsafe accommodation (DCLG 2008).

Taken together, these elements suggest that, like for like, the vast majority of newly arriving migrant households almost certainly consume considerably less housing than the equivalent UK-born household even after accounting for their lower household formation. Taking numbers and density of occupation together, the overall impact on demand depends crucially not just on the numbers of migrants but also on how long migrants stay in the country. Even those who have higher incomes are likely to consume less housing than UK-born households, at least to begin with. The majority of those from poorer countries consume far less housing when they first arrive but they do, on average, stay longer so that ultimately their demands are similar to indigenous households.

To the extent that additional migrants do increase market demand, the most immediate question is the impact of that demand on house prices and rents. NHPAU's estimate, given in evidence to the House of Lords' Select Committee, suggested an additional price increase of around one-half of 1 per cent per annum if 2008 levels of net immigration were maintained (House of Lords 2008a: para. 172). This would be modified downwards if the adjustments discussed above were taken into account—but the effect would still be significant. The impact on private rents has been addressed in less detail. Figure 4.1 suggests that private rents have not risen greatly since 2000 at the lower end of the market, even in London where the pressures have been

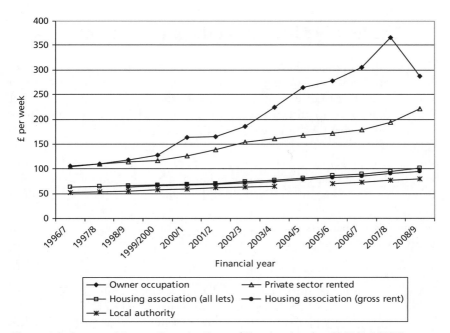

Figure 4.1. Rents and Owner-Occupier Costs of Housing, London 1996/7–2008/9
Source: Dataspring.

greatest. This is partly because the supply of private rented accommodation has been able to expand quite rapidly in response to increased demand. But it also almost certainly reflects a decline in the quantity and quality of what is being consumed, as densities of occupation have risen.

This analysis does not detract from the argument that housing is an important element in estimating the net benefits of migration. Rather there is an undoubted cost associated with increased demand, higher prices, and less availability. But this cost is less than is often suggested and less than for an equivalent UK-born household. So the relevant question in terms of value to the economy comes back to whether migrant workers are making an additional contribution to the productive economy rather than simply substituting for local workers (Wadsworth, Chapter 3 of this volume). The review of the evidence on the impact on the economy and public finances undertaken by LSE for the Greater London Authority which concentrated on irregular migrants suggested that there were indeed positive benefits to both the economy as a whole and to the public purse although these were reduced in the long term by the costs of housing lower-income households (Gordon et al. 2009).

4.4. **The housing impact on the public purse**

The most direct potentially negative impact of long-term immigration lies in the potential costs of housing support which is provided in the form of income-related assistance[4] and access to subsidized social housing. Here it is important to distinguish between refugees and asylum seekers and those who come to work. Asylum seekers, if they are accepted as refugees, have rights to housing assistance immediately. This will nowadays normally be provided by the National Asylum Support Service (NASS) and will, initially, be in the form of relatively cheap rented housing outside London. Those who do not ask for assistance often live with friends and family. Once given indefinite leave to remain these households have immediate rights to access income-related benefits and social housing in the same way as a UK-born citizen. An unknown proportion of accepted refugees will require long-term housing assistance depending on how easy they find it to obtain reasonably paid work.

Migrants from the European Union have the same rights as UK citizens, except that those from accession countries must not make any charge on the public purse for the first year. Those coming from outside Europe have no rights to public assistance at all until they receive unlimited right to remain, or become citizens. In the context of housing this means they have no access to income-related benefits or to local authority owned housing. Housing Associations may let to such households, but will generally not do so because of the lack of Housing Benefit.

Government statistics suggest that perhaps 6 per cent of mainstream lettings to new social housing tenants in England went to foreign nationals in 2006–7. They also suggest that most of those who were housed were either the spouses or children of UK nationals or had been living in the United Kingdom for a number of years. There is almost no instance of economic migrants gaining access to social housing, until they are fully established as citizens (DCLG 2008).

While these limits on eligibility constrain the cost to the public purse as compared to equivalent UK-born households until migrants gain unlimited right to remain, a more fundamental question is whether those who do remain and gain these rights will require housing assistance.[5]

The evidence on tenure presented in Table 4.3 suggests that a significant proportion of those coming from poorer countries are able to access social rented housing, especially in London. Indeed, for those who have been in England for three or more years, almost 30 per cent of migrants identified in the LFS as living in London are in the social rented sector as compared to just over 20 per cent of UK-born individuals. This partly reflects the likelihood that such households will have children and therefore be classified as in priority need and partly the concentration of refugees in this group who move to London as they become more settled. As importantly, it reflects the extent to which these groups remain on low incomes (Table 4.2). To this extent, migrants from poorer countries, who are anyway more likely to stay in the country longer, will indeed put disproportionate additional pressure on housing assistance, particularly on social housing. Moreover, the needs of this group of poorer migrant households are expected to increase over the next decade, as more of those who entered in the 'boom' years of the late 1990s and early 2000s become eligible for assistance.

There are no up-to-date estimates of the potential costs from low-income migrant households who settle in England. One relevant estimate was that made by LSE, London, in relation to the regularization of irregular migrants. This suggested that perhaps as many as 70,000 additional social homes would be required if those already in the country irregularly achieved permanent rights to remain (Gordon et al. 2009). This is roughly equivalent to adding one year's requirement for affordable housing to current government estimates. If these social sector homes actually are provided, the costs to the public purse would be very significant indeed. If they are not provided (which is much more likely, given current building rates and public expenditure cuts), there would instead be increased competition for scarce social housing and continued local housing allowance costs associated with the higher rents in the private rented sector.

This analysis clearly raises issues about the value to the British economy of continued migration from what have been called poorer countries. In this context it should be remembered that the analysis uses 'rich' and 'poor' countries as a simplification for the relative probability that households will access low-paid jobs and remain on low incomes into the longer term. It should also be remembered that those who will need assistance, apart from refugees, cannot be directly identified and the majority of migrants from these countries will successfully obtain adequate housing and pay for it themselves either as owner-occupiers or as private tenants.

The evidence on potential housing costs to the public purse is also relevant to understanding the implications for housing demand of the points system for working migrants, the tougher rules being applied with respect to refugees and asylum seekers, and the potential impact of regularizing irregular migrants. The points system and the tougher rules mean that both the absolute numbers and the proportion of migrants from poorer countries can be expected to decline—especially if a cap on overall numbers is introduced. Regularizing irregular migrants on the other hand would increase the demand for housing in general and for lower cost and social housing in particular (Gordon et al. 2009). However, although it was part of the Liberal Democrat manifesto and is supported by the Mayor of London, it is currently not on the political horizon. The evidence presented here on the potentially high housing costs of additional migration thus, in many ways, reflects the legacy of the very high levels of immigration of the late 1990s and early 2000s rather than any likely future scenario.

4.5. **Migrant housing and social cohesion**

The increase in net immigration over the last decade is perceived to have had adverse effects on social cohesion and integration, particularly in areas where the pace of change has been rapid and the results have been high concentrations of migrant households.

Housing, particularly social housing, is understandably a focus for concern, especially with respect to whether people are being treated equitably. Moreover, there is a strong historical basis for those living in the community to regard residential qualifications as a reasonable basis for the allocation of social housing. Local authorities often support this view. Since 1997, waiting lists for social housing have risen by 80 per cent in the country as a whole and by 100 per cent in London (DCLG, Housing live table 600)—so it is not at all surprising that this is an area of particular concern.

Much of the discussion on these negative impacts does not distinguish carefully between different sources of tension including those relating to transience, to inter-area mobility, to ethnicity, to race, to international migration, and to more general issues of culture, religion, and language (Travers et al. 2007). In particular, most of the data relating to migration does not differentiate between new migrants and those who have been settled in the country for many years. Equally the data on social problems often relates more to ethnicity and the concentrations of particular racial groups, even if they (and indeed their parents) were born in the United Kingdom, rather than specifically to migrants.

Survey evidence suggests that the vast majority of people feel that they get along with each other in their local area even if they come from very different backgrounds. It also suggests that that proportion is increasing. On the other hand, the proportion of adults mentioning immigration and race relations as their most important concern has risen from less than 5 per cent in 1997 (DCLG 2009a) to over 40 per cent in 2008 (Ipso Mori, quoted in House of Lords 2008b). There is also evidence that competition for social housing is seen as one of the most important areas of tension between established households and new entrants. This is reflected in general perceptions, against the statistical evidence, that large numbers of non-UK nationals jump the queue for social housing. One example of this is in Barking, where the statistics suggest that hardly any foreign nationals have been allocated social housing over the last few years but where the issue has been the subject of continued political tension. In this context, for instance, Margaret Hodge MP for Barking has suggested that established British families should be given priority over migrant households (Hodge 2007).

More qualitative surveys also point to the importance of competition for social housing in generating tension (Robinson and Reeve 2006; Markova and Black 2007; Chartered Institute of Housing 2008). However, these surveys also suggest that the concern may be more about 'incomers'—whether from the next locality or from overseas—rather than about international migrants as such (Travers et al. 2007).

An issue of particular importance is that of access to family housing. There is a growing problem of overcrowding in the social rented sector, especially in London, and very small numbers of larger houses are built or come free for reletting. In this context even a small number of such units being let to migrant households can cause tension—especially as many people do not distinguish between ethnicity and nationality.

Overall, there is no doubt that the shortage of housing, especially social housing, is a source of tension in many localities. Equally many people blame migration for exacerbating the obvious problems. Yet the statistical evidence on social housing allocations does not support this view. Moreover, economic migrants generally put far less pressure on the housing system than the equivalent UK-born population and this is true not only for housing but for other local services (Gordon et al. 2009).

4.6. Implications

The evidence presented here suggests that housing should indeed be an important element in assessing the net benefits of migration. However, it also suggests that the costs may have been overestimated and that migrants generally use the existing stock more effectively than the indigenous population. The core issue with respect to whether migration benefits the economy therefore remains that of additionality, because migrants who help fill gaps in the labour market also generally do so at lower than average housing costs.

In the current economic environment it is likely that, whatever government policy, net immigration will fall. Even so, there are structural reasons to expect a continuing significant inflow over the medium to longer term (Gordon et al. 2007).

Whatever the level of net immigration, the impact on housing requirements is almost certainly less than suggested from government projections of the number of households and the need for affordable housing. Even so the longer term impact of migration by lower income households on government housing costs is likely to be significant. Moreover, there are real social and resource costs, particularly to local communities which experience rapid change, that must be addressed. More generally, migration, like any other increase in demand, also impacts on house prices because of the extreme inelasticity of new supply. The most likely outcome of higher levels of migration is therefore higher house prices, higher densities—and greater costs to government for achieving adequate standard housing for all. Thus, even those migrants who pay their own housing costs have negative impacts on other households.

The fundamentals that make the impact on housing so important are thus:

- inelasticity of supply;
- the high public cost of adding to the social housing stock; and
- the structure of income-related housing benefits.

These are issues that must anyway be addressed if the overall housing system is to work better. Reducing migration is seen as an easy answer, but restricting migration simply for housing-specific reasons would be highly undesirable. Government policy on migration should take account of the full range of economic and social benefits and costs, as well as our moral commitments across the world. The consequences for housing, local services, and social inclusion should be carefully measured and addressed—but not through discriminatory policies.

One issue here is the treatment of irregular migration. If, as seems almost certain, most will not be deported the case for regularization is very strong. The result would be higher productivity, a boost to public funds, and a more integrated population. It would impose additional costs on housing but only those that come from higher incomes and higher standards.

The main costs specific to immigration are the rapid changes in population that localities may have to absorb. Yet there is little evidence that forced dispersal significantly improves conditions for either migrants or established households. There is, on the other hand, evidence that it reduces the chances of refugees obtaining suitable employment when they are legally enabled to do so and this must be bad for cohesion and integration as well as productivity.

The most obvious approaches to improving the situation for migrant households are the same as for established households—making the private rented sector work more effectively to provide easy access but adequate standard housing. This would require a re-examination of regulation which currently gives no more than six months security of tenure. It would also need a more transparent and simpler regulatory structure for Houses in Multiple Occupation—something which the Coalition government is already addressing. More fundamental restructuring of the local housing allowance system, as well as of income support more generally, is also envisaged. These may make it tougher for individual households but would undoubtedly improve the relative position of migrants who have to pay their own way.

With respect to additional provision, the most obvious approach of involving employers has generally worked poorly. If it is to work better there must be more transparent contracting so that housing and wages are clearly distinguished and migrant workers have some choice as to where they live. Hostels and short-lease accommodation solutions could also be enabled more effectively—especially for those expecting to stay for relatively short and well-defined periods. This is now being better achieved in the context of student housing.

Accommodating larger migrant families, many of whom are refugees, must involve additional socially organized provision. Building large numbers of social sector dwellings is not feasible within the current financing and benefit framework, especially in London where the shortage is most acute. Nor is it likely to be the best option. Leasing from the private sector is more cost-effective. Again, however, the solution to the housing problem may well lie in increasing the opportunities for all adult members of the household to work and therefore pay their way.

The now well-established points system brings with it a reduction in lower skilled immigration from non-European countries and therefore less pressure on the lower end of the housing market and ultimately on social housing and government funds. However, immigration is not simply about filling gaps in the UK labour market. It is also about supporting an efficient export market in education; meeting our commitments to established households who originally came as migrants; playing our role in ensuring well operating and equitable asylum systems; meeting our EU commitments; and many other objectives. Adequate affordable housing is an important element in ensuring that these objectives can be achieved. In the short run there is a need to defuse the tensions associated with housing new migrants by developing a better evidence base; ensuring greater transparency about rights, responsibilities, and outcomes; and enabling the private rented sector to be more responsive. In the longer term it is about a much better operating housing system, where migrants like any other household have options which reflect the true costs and benefits to society.

☐ NOTES

1. The author wishes to thank Alan Holmans (University of Cambridge) and Ian Gordon (LSE) for their input into this chapter.
2. The new government's policy is to remove national targets. However, they will still use these projections when negotiating with local authorities (Conservative Party 2010).
3. Headship rates are defined as the proportion of a given category of the population with particular attributes (e.g. men aged 25–34) who live as separate households.
4. This includes Housing Benefit in the social sector which is based on actual rents and Local Housing Allowance in the private rented sector which relates to average rents in the area.
5. In this context it should be noted that the Labour government had moved to introduce Earned Citizenship proposals which would both clarify and strengthen the conditions that must be met before becoming eligible for assistance (Home Office 2008).

☐ REFERENCES

Barker, K. (2003) *Delivering Stability: Securing our Future Housing Need, Barker Review of Housing Supply*, Interim and Final Reports, London: HM Treasury.

Chartered Institute of Housing (2008) *Allocation of Social Housing to Recent Migrants*, Birmingham: CIH.

Department of Communities and Local Government (2008) *Managing the Impacts of Migration: A Cross Government Approach*, England: DCLG, June.

—— (2009a) *Household Projections to 2031*, England Housing Statistical Release 11, England: DCLG, March.

—— (2009b) *Citizenship Survey: April 2008–March 2009*, England: DCLG, July.

Gordon, I., Travers, T., and Whitehead, C. (2007) *The Impact of Recent Immigration on the London Economy*, Corporation of London.

—— Scanlon, K., Travers, T., and Whitehead, C. (2009) *Economic Impact on the London and UK Economy of an Earned Regularisation of Irregular Migrants to the UK*, London: LSE.

Green, Sir Andrew (2009) 'We must Halt this Conspiracy of Silence over our Immigration Crisis', *Daily Mail*, 22 October 2009.

Hodge, M. (2007) 'A Message to My Fellow Immigrants', *Observer*, 20 May 2007.

Holmans, A. (forthcoming) *Immigrants to London from Outside the United Kingdom: Their Housing and Subsequent Moves*, Cambridge: Cambridge Centre for Housing and Planning Research (CCHPR).

—— and Whitehead, C. (2008) 'New and Higher Projections of Future Population in England—A First Look at their Implications for Households and Housing', *Town and Country Planning Tomorrow Series Paper 10*, September 2008.

—— Monk, S., and Whitehead, C. (2008) *Homes for the Future: A New Analysis Technical Report*, Cambridge: CCHPR.

Home Office (2008) *The Path to Citizenship: Next Steps in Reforming the Immigration System*, London: Home Office.

House of Lords (2008a) *The Economic Impact of Immigration, 1st Report of Session 2007–08*, Vol. 1, HL 82.1, April.

—— (2008b) 'The Economic Impact of Immigration, The Government's Reply to the First Report from the House of Lords Committee on Economic Affairs Session 2007–08', *HL Paper 82*, June.

Markova, E. and Black, R. (2007) *East European Immigration and Community Cohesion*, York: JRF.

NHPAU (2009) *More Homes for More People: Advice to Ministers on Housing Levels to be Considered in Regional Plans*, National Housing and Planning Advice Unit (NHPAU).

ONS (2009) *National 2008-based Population Projections*, Office for National Statistics (ONS).

—— (2010) *Migration Statistics Quarterly Report*, No. 4, February 2010 and No. 5, May 2010 (ONS).

Robinson, D. and Reeve, K. (2006) *Neighbourhood Experiences of New Immigration: Reflections from the Evidence Base*, York: JRF.

Ruth, J. and Latore, M. (2009) *Social Housing Allocation and Immigrant Communities*, Research Report 4, London: Equalitiy and Human Rights Commission.

Shelter (2009) *Homes for the Future: A New Analysis of Housing Need and Demand in England: An Update*, Research Report, London: Shelter.

Travers, T., Tunstall, R., Whitehead, C., and Provot, S. (2007) *Population Mobility and Service Provision*, London: London Councils.

Wadsworth (2010) *Immigration and the UK Labour Market*, Chapter 3 in this volume.

5 Job Guarantees for the Unemployed: Evidence and Design

PAUL GREGG

5.1. Introduction

As part of the 2009 budget, the Chancellor announced plans for a job guarantee for the young unemployed, under the dual pseudonyms of the Young Persons Guarantee and Backing Young Britain. The core proposal was for an offer of six months full-time activity for all those reaching six months unemployment on the Job Seeker's Allowance (JSA) and aged 18–24 years old. This offer would become mandatory after nine months of claiming JSA. The full-time activity will cover a number of options. There were to be two main options and two less common ones. First, Sectoral Routes would offer young people training in specific employment growth sectors with active employer engagement. The major sectors were in hospitality and care. The second major element was the Future Jobs Fund. Here employers and charitable organizations bid for the provision of six-month part-time jobs. These pay the minimum wage but these costs are entirely met by the government. The providers do not bid with cash but with evidence of the potential benefit to the participant in improving employment prospects. These types of positions are sometimes called transitional jobs and will be assessed later. The other elements that were less widely used were regular apprenticeships where it is hard to increase the numbers of places with employers and finally a Community Taskforce. The incoming government elected in June 2010 has announced that the Future Jobs Fund will not recruit any new placements and hence, whilst existing placements will proceed, this element of the Young Persons Guarantee has been stopped. However, the government has intimated that the Guarantee will remain in place and will commence at six months duration on JSA. The scheme will thus make more use of Sectoral Routes and apprenticeships and the Community Taskforce.

There is now much evidence highlighting how long-term unemployment leads to lifetime scarring effects of lower wages, frequent joblessness, and poor health, which I will briefly summarize below. This provides much of the motivation for such programmes and there have been many over the years. It is crucial that the current initiative learns as much as possible from past failures as well as the moderate successes. This chapter discusses the evidence whether active labour market policies which include training and work experience are successful, and draws out some lessons for the design of Job Guarantees.

5.2. THE CASE FOR ACTION

Britain has just experienced the worst recession since the Second World War and the full effects of this on the economy may not have yet been felt. Despite the depth of the recession the impact on the labour market has produced a number of surprises given previous patterns. In both of the recessions in the early 1980s and 1990s, around 6 per cent of all jobs were lost before employment levels turned the corner (see Figure 5.1). Furthermore, the job loss continued for two years or so after the recovery in output started—some thirteen or fourteen quarters after the onset of recession.

In this recession the scale of employment loss has been just over 2 per cent and employment stabilized in the summer of 2009, before the fall in output

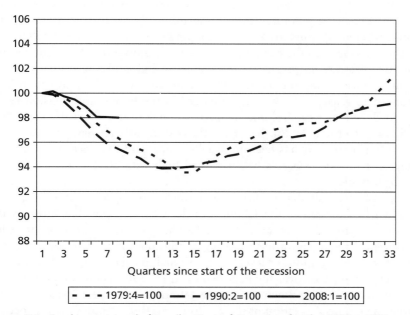

Figure 5.1. Employment Levels from the Start of Recession for the 1980s, 1990s, and 2008/9 Recessions

Source: ONS.

had been completed. This is most extraordinary and does not appear to reflect greater labour market flexibility as there are no signs of extra adjustment in wages or hours worked compared with previous recessions. Nor is the pattern shared by the United States which is commonly seen as the most flexible labour market (see chapter 2 by Nickell in this volume). This extraordinary performance appears to rest on three main pillars; the first is that profitability going into this recession was very high. Firms do not engage in drastic workforce reductions in the teeth of the recession unless they fear the company will go under or, of course, if the company does indeed go bankrupt. The high levels of profitability gave some protection from this emergency job cutting. Furthermore, profitability has held up surprisingly well through the recession with the bulk of the fall in GDP coming in the form of declines in government revenues rather than profits, with the profit share of GDP actually rising, although small businesses and the self-employed have suffered. The fiscal stimulus package through 2009 and keeping the banks afloat through the crisis has been costly but clearly has made a large contribution to saving jobs. Finally, the sharp fall in nominal interest rates has made the cost of servicing existing debt low but the ability to secure extra credit for investment and so on has been squeezed severely. This has knocked on heavily to investment but the upshot is that firms have not been as cash strapped as might have been the case. Finally, firms in past recessions widely used early retirement as a less painful form of job shedding. This is usually voluntary and workers get good compensation for stopping work, so it creates less ill feeling in the workforce. In the past, if a company's pension fund was in good shape the full cost was not borne by the company and could be passed into the future pension funding needs. The rules around early retirement have changed to make the costs fully apparent in the books, and pension funds are in deficit or have become defined by contributions to each individual rather than a fund. All this has made the cost of early retirement greater and more transparent. It has been unusually marked in this recession that employment of older workers has remained high with all the falls focused on younger workers.

As staff are valuable to firms, with their firm specific knowledge and productive experience, the labour is held wherever possible through the recession, with firms preferring to take shorter term hit on profitability. However, if the medium-term trading conditions continue to look difficult, then firms engage in lower level but continued job shedding to align staffing with expected needs over the next two or three years. There remains the risk that firms will revise down these expectations in the face of weak demand, given the financial position of the government, thus creating the prospect of a sustained period of flat or gradually falling employment over the next two years or so.

The overall picture for employment has been surprisingly good but whilst job shedding has been less common than before, firms have still frozen recruitment and those trying to enter the labour market, especially the young, are facing a bleak prospect. The extent to which employment loss has fallen on the young has been incredibly stark. For a long while now more young people have been staying on at school after the age of 16 and also more are going through to higher education. By 2007, 76 per cent of 16–17 year olds and around 28 per cent of 18–24 year olds were in full-time education, and one consequence of the recession has been a sharp increase in young people staying on in education, and so in autumn 2009 some 82 per cent of 16–17 and 31 per cent of 18–24 year olds were in full-time education (Goujard et al. 2011). Figure 5.2 shows the employment rates for young people according to whether they are in full-time education or not. The figure makes three very important points. First, the employment rate of both groups of young people not in education has fallen by some 8 percentage points, far more than for any other age group. Second, the decline precedes the current recession which has accelerated a longer standing trend. Over this period, as already noted, this is a shrinking group as continued education has increased but the numbers involved are still large. Third, that as of early 2010, despite a lot more young people staying on in full-time education, around one in five 18–24 year olds and around one in ten 16–17 year olds is neither in work or full-time

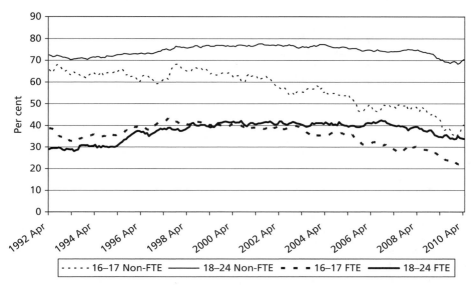

Figure 5.2. Employment Rates among Young Adults According to Whether in Full-Time Education, 1992–2009

Source: ONS.

education. Britain continues to have a very disorganized school-to-work transition, despite many initiatives in this area.

Britain has a number of birth cohorts where all children born in a short-time window are tracked for the rest of their lives. The National Child Development Survey of 1958 has tracked a group who reached 21 at the onset of the severe 1980s recession. It is thus possible to follow those who experience long periods without work from this period right through to when they are aged around 44. Studies have highlighted how those men with more than a year out of work before age 24 go on to experience massively more time out of work right through to the age of 44, receive substantially lower wages, and also suffer from poorer health (e.g. see Gregg 2001; Gregg and Tominey 2005). Studies suggest that only part of this is due to lower educational attainment or aspects of family background. Rather those experiencing extended worklessness when young suffer very long-term scars through low wages or unemployment. Table 5.1 shows this data for young men in the National Child Development Survey in 1981. It shows how just under 10 per cent of these young men experience more than a year out of work by age 23 with more than half experiencing no unemployment at all. Those with long exposure to unemployment often had more than one spell rather than being long-term unemployed for a single spell. The table shows how those with long periods of worklessness went on to spend nearly 20 per cent of their time unemployed, between the ages of 28 and 33, and another 20 per cent were

Table 5.1. The Effect of Unemployment on the Later Experience of Unemployment (National Child Development Survey Cohort Aged 23 in 1981)

	Average percentage of time spent unemployed, aged 28–33 (percentage with any unemployment)	Average percentage of time spent inactive, aged 28–33 (percentage with any inactivity)	No. in samples
Total			4064
No unemployment, aged 16–23	1.4 (7.5)	2.3 (9.6)	2382
At least 1 but <6 months unemployment, aged 16–23	2.6 (13.8)	3.7 (15.6)	916
At least 6 but <12 months unemployment, aged 16–23	5.3 (21.4)	7.1 (24.6)	411
12+ months unemployment, aged 16–23	18.5 (40.0)	22.9 (46.8)	355

inactive, that is, out of work but not seeking a job. So in total they spent 40 per cent of their time workless. Gregg (2001) suggests that around half of these scars are due to the long exposure to unemployment itself and the rest due to poor education and living in a depressed neighbourhood. The picture that emerges is of a failure to connect to stable employment and hence to jobs offering experience and training that lead to higher wages.

So the justification for intervention to prevent long or frequent periods out of work or education among young people does not rest just on current unemployment but on the long-term scars that these young people experience and potentially pass on to the next generation. These scarring effects are not confined to young people (see Gregory and Jukes 2001; or Arulampalam 2001 for the United Kingdom) but they are far more common in this age group and will affect a person for longer, as they are yet to gain much labour market experience. The evidence set out below seeks to explore the potential for support services and the relative merits of job search, training, and work experience. A key aspect is whether the tensions between early job entry and skills/experience, which have been found in many previous programmes, can be reduced when addressing youth unemployment.

5.3. **Potential benefits of a job guarantee**

The first argument for such schemes is simple common sense: if there is work needing to be done and people wanting to work, the government should organize it (if the market fails). Thus, the first benefit does *not* depend on the subsequent benefits to someone of going on the scheme, but on the *contemporaneous* benefits that someone is undertaking useful work rather than being unemployed and for people to have a wage and the satisfaction of making a contribution. The wider social benefit also relates to the effect of the scheme *before* people reach the time limit for a Guarantee. All the evidence suggests that compulsory full-time activity encourages some people to find other solutions *before* a part-time minimum-wage job becomes compulsory. The third potential benefit relates to the *subsequent* activity of people who have gone through a guaranteed job. The argument here is that work experience and full-time activity will help people get work more easily. This is perhaps the acid test for any government intervention.

The major criticisms often levelled at job-creation schemes that have been run in the past is that they have produced rather little in the way of useful output and that they have in some instances actually delayed job entry and subsequent job retention rather than enhanced it. The main aim of this chapter is to assess the evidence for these kinds of employment effects.

5.4. **Policy evidence and policy evolution**

Following the economic and employment 'shocks' of the 1970s, most OECD countries made use of temporary job creation and employment programmes. The important difference with the 'public works' programmes that character-ized the 1930s was that the new generation of programmes was usually, but not always, targeted at the long-term and young unemployed. The challenge was to provide temporary jobs but in a way that did not undermine the regular labour market, hence they were in activities not normally undertaken in the market or public sectors. Those given jobs were usually employees and would be employed at either the minimum wage or the 'going rate'. As economies recovered, attention turned to the role that these programmes played in assisting participants to obtain regular jobs, and by 1994 the OECD 'Jobs Study' pointed to an increase in evaluation evidence which was generally negative about the impact on future employment chances. David Card's recent review suggested that public job creation was among the least effective programmes in helping people's future job chances (Card et al. 2009). Sianesi (2002) concludes that 'all the programmes initially reduce their participants' employment probability in the short term' through what is called the lock-in effect, whereby people delay looking for an alternative job because they already have one, albeit often temporary. Hence Relief Work was associated with lower employment rates and more time spent claiming benefits than if the person had been unemployed and searching for regular work.

By the mid-1990s, the OECD reported that many member states were 'abolishing' or 'scaling back' public sector job-creation programmes and concluded that 'job creation in the public sector has not been successful'. This finding was reinforced by John Martin, in an influential and often cited OECD survey, where he suggested that the evaluation evidence 'showed fairly conclusively that this measure has been of little success in helping unem-ployed participants get permanent jobs' (Martin 2000).

5.5. **The reform of temporary employment programmes**

5.5.1. WORKFARE

The first wave of reforms attempted to reduce lock-in effects but in two very different ways. One direction was to reduce the comfort factor of working on temporary jobs by reducing pay below minimum-wage levels, either to the level of benefits plus a small allowance or in Workfare-type programmes, to benefit levels. For instance, in Germany, wage levels were set below the minimums available in regular jobs, and in programmes such as the French CES (Contrats Emploi Solidarité) and the British Community Programme wages were restricted by limiting the number of hours so that participants' wages were only just above benefit levels. These reductions in the 'comfort' factor often have been linked to increased requirements for groups of long-term benefit recipients to engage in employment programmes where claimants are required to work for their benefit payments. The Community Programme, Employment Action, and Project Work were UK schemes of this type.

This direction of redesign for temporary employment programmes was evident too in the implementation of 'Workfare' programmes which, in the United States, Australia, and New Zealand, eclipsed conventional temporary employment or job-creation programmes. 'Workfare' is often used as a general term to characterize a broad approach to welfare reform but originally it applied to those US programmes where mandated individuals were required to 'work off' any benefit payments received, through undertaking marginal public or community sector activities. In Australia and New Zealand, this has taken the form of 'Work for the Dole' programmes where many of the long-term unemployed have been required to fulfil their 'mutual obligation' by undertaking unpaid part-time work in the community. Evaluations show that the activity requirement can 'shake out' people from claiming benefits, some of whom will get jobs whilst others move on to other benefits such as those related to illness, but participation in the core programmes provide little or no direct employment assistance. The evaluation evidence shows that these programmes have little impact on participants' subsequent employment rates and in New Zealand, for example, a large-scale work-for-the-dole programme was terminated when econometric evidence confirmed it was 'locking' unemployed people into longer unemployment durations.

5.5.2. JOB SEARCH

The other very different approach was to emphasize job search. Participants were given more job-search assistance and job-search effort was often monitored. Providers and programme job-entry performance were also monitored and in many cases payments to providers were increasingly related to job-entry performance. The work experience (via temporary jobs) element here was usually marginal. The United States undertook a sizable number of randomized control trials of welfare-to-work policy in the 1990s. MRDC, a company that undertook most of these evaluations, in a synthesis report of twenty-nine such schemes, found that just eight were both focused on early job entry but also contained mandatory activity periods. These schemes therefore combined both major elements of work experience and job-search support and all of them led to increased job outcomes with magnitudes averaging at levels similar to the UK New Deal programmes.

5.5.3. WORK TRIALS

In the United Kingdom, one of the most successful work experience programmes has been Work Trials. Formerly part of the Job Interview Guarantee scheme (which started nationally in 1990), Work Trials became a separate national programme from April 1993. Work Trials encourage employers to take on unemployed and inactive benefit claimants for a trial period of up to three weeks. Applicants on a Work Trial continue to receive benefits and get travel and meal expenses. Overall, the evidence (which has serious limitations) suggests that Work Trials are both effective at helping people gain work and cost-effective, as the costs are very low. A previous report showed additional job-entry rates to vary between 34 and 40 per cent and the Department of Work and Pensions (DWP) believes that Work Trials was its most cost-effective programme. The problem has always been securing enough private sector job placements.

5.5.4. NEW DEAL FOR YOUNG PEOPLE

In 1995, Gordon Brown's team started working on the design of the New Deal Programme for the Unemployed. The intervention was driven by the emerging evidence of the scarring effects of long-term unemployment. But there were also two other objectives: to address the sense of abandonment and alienation that young unemployed felt, and to highlight the social waste of long-term unemployment.

The programme was designed to take on board evidence of previous poorly achieving programmes and best international practice. The first key element was a four-month period of intensive and supported job search—the Gateway period. This was followed by entrance into one of four options: a placement with an employer, self-employment start up, an education/training course, or charitable sector-led placements. There was to be 'No Fifth Option' of continued benefit receipt. The New Deal for Young People (NDYP) was built to avoid the poor results from the Community Programme and training schemes in the 1980s.

NDYP has been evaluated using a number of approaches, the most convincing being a technique known as 'regression discontinuity design', which took advantage of the fact that NDYP applied to those aged 18–24 after six months of unemployment, whereas the New Deal for those aged 25 and over

(ND25+) applied after 18 months. The small age difference between those just under or over 25 at six months duration creates a convincing comparison group for what would have happened if the scheme had not been introduced. Studies by Van Reenen (2004) and more recently De Georgi (2005) find that NDYP raised outflows into work by 5 percentage points (a 20 per cent increase) and that the costs (net of benefit payments) were more than justified by the savings. The net cost was around £4,000 per market job and this does not include any value from the activities undertaken.

The assessments of NDYP do not distinguish between the effects of the Gateway intensive search, the threat of mandation, and the impact of the different options. The impact of the options element of the package can be seen in pilots for the New Deal 25+ where for those aged 50 or over the Intensive Activity Period (IAP), which was akin to the options element for NDYP, was initially voluntary and then became compulsory in pilot areas on a random basis, before finally going compulsory nationally. Pilots ran in fourteen Jobcentre Plus districts between 2004 and 2006, and comparing the outcomes of those in areas where it was or was not compulsory provides a robust estimate of the effect of making IAP compulsory. The main findings were that the requirement to participate in the IAP caused a sustained increase in employment and, in the longer run, a similar-sized reduction in claimant unemployment. Two years after ND25+ entry, those over 50 required to participate in the IAP had an employment rate of 27.3 per cent, some 5 percentage points higher than the rate for similar people in areas where no such requirement existed (Dorsett and Smeaton 2008).

5.5.5. INTERMEDIATE LABOUR MARKETS

It was in this overall programme context that the concept of creating Intermediate Labour Markets (ILMs) emerged and was developed by local providers and partnerships in Britain. In contrast to the marginal economic activities that characterized conventional temporary employment programmes, ILMs sought to provide more realistic work experience by integrating their projects with local regeneration programmes and with initiatives that sought to stimulate job creation through an expansion of the social economy. Providers suggested that the experience of 'real work' and personal support was a more effective way of tackling the employment barriers facing the long-term unemployed. Early case studies suggested that although costs were greater, their job entry and job retention rates were also higher than those of mainstream programmes.

In the early phase, ILMs characteristically were small scale. By the mid-1990s, however, a viable network existed in Britain bringing together a range of providers sharing some key features. They:

- recruited long-term unemployed people on temporary contracts;
- paid wages to participants for at least part of their stay;
- gave access to off-the-job training and personal development activities; and
- provided assistance with job search and job placement.

They are thus a hybrid between job creation and job search focused schemes. Whilst the New Deals were also hybrids, the difference is that under the early ND schemes the job search focus came in a distinct phase before and after the placement, rather than running alongside it, thus the claimant was not required to search and providers were not incentivized to secure jobs for participants in the work-experience phase. This was especially marked in the early versions.

The most substantial and best-evaluated UK ILM project was Step Up. The Step Up pilot provided a guaranteed job and support for up to fifty weeks. It was available to those in the twenty pilot areas who remained unemployed six months after completing their New Deal Option or IAP. An independent Managing Agent sourced jobs from employers in the private, public, or voluntary sectors, and Jobcentre Plus placed participants into the jobs. Employers were paid a wage subsidy for fifty weeks of at least the minimum wage and a fee to reflect their additional costs. The subsidized job was of 33 hours a week to enable job search within a normal working week. Support to participants was provided through a Jobcentre Plus Personal Adviser, a Support Worker from the Managing Agent, and a workplace buddy.

Overall, for young people job outcomes were 3.2 per cent points higher in Step Up areas. The scheme was more successful for those aged over 25 with 6 percentage points employment gains. Step Up was only partially successfully in mixing the message of both current work and job search for the follow-on job. The report suggests that many expected to be taken by the Step Up employer which often did not come to pass. Certainly, the cost of Step Up can be greatly reduced.

5.6. **Lessons**

Following the worst recession since the Second World War, unemployment is once again a key policy issue for governments. Whilst in the United Kingdom overall unemployment has risen relatively modestly, the picture for young people is every bit as bleak as in previous recessions and so it is valuable to ask what lessons we have learnt that might address youth unemployment.

First, for young people the potential benefit of support into work is only one part of a plausible response. Encouraging continued education is a valuable, indeed crucial, additional response, especially for those aged under 20. The outgoing Labour government introduced a September Guarantee which gave a guaranteed place in education or on an apprenticeship for 16 and 17 year olds and outlined plans to raise the school-leaving age to 18 over the next five years. The imminent prospect of substantial spending cuts means that there must be serious concerns about the abolition of the Education Maintainance Allowance and the availability of places in higher education in the near future.

For programmes aimed at helping unemployed young people who have left full-time education, the discussion above gives a set of desirable design features. The first is that work replacement and short-term, low-cost training that are unconnected to specific vacancies run a serious risk of being unhelpful in aiding the move into regular employment. This is because of a lock-in effect whereby people reduce or stop regular job search whilst on the programme, which delays the chances of securing employment. This risk can be overcome with intelligent design and implementation where:

1. Training is employer-supported with employer agreement to consider programme participants favourably. This can be through guaranteed interviews, work trials, or job offers on course completion.
2. Long-term training for recognized qualifications in shortage areas—Level 3 or 4 apprenticeships fall into this area.
3. Work experience or subsidized employment with private sector employers has a proven track record.
4. Work experience or work replacement in public or charitable settings that is embedded in a setting of supported job search/matching has a good chance of success.

In the above list, elements 1, 3, and 4 all offer different ways of overcoming the lock-in effect. The first involves employers in training and secures agreements for employers to offer available vacancies to graduates of the training programme. The fourth element places people with employers who, having detailed experience of working with the individual, will often take the person on, or where this does not happen the person can offer a reference and clear recent evidence of good work practices. This information is highly valued by potential employers. The fourth element seeks to match the work experience with continued job search and places a clear requirement, often including a financial incentive, for providers to help the participant secure work. The second element which focuses on high-value skills does not seek to overcome the lock-in effect but tries to offer longer term success in employment and wages.

The outgoing Labour government created the Young Persons Guarantee which was looking to work through all four of these vehicles. The programme offered a placement onto one of four options. The first, called Sectoral Routes, fits into the first grouping in the above typology of potentially useful elements. This was a training programme for jobs in industries with high levels of recruitment such as hotels and social care but employers agreed to offer participants a job on completion of the training course. The second option is the use of apprenticeships, which is part of wider aim to increase the numbers of young people with higher level 3 and 4 vocational qualifications, and securing enough employers to offer the essential work-based learning environment has been a long-standing problem. The Future Jobs Fund was to have elements of both typologies 3 and 4 above. For this element to work, the embedding in a regime to maintain job search and employer engagement was crucial. Employers and charities seeking to run placements on the programme had to bid using a currency of the value of the placement to the participant; that is, only the best bids in terms of offering support for future job entry would be selected. However, no financial inducement was built-in and hence it was essential that the best placements were identified *ex ante* according to whether they had a clear capability to engage potential future employers and support job search by the participant at least in the later half of the placement. Furthermore for those who fail to secure work at the end of the placement need immediate support with job search of the kind offered in the Flexible New Deal to the long-term unemployed. This would be akin to the follow-through stage of the old New Deals but this aspect was never developed before the Future Jobs Fund was abolished. The final option on the Young Persons Guarantee is a Community Taskforce placement. The details of how this will operate remain vague. It was planned initially to be rarely used and just to make sure the Guarantee was guaranteed, but with the demise of the Future Jobs Fund it is likely to be increasingly important. The likelihood is that local authorities or charities will create temporary placements rather like the Taskforce elements of the old New Deal programme. However, these were widely thought to be the least successful elements and that they needed a great sense of undertaking useful work and to increase the focus on securing a job at the end of the placement. This might be achieved if a system is created whereby social enterprises and local community groups (from Scout Groups to Tenant Associations) bid for the time of the programme participants. The bid is not with money but with social value (although a contribution of volunteer time and materials could be asked for). It is also vital to the participant, a future employer, and the community as a whole, for clear social value. Community involvement in this is a very powerful signal. The lack of a clear system to promote ongoing job search by the participant and engagement of potential future employers by the agencies offering the placements remains a major concern.

Overall the evidence would support a programme structure broadly as follows. At around six months duration, a period of intensive job search monitored by a provider or Job Centre Plus would be started with the aim of helping as many as possible to enter into work before the more costly Job

Guarantee phase starts. It also offers the chance to address basic skills problems which may reduce the effectiveness of any placement. In the placement phase, the Sectoral Routes option offers training and a guaranteed job offer, and apprentices have a high success rate of securing jobs on completion. For those not going into these elements, the provider needs to identify clearly the next step into work for the participant, engaging with employers and helping or motivating the participant to look for this next step. Future employers will be looking for relevant experience, a good reference, evidence of good work habits, and self-motivation from the participant. The placement needs to be able to offer credible evidence of these. This means the placements have to be as close to normal work as possible, with a wage and all that implies in terms of turning up on time and good work habits. In the past this has been best produced by wherever possible using regular private sector employers. The ending of the Future Jobs Fund, before any evidence of success or failure was possible to ascertain, is strange and probably a mistake. If the Community Taskforce becomes the major alternative placement then this focus on getting the participant into a regular job may be secured through outcome-related fees, as has been widely used in the past with clear evidence of success. Incentive payments for participants to secure follow-on jobs and the role of Golden Hellos to the new employer should also be considered. When a placement finishes, a follow-up phase to make the most use of the recent experience is essential. The value of the output is also important in terms of the overall value of the programme and it is also rewarding to participants. The more the work is seen as valued by the community, the better.

☐ REFERENCES

Arulampalam, W. (2001) 'Is Unemployment Really Scarring? Effects of Unemployment Experiences on Wages', *Economic Journal*, 111(475), 585–606.

Bivand, P., Brooke, B., Jenkins, S., and Simmonds, D. (2006) *Evaluation of the StepUP Pilot: Final Report*, DWP Research Report No. 337 (http://research.dwp.gov.uk/asd/asd5/report_abstracts/rr_abstracts/rra_337.asp).

Card, D., Kluve, J., and Weber, A. (2009) 'Active Labor Market Policy Evaluations: A Meta-Analysis', *IZA Discussion Paper* No. 4002.

De Giorgi, G. (2005) 'Long-term Effects of a Mandatory Multistage Program: The New Deal for Young People in the UK', *Institute of Fiscal Studies Working Paper* 0508.

Dorsett, R. and Smeaton, D. (2008) *Mandating an Intensive Activity Period for Jobseekers Aged 50+: Final Report of the Quantitative Evaluation*, Report to: Department for Work and Pensions Research Report 500.

Goujard, A., Petrongolo, B., and Van Reenen, J. (2011) 'The labour market for young people', in P. Gregg and J. Wadsworth (eds.) *The Labour Market in Winter: The State of Working Britain 2010*, Oxford: Oxford University Press.

Gregg, P. (2001) 'The Impact of Youth Unemployment on Adult Employment in the NCDS', *Economic Journal*, 111(475), F623–53.

—— (2008) *Realising Potential: A Vision for Personalised Conditionality and Support*, DWP (http://www.dwp.gov.uk/welfarereform/realisingpotential.asp).

—— and Tominey, Emma (2005) 'The Wage Scar from Youth Unemployment, Labour', *Economics*, 12 (4), 487–509.

Gregory, M. and Jukes, R. (2001) 'Unemployment and Subsequent Earnings: Estimating Scarring among British Men 1984–94', *Economic Journal*, 111(475), 607–25.

Martin, J. (2000) 'What Works among Active Labour Market Policies: Evidence from OECD Countries' Experiences', *OECD Economic Studies* No. 30, 2000/I, Paris: OECD.

Sianesi, B. (2001) 'Differential Effects of Swedish Active Labour Market Programs for Unemployed Adults during the 1990s,' *IFS Working Paper* W01/25, London.

—— (2002) 'An Evaluation of the Swedish System of Active Labor Market Programs in the 1990s', *The Review of Economics and Statistics*, February 2004, 86(1), 133–55.

Van Reenen, J. (2004) 'Active Labour Market Policies and the British New Deal for Unemployed Youth in Context', in Richard Blundell, David Card and Richard Freeman (eds.) *Seeking a Premier Economy*, Chicago: University of Chicago Press.

Part II

New Institutional Patterns in Labour Markets

6 Individualization and Growing Diversity of Employment Relationships

WILLIAM BROWN AND DAVID MARSDEN

6.1. Introduction

One of the most striking features of the recession of 2009–10 has been the apparent willingness of employees to accept changes in their terms and conditions of employment in order to retain their jobs. By early 2010, a number of observers had begun to ask whether this new adaptability of pay and working patterns to accommodate the drop in demand had contributed to the relatively small impact of the first wave of the recession on employment compared with previous major recessions (see Chapter 5 by Gregg). In this chapter, we examine the current evidence behind this claim, albeit fragmentary, and argue that this new-found adaptability has its origins in a number of institutional changes that have been gathering momentum over the past two decades. We also consider the winners and losers.

The chapters by Nickell and Gregg show that the initial impact of recession on employment had been much less severe than expected. The Office for National Statistics (ONS) has produced a detailed comparison with the early impact on employment of the current recession compared with previous deep recessions, and although it is too early to rule out a 'double-dip', there is reasonable *prima facie* evidence that labour market adjustment has changed (ONS 2010). The other notable observation, which may be related, is that pay reductions absorbed a good deal of the recession's initial impact, with average weekly earnings for the whole economy crashing at an annualized rate of 5 per cent in the early months of 2009 (Figure 6.1).

These aggregate statistics are reflected in the experience of many individual companies, according to reports in the press. In February 2009, Toyota attracted national attention by announcing a freeze of pay and bonuses shortly after BMW and Vauxhall announced stringent cut backs in their UK plants (*Financial Times* 19/02/2009). Honda followed with similar announcements of pay cuts in March (*The Times* 24/3/2009); in July, the BBC

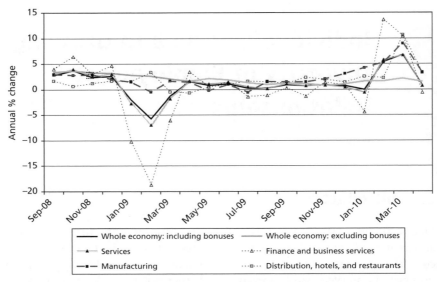

Figure 6.1. Weekly Earnings Growth by Sector (Annual Rate %): Effect of Bonuses

Source: ONS online: AWE Supplementary Tables.

Note: Average weekly earnings include bonuses unless stated otherwise.

reported that BT was seeking pay cuts in exchange for more holidays (BBC 04/ 07/2009); and in January 2010, the *Guardian* reported that some employers were using the recession to claw back paid leave arrangements (*Guardian* 07/ 01/2010).

Some of these adjustments may be accepted voluntarily. Some workers may prefer a temporary pay cut in order to keep their jobs for the longer term. It is possible that, after a decade of policies to foster employee commitment in many organizations, employees' attitudes have changed, and that they trust their employers that short-term pain will be rewarded by long-term gain. However, it may not be that simple: a recent CIPD survey shows that as few as one-third of British employees trust their senior managers (CIPD 2010). It may be that weakened unions no longer offer their traditional opposition to pay cuts. There may also be a greater readiness by employers to cut benefits in a way they did not in the past. The degrading of superannuation schemes has, for example, been a feature of this period. At a time when the economic recession is more severe, and trade unions are weaker, than at any time since the war, it would be unproductive to speculate about the extent to which these changes have been imposed, acquiesced to, or agreed by the workers concerned. Instead, we focus on recent changes in employment relationships in Britain, and their consequences, and then on the winners and losers, which provides a cue for considering the longer term desirability of some of these developments for social justice and cohesion.

6.2. **Recent changes in British employment relationships**

The changes to be reviewed might be categorized broadly into those of substantive and of procedural individualization (see Brown et al. 1998). The first concerns the extent to which the actual content of employment contracts has become more diverse in terms for example of hours worked, pay received, job descriptions, and contractual status. The second concerns the extent to which the procedures whereby these contracts are determined has become less a matter of collective bargaining and more one in which the employer deals with the employee as an individual, frequently imposing the terms without negotiation.

A powerful driver of change in recent years has been structural change. Over the quarter century of trade union collapse since 1980, the proportion of all employees in manufacturing, the heartland of private sector collectivism, fell from 38 to 15 per cent in 2004. The proportion employed in the heavily collective public sector fell from 36 to 28 per cent. The proportion of the workforce employed in the thinly unionized private services sector rose from a quarter to over a half (Brown and Edwards 2009: 13). The size of the workplace in which people were employed, commonly associated with collectivism, fell in manufacturing, although it rose in private services.

The diversity of employment contracts has increased substantially. The proportion of the workforce who were primarily self-employed rose from 8 per cent in 1980 to 13 per cent in 2010. The increase in part-time employment was from 14 to 27 per cent over the same period, closely linked to the rise in female employment. The proportion of workplaces where at least half the workers were part-timers rose from 13 to 28 per cent of the total. The use of fixed-term contracts rose. The proportion of workplaces using fixed-term contracts of less than a year rose from about one in five to one in three (Brown and Edwards 2009: 17). There has also been a rise in employment through agencies. Both these trends have been particularly marked in the public sector. The proportion of workers on contracts without any defined working hours has risen, as has that of those on annualized hours. Overtime working, typically with a high degree of employee discretion, has diminished. Overall, the employment contract has, in summary, become more flexible and, with this flexibility, more under the control of the employer.

It is not only that there is greater variability of contract but also of pay within those contracts. During the 1980s, there was a sharp rise in the practice of making some components of pay contingent on outcomes: linking pay to individual or work-group performance, or to company profits, or introducing employee share ownership schemes. And although enthusiasm for such schemes has waned somewhat more recently, for the economy as a whole the proportion of workplaces with some sort of contingent pay scheme rose from 41 per cent in 1984 to 55 per cent in 2004. For the private sector alone that increase was from 52 to 67 per cent. The growth in profit-related pay was a particularly notable feature of the 1980s. It had been officially encouraged for a time by tax incentives, but continued after they were withdrawn. By 2004, profit-related pay covered 45 per cent of private sector workplaces, more than twice the 20 per cent it had stood at in 1984. In brief, a major reason for pay becoming more flexible in the present recession is simply that pay systems had been introduced which made it contractually more flexible and contingent upon individual and company performance. Another feature of recent years is one of the increased diversity of contingent pay schemes within single workplaces; incentives are being shaped more specifically to the potential of particular jobs and technologies (Pendleton et al. 2009). No negotiation or managerial diktat would have been necessary to achieve many of the pay cuts of the past couple of years (Figure 6.1). They would have been simply an intended and expected consequence of the tougher product market.

6.3. **The collapse of procedural collectivism**

The recent increase in the diversity and flexibility of employment contracts, and in the extent to which they are employer-designed, is both a consequence and a cause of the decline of organized labour. The scale of that collapse is hard to exaggerate. The proportion of the employed workforce in trade unions collapsed from around 55 per cent to around 30 per cent between 1980 and 1996, after which it drifted slowly down to 28 per cent in 2007. But the decline in the coverage of collective bargaining has been both more extreme and more remorseless. If we look just at the private sector, the proportion of workplaces where management engages in any collective bargaining fell from 47 to 38 per cent between 1984 and 1990, the main period of anti-union legislation and public confrontations. But it fell further to 24 per cent in 1998, and it continued its fall at an undiminished rate after New Labour was elected, to 16 per cent in 2004. Relatively little of this retreat can be attributed to structural change in the economy and to the contraction of traditionally highly unionized sectors. It has been clearly demonstrated that the overwhelming driver has been increased competition within individual product markets (Brown et al. 2009). Firm by firm and sector by sector, employers have responded to tougher competition by tightening controls over work, and either refusing to deal with trade unions at all or doing so only on the basis that their role is one of passive consultation or of positive contribution to improved productivity.

Trade unions have responded in kind. It is not just that strike levels had tumbled by the end of the 1980s to lower levels than in recorded history and stayed there: the annual number of strikes recorded per million union members had averaged around 250 in the 1950s, 1960s, and 1970s; halved in the 1980s; and fell to and remained at a tenth of it in the 2000s. The sectoral location of strikes also changed. Over the past decade the vast majority of working days lost in strikes are in the public sector; in the private sector strikes have become a rarity. Trade unions in the private sector have increasingly sought survival by cooperating with employers in their desire to enhance productivity and competitiveness. The officially encouraged 'workplace partnership' deals of the turn of the millennium were not a passing fad, although the terminology became electorally unattractive to union leaderships and fell from use. But *de facto* partnership deals are now the essence of private sector collective bargaining—and also a growing feature of the public sector.

So far we have drawn attention to the fact that competitive pressures have transformed the form and content of employment contracts in the private sector, emphasizing that this has been a substantially greater change than in the public sector. But this is not to say that the public sector has been unchanged—very far from it. For one thing the privatizations of the past thirty years have removed to the private sector some of the most renowned strongholds of trade union power, such as steel, car assembly, aerospace, shipbuilding, docks, airports, and coal mining. The evidence suggests that, far from unions preserving some of their traditional authority in these sectors, management withdrew from collective bargaining even more than in comparable sectors that had never been in state ownership (Brown et al. 2009: 44). It is true that unions have retained a solid foothold in some privatized sectors—typically those characterized by 'natural monopolies' where there are official regulators: gas, water, electricity, communications, and rail. But union influence over daily work organization is nonetheless much diminished.

Indeed, union influence has also diminished substantially in sectors that have remained public. In health, education, and local and central government, quasi-market pressures such as league tables, outsourcing, trusts, competitive tendering, and other resource competitions have greatly reduced union influence. In some sectors where union control was substantial it has taken a struggle. For the prisons it took the introduction of private prisons to trigger a sea change. In the fire and emergency services and the postal service, it has been the failure of national strike action. The public sector remains distinctive in its attachment to collective bargaining. But the past twenty years have seen, for both pay fixing and wider management, a radical shift away from centralized, standardized arrangements, and towards greater discretion for local management and lesser involvement for unions (Bach et al. 2009).

6.4. Consequences of change

A reflection of the decline in union influence is the change in the way that employers communicate with workers. Some sort of arrangement for this has been in place for over 80 per cent of workplaces at least since the 1980s. But whereas at that time 66 per cent of those communication methods involved trade unions (and of that 24 per cent involved unions exclusively), by 2004, only 38 per cent involved trade unions (and a historically tiny 5 per cent trade unions exclusively). Management had come to dominate the communication process, through means such as consultative committees open to all employees, through problem-solving groups, through employee opinion surveys, and, notably, the use of team briefing, the use of which doubled from 36 per cent of workplaces in 1980 to 71 per cent in 2004. The representative role of unions, even where they are recognized by management, had been substantially reduced (Willman et al. 2009).

The implications of these developments for employment contracts have been massive. Much more is at the discretion of the employer alone: what employees are paid, what hours they work, when they work, whom they work with, and what they do. Contracts, which in the 1980s might have had quite specific job descriptions carefully negotiated with trade unions, are now typically left vaguer, with letters of appointment describing the worker's duties giving renewed emphasis to catch-all clauses of the sort '. . . and any other duties for which your manager considers you to be competent'. Between 1984 and 2004, the proportion of British private sector employees (in workplaces with twenty-five or more) whose pay was determined by management acting alone rose from 59 to 85 per cent. For many of these workers, this would not in practice have meant 'individual negotiation' of any substance, or even 'take it or leave it', but 'take it or leave'.

Quite apart from institutional change, the extraordinary growth over this period of electronic surveillance capability—whether email records, CCTV, 'satnav' location techniques, electronic payment recording, or mobile phones—has immeasurably increased employers' ability to monitor their employee's conduct of work. For a wide swathe of jobs, technology has transformed the employer's knowledge of and control over the worker's execution of the employment contract. It is not that employers have the capacity routinely to analyse this unimaginable volume of data; what matters is that they have potential access to individual evidence to enforce contractual compliance through disciplinary procedures. That said, a potential casualty of undue monitoring of employees is the basis of trust between employer and employee upon which much work pride and quality depends.

The shift in power towards employers has been reflected in some aspects of the experience of the workers. While pay has generally improved steadily in real terms over the past thirty years, it has also become more unequal, with consequent increases in dissatisfaction provoked by increased relative deprivation for many (see Chapter 11 in this volume by Machin). Job security, measured in terms of involuntary job separations, has generally increased, and despite a long period of deregulation, job tenures have proved relatively stable in the United Kingdom as in other major advanced economies (OECD 1997: ch. 5).[1] But some aspects of work have, overall, become less attractive to the employee. Workplace autonomy has tended to decrease (Gallie et al. 2004; Green and Whitfield 2009). The perception that stress and work intensity are increasing, which was marked in the 1990s, has continued (Green 2004, 2008).

What about the growth of individual employment rights, it might be argued. Has not the several score of employee protections and entitlements that have been introduced in the past thirty years, around half as a result of EU influence, compensated for the decline in trade union influence and introduced new inflexibilities from the employer's point of view? The answer is that, while these have indeed provided some compensation in terms of employee entitlements, there has been no substitution for the decline of trade union influence over the conduct of work. Rights against sexual, racial, and disability discrimination, against bullying and mispayment of wages, rights for maternity leave, family friendly policies, unfair dismissal entitlements, information and consultation rights, and so on, all increase the cost of employment. This has been manifest in the sharp growth in specialist human resource management: present in two-thirds of workplaces in 2004 compared with one-half in 1980 (Guest and Bryson 2009: 125). Overall, these rights have probably favoured employers with greater initial command of their workforces; the National Minimum Wage, for example, has probably shifted employment and market share away from employers who relied upon low pay to compete towards employers who rely more on competent employee management (Metcalf 2008). But, for all but the more authoritarian and unscrupulous employers, these new employment rights do not compromise the power to manage.

There is a sharp contrast with the collective bargaining practices of the past. We shall come in a moment to what trade unions achieved for their members in terms of wages and substantive conditions. But their achievements in terms of modifying the employer's power to manage were considerable. British collective bargaining has always been distinctive by comparison with other

European countries or, for example, the United States, Canada, or Japan, in the extent to which it offered union members influence over the immediate conduct of work (Fox 1985). By the 1970s, in both public and private sectors, more or less tacit negotiations at the workplace over manning levels, work rates, overtime, bonus payments, and even work methods were commonplace. Conducted with employee representatives, commonly called 'shop stewards', and backed by an awareness of the capacity for very local workplace collective action, these exercised substantial constraint over management. It is this distinctive characteristic of local control over the conduct of work which has diminished dramatically. For example, in 1980, of a representative sample of works managers responsible for manufacturing plants with 100 or more employees where trade unions were recognized, 40 per cent said they would normally negotiate with union representatives over the reallocation of work. In 1998 the comparable proportion reporting this was 4 per cent (Brown and Nash 2008). Similar but more specific examples could be given across a wide range of sectors. It is not that local union influence over the conduct of work has diminished sharply everywhere—there are odd groups such as long-haul passenger aircraft pilots and theatrical stagehands where it is still notable—but it has become very much the exception rather than the norm. Changes in employment laws have done nothing to sustain it.

The shift in the character of trade unions, of collective bargaining, and of the control of work is clearly reflected in evidence of the economic consequences. It is reflected in wages. The 'mark-up' or apparent wage premium enjoyed by union members over non-members had been around 10 per cent in the 1970s up to the early 1980s, falling to (according to Labour Force Survey data) 6 per cent for 1993–9, and further to 3 per cent for 2000–6. It was, interestingly, more resilient in small workplaces of under twenty-five employees (where unionization is relatively rare), standing at around 8 per cent in 2004 (Blanchflower and Bryson 2009: 61–3). It was not only with wages that union influence diminished. In the early 1980s, the evidence suggested that the presence of unions in an establishment was associated with relatively low employment growth there, possibly indicating an effect in discouraging investment. Whatever the reason, this disappears after 1990 (op. cit.: 65). And there is a similar pattern with regard to the financial performance. 'Unions were associated with poorer financial performance in the early 1980s. But this difference has since disappeared, and it has been due to an improvement in the relative position of unionised workplaces rather than any deterioration among non-unionised workplaces' (op. cit.: 68). More subjectively, managers' perceptions of the rather fuzzy notion of 'industrial relations climate' followed a similar track, with unions being seen as detrimental in the 1980s, but with such an effect disappearing from the later 1990s (op. cit.: 71).

In summary, Britain entered the recession of 2009 with employment relationships that were remarkably altered by comparison with those prevailing in the recession of 1991, and even more with those of the recession of 1980. Contracts of employment had become more diverse in form, more contingent upon economic circumstances, more individualistic procedurally, and above all, far more under the control of employers. Little wonder that in 2009 they permitted a more flexible response to the demands of product markets than at any time since the Depression of the 1930s. And because the driving force behind their change has been toughening product market competition, which has, more than anything else, undermined collective bargaining and the influence of trade unions, there is every reason to believe that this change has been irreversible.

6.5. **Winners and losers of the change**

The gap left by the erosion of the old system of joint regulation of the workplace and more generally of labour markets by collective actors is gradually being filled. In its place is a different system of regulation which gives primacy to the needs of individual organizations and their employees, and in that respect is more 'market-oriented'. It is also less egalitarian, and many of the developments described above have disproportionately affected the workers who had gained most from joint regulation. Whether it is any more sustainable in the long run than the system it had displaced can be debated. Below, we set out some of the key elements, which also give the lie to some of the winners and losers of these changes.

First, the flexibility of nominal wages shown in Figure 6.1, if sustained into the future, stands in stark contrast to views of practitioners and labour economists of earlier generations. Keynes and Hicks both noted the received wisdom that the structure of relative wages in Britain's unionized economy was a major obstacle to the downward flexibility of money wages. It was for this reason that Hicks (1955) argued that modern economies had moved from the gold standard to the 'labour standard' in which currency fluctuations had to bring about the adjustments in real wages that the labour market could no longer provide. Although it is too early to say definitively, it is hard to avoid drawing a connection between the fall in money wages in early 2009 and the apparent robustness of employment levels at the onset of the recession. Although financial and business services showed the biggest drops, they also occurred on a smaller scale in manufacturing and other services. The link with variable pay also seems highly plausible: the pay practice has been steadily spreading over the past two decades; and comparison of pay trends with and without bonuses shows clearly that bonuses provided nearly all the pay flexibility displayed in Figure 6.1.

Before hailing this as the dawn of a benign new era, one should consider other evidence on the incidence of bonuses. One reason why workers have often opposed variable pay is that they have no cushion of savings and discretionary income to absorb drops in pay. A steady rate of pay, supplemented with overtime, made it possible to plan family budgets. Worker preferences such as these influence the kind of pay system employers will offer when they compete to attract labour. Low-income workers prefer the certainty of stable rates of pay. In contrast, high-income workers, who can afford the associated risk, may well prefer variable pay, especially if they believe it will reward the success of their own efforts and that of their organization. In fact, this is borne out in recent British earnings statistics. There is a strong correlation between the *level* of annual pay and the *percentage* annual bonus. This can be seen in median pay and bonus per cent for detailed occupations shown in the ONS 2008 and 2009 Annual Surveys of Hours and Earnings (ASHE).[2] In other words, the much sought after flexibility of money wages in order to give greater job security can be found in today's labour market, but mainly for higher paid occupations.

Another notable feature of the emerging pattern of regulation is a change in the nature of employee voice. Again, we suggest this gives greater market flexibility, and also that it benefits mainly the better qualified and better paid. As collective union voice has declined in Britain since the early 1980s, so a new configuration of voice channels has developed. Occupational licensing and its related interest associations, as argued in chapter 7 by Humphris, Kleiner, and Koumenta, have expanded in the United States while trade unionism has declined. Their data suggest that British labour markets are experiencing a comparable change. Although the jury is still out on the net public benefits of licensing, there are notable parallels with old-style craft unionism which controlled entry in order to regulate pay and working conditions. Licensing establishes common standards of training and performance, and in doing so it helps to create more flexible labour markets with a large pool of skills for employers, and it ensures that workers' qualifications have wide currency across the labour market. In contrast, much employer-provided training is not transferable, so that when people lose their jobs they often have to step down the skill hierarchy. However, as Humphris and her co-authors point out, licensing benefits primarily higher paid workers.

In their classic defence of the benefits of trade unions to the economy, Freeman and Medoff (1984) emphasize how employers can gain if their employees will share information with them about their jobs and the general functioning of the company. It helps to balance the one-sidedness of much information that filters up the managerial hierarchy, and so can boost productivity. Willman et al. (2009) show that employers' demand for voice has not diminished, but to use Freeman and Medoff's metaphor, it has emphasized only one of the 'two faces of unionism': assisting the flow of information in the workplace, but not bargaining over pay. Thus we have seen an expansion of employer-led voice, such as consultation, quality circles, and workplace briefings, but these are all management-led, and their agenda is usually set by management. Part of the price of union-led voice is that the organizational imperatives of collective bargaining, which include building coalitions among disparate groups of workers, inevitably involve trade-offs in which the strong demonstrate solidarity with the weak. Metcalf et al. (2001) show that typically, in Britain, unions have reduced pay inequalities among the groups they represent. Detaching 'productivity' voice from 'bargaining' voice should in principle enable employers to raise productivity, and they may then use this to reward the workers whose skills and continued loyalty matter most. In addition, as electronic personal communications become ever more potent as means of mobilizing worker discontents, there are dangers for both employers and the wider society in the contraction of the representative infrastructures of unions which might permit elected representatives to manage those discontents.

Although trends in *individual* employee voice are not available for the quarter century of union decline, the most recent Workplace Employment Relations Survey (WERS) (2004) indicates that it is strongly associated with the effectiveness of their outside option. Thus, individual voice is greatest for employees with high levels of education, in skilled and professional occupations, who have been recently mobile, and who are highly paid in their occupation: factors that indicate a strong external labour market. Such workers were more likely to express confidence in the power of their individual voice in the workplace (Marsden 2010a). The same data suggest that effective individual voice is inversely related to collective union voice, whether in the form of workplace collective agreements, or workplace representatives, and is negatively related to measures of management-led voice, except for appraisal being linked to pay. Whether workers can literally choose between individual and collective voice is not clear. However, if they have limited time and effort to devote to voice activities, and union coverage has become patchy, it seems entirely logical that they should hone their individual voice skills and ensure they maintain a strong outside option. As noted in the CIPD survey cited earlier, most British workers do not trust their managers. Once again, in this new more market-driven environment, the advantage lies with those employees who have the most marketable skills.

A final institutional change that may lie behind greater pay flexibility has been the decline of strongly institutionalized entry routes to a number of occupations. This change may liberalize access, but it too has come with a price tag of increased inequality. Although these channels may have restricted increases in labour supply, one important advantage was that competition for entry took place over a relatively short time period. Those who did not get a training position with a top local employer were still young enough to try another company or a different occupation, and to start earning their living. Today, in a number of occupations such channels have declined and have been replaced by a prolonged period of competition in unstructured labour markets. Aspirant entrants to these occupations have to build up their personal networks, negotiate deals, take on low paid work or even unpaid internships to get known, and achieve the break that will bring them peer recognition and status as full members of the occupation (Marsden 2010b). Such prolonged entry tournaments open up supply, and also require financial support from families. As the Sutton Trust (2006) observed in the case of journalists, loss of the traditional entry routes meant that aspirants were dependent on family wealth, and so the occupation had become more elitist in recent years. Another feature of the extended competition for entry is that a number of workers become trapped in the fringes of these occupations not only having failed to gain entry to the prestigious core but also having left it too late to train for a different occupation. Such people continue to depress the pay and conditions of those competing for entry. Thus once again, a move to more flexible and less institutionally regulated labour markets may be good for adjustment to shifts in demand, but they can also be socially regressive.

In conclusion, the decline of organized union voice in Britain and of collective regulated employment practices may well have enabled pay and work practices to absorb some of the shock of the first wave of the recession, and so to protect employment levels, at least initially. As unemployment has such a scarring effect as noted in other chapters, this must be a significant gain. However, it has to be set against the price in terms of inequality. As chapter 12 by Vignoles shows, inequality also scars as young people from deprived homes fare much worse in the educational system than their peers from better-off homes. This is not an easy trade-off to decide, and without collective voice many of those most affected probably have little or no voice in this decision. The trade-off is not just one for national politicians but also for employing organizations. The CIPD's concern that so few British workers trust their employers was justified because many of the modern methods of human resource management depend upon winning employee motivation so that managers can rely on them to make good decisions that benefit their organizations. This requires a reasonable degree of trust on both sides. If workers feel that their managers' willingness to listen to them depends upon their marketability, then the price that organizations pay will be more limited cooperation and commitment. Traditional forms of union-based collective voice may often have been adversarial, but they were not always so, and it is perhaps a mistake to let the experience of the 1970s and early 1980s colour one's judgement for all time. These were years of intense social conflict as inflation undermined social cohesion.

☐ NOTES

1. For an annual update, see OECD Stat Extracts at http://stats.oecd.org/Index.aspx
2. The correlations were 0.80 and 0.63 for 2008 and 2009, respectively, for four-digit occupations, both significant at <1 per cent. The 2009 figure may be lower because of the sharp fall in bonuses in February–March that year. The ASHE data relate to April.

☐ REFERENCES

Bach, S., Givan, R.K., and Forth, J. (2009) 'The Public Sector in Transition', Ch. 13 in Brown et al. (2009).

BBC News (2009) 'BT Offers Holidays for Pay Cuts', 7/4/2009.

Blanchflower, D.G. and Bryson, A. (2009) 'Trade Union Decline and the Economics of the Workplace', Ch. 3 in Brown et al. (2009).

Brown, W., and Nash, D. (2008) 'What has Happened to Collective Bargaining under New Labour?', *Industrial Relations Journal*, 39(2), 91–103.

—— and Edwards, P. (2009) 'Researching the Changing Workplace', Ch. 1 in Brown et al. (2009).

—— Deakin, S., Hudson, M., Pratten, C., and Ryan, P. (1998) *The Individualisation of Employment Contracts in Britain*, Research Paper for the Department of Trade and Industry, London.

—— Bryson, A., and Forth, J. (2009) 'Competition and the Retreat from Collective Bargaining', Ch. 2 in Brown et al. (2009).

—— Bryson, A., Forth, J., and Whitfield, K. (eds.) (2009) *The Evolution of the Modern Workplace*, Cambridge: Cambridge University Press.

CIPD (2010) *Employee Outlook: Emerging from the Downturn*, London: Chartered Institute of Personnel and Development.

Financial Times (2009) 'Toyota Freezes Pay and Bonuses to Stem Losses', 2/19/2009.

Fox, A. (1985) *History and Heritage*, London: Allen and Unwin.

Freeman, R. and Medoff, J. (1984) *What do Unions do?*, New York: Basic Books.

Gallie, D., Felstead, A., and Green, F. (2004) 'Changing Patterns of Task Discretion in Britain', *Work, Employment & Society*, 18(2), 243–66.

Green, F. (2004) 'Why has Work Effort Become More Intense?' *Industrial Relations*, 43(4), October, 709–41.

—— (2008) 'Leeway for the Loyal: A Model of Employee Discretion', *British Journal of Industrial Relations*, 46(1), 1–32.

—— and Whitfield, K. (2009) 'Employees' Experience of Work', Ch. 9 in Brown et al. (2009).

Guardian (2010) 'Snowed in, out of Pocket. Store Staff Face a Wage Freeze', 1/7/2010.

Guest, D. and Bryson, A. (2009) 'From Industrial Relations to Human Resource Management: The Changing Role of the Personnel Function', Ch. 6 in Brown et al. (2009).

Hicks, J.R. (1955) 'The Economic Foundations of Wages Policy', *Economic Journal*, 65(259), 389–404.

Marsden, D. (2010a) 'Individual Voice in Employment Relationships: A Comparison under Different Collective Voice Regimes', *Working Paper* 1798, Centre for Economic Performance, London School of Economics.

—— (2010b) 'The Growth of Extended "Entry Tournaments" and the Decline of Institutionalised Occupational Labour Markets in Britain', *Discussion Paper* 989, Centre for Economic Performance, London School of Economics.

Metcalf, D. (2008) 'Why has the British National Minimum Wage had Little or no Impact on Employment?', *The Journal of Industrial Relations*, 50(3), 489–511.

—— Hansen, K., and Charlwood, A. (2001) 'Unions and the Sword of Justice: Unions and Pay Systems, Pay Inequality, Pay Discrimination and Low Pay', *National Institute Economic Review*, 176 (1), April, 61–75.

OECD (1997) *Employment Outlook 1997*, Paris: Organisation for Economic Cooperation and Development.

ONS (2010) *GDP and Unemployment: Recessions Compared*, May 2010, Office for National Statistics, http://www.statistics.gov.uk/cci/nugget.asp?id=2294

Pendleton, A., Whitfield, K., and Bryson, A. (2009) 'The Changing Use of Contingent Pay at the Modern British Workplace', Ch. 11 in Brown et al. (2009).

The Sutton Trust (2006) *The Educational Background of Leading Journalists*, The Sutton Trust, London.

The Times (2009) 'Pay Cuts and Freezes Spread as Inflation Plunges to 50-Year Low', 3/24/2009.

Willman, Paul, Gomez, Rafael, and Bryson, Alex (2009) 'Voice at the Workplace: Where do We Find it, Why is it there and Where is it Going?' Ch. 5 in Brown et al. (2009).

7 How Does Government Regulate Occupations in the United Kingdom and the United States? Issues and Policy Implications

AMY HUMPHRIS, MORRIS M. KLEINER, AND MARIA KOUMENTA

7.1. Introduction

One would be hard-pressed to think of a major labour market institution that is growing faster than occupational regulation in both the United States and the United Kingdom. Yet there has been little coverage of the policy issue in either the academic or public policy publications (Stephenson and Wendt 2009). The regulation of occupations by government has a long and varied history in the United States and the United Kingdom. In the United States, systematic licensing of occupations began at the state level in the late nineteenth century with the regulation of traditionally licensed occupations such as doctors and lawyers (Council of State Governments 1952). In the United Kingdom, there has been a long tradition of guilds and charters given by the Queen or by Parliament. More recently, occupational regulation has grown in both the United States and the United Kingdom and so has the economic influence of this institution.

Occupational regulation refers to the process where entry into an occupation requires the permission of the government or a relevant professional body (Kleiner 2000). Economists have long recognized the potential economic effects of occupational regulation. In *The Wealth of Nations*, Adam Smith comments on the ability of the crafts to lengthen apprenticeship programs and limit the number of apprentices per master, thus ensuring higher earnings for people in those professions (Smith 1937). Explicit in his argument is the idea that such institutions were not necessarily associated with increases in the quality of the output, rather they served as a restrictive mechanism. Similarly, in the United States, Nobel Laureate Milton Friedman stated that 'there has been retrogression, an increasing tendency for particular occupations to be restricted to individuals licensed to practice them by the state' (Friedman 1962).

One of the major reasons occupational regulation has grown is because it serves the interests of those in the occupation as well as in the government. Members of an occupation benefit if they can increase the perceived or the real quality and thus the demand for their services, while restricting supply simultaneously. Government officials benefit from the electoral and monetary support of the regulated as well as the support of the general public, whose members think that regulation results in quality improvement, especially when it comes to reducing substandard services or protecting public health and safety.

7.2. Occupational regulation in the United States

In the United States, more than two-thirds of occupational regulation takes place at the state level. In general, state regulation of occupations takes three forms. The least restrictive is registration, in which individuals file their names, addresses, and qualifications with a government agency before practicing the occupation. The registration process may include posting a bond or filing a fee. In contrast, certification permits any person to perform the relevant tasks, but the government or (more often) another non-profit agency administers an examination and certifies those who have passed the level of skill and knowledge for certification. For example, travel agents and car mechanics are generally certified but not licensed. The toughest form of regulation is licensure; this form of regulation is often referred to as the right to practise. Under licensure laws, working in an occupation for compensation without first meeting state standards is illegal.

For the members of the occupation, obtaining licensing is generally the objective, because it imposes state sanctions on new entrants from within a state or for those moving in from another jurisdiction. For the administrators of the professional association, the resulting increase in responsibility and revenue from dues and continuing education usually results in an increase in pay. Moreover, most licensing provisions require continuing education classes for fees, which raise the revenue for the occupation association. Greater revenue for the occupation association, increased responsibility, and revenue from dues and continuing education usually result in an increase in pay for leaders of the occupational association.

For the occupational association, obtaining licensing legislation requires raising funds from members to lobby the state legislature, particularly the chairs of appropriate committees. In addition, the occupation association often solicits volunteers from its membership to work on legislative campaigns. With both financial contributions and volunteers, the occupational association has a significant ability to influence legislation, especially when opposition to regulatory legislation is absent, diffuse, or minimal.

7.3. Occupational regulation in the United Kingdom

The UK model of occupational regulation bears many similarities with those found in other Commonwealth countries such as Australia and Canada but has some marked differences from the US model. It involves a variety of diverse institutional structures including general and industry-specific law as well as practices based on custom. As a result, it can vary along the following key dimensions. First, it can be statutory, meaning that the requirement for a licence is set down in statute, or it can be voluntary. In the former case, it largely follows the Victorian model in that professions are granted such status with an Act of Parliament so regulation is at the national level. Second, it can vary depending on the range of products or services that are licensed. As such, an individual with a specific job title can provide all products and services covered by that occupation (known as protection of title), or a specific job title enables the individual to undertake certain activities or provide only specific services (known as protection of function). This latter form of regulation does not restrict individuals from entering the profession, but it places restrictions on the activities they are allowed to perform as part of the profession. For example, one can practise as an electrician and can carry out electrical installations but a certified electrician has to inspect these installations and certify their safety. Third, it can vary depending on whether the licence is issued by an occupational body, a government organization, or whether the licence is issued on a local basis usually by a local authority. Regulatory bodies in the United Kingdom are independent of any branch of government but they work closely with government departments when reviewing occupational regulation issues. The majority of occupations in the United Kingdom are licensed nationally with the exception of taxi drivers who are issued a licence at a local authority level. Requirements for obtaining a licence or becoming registered with a professional body can include passing an industry-specific exam, the demonstration of work practices, and passing a medical or criminal record check. Finally, a licence in the United Kingdom can either be for life or might have to be renewed periodically to demonstrate continued fitness to practise (Frontier Economics 2003).

Based on these dimensions, occupational regulation in the United Kingdom can take the following forms. *Certification or accreditation* is the process in which a relevant authority assesses whether practitioners meet at minimum a set of predetermined criteria that demonstrate competence and knowledge in a specific area. A private non-profit industry body is usually responsible for overseeing the process and granting the certificate. Certification is not mandatory; therefore a non-certified practitioner also may provide similar services. However, given that certification indicates the achievement of a certain level of skill, some consumers might be prepared to pay a premium for using a certified practitioner as opposed to a non-certified one.

Registration, on the other hand, may be voluntary or mandatory (law requires practitioners to be registered, e.g. doctors), and it involves practitioners meeting certain standards before they can enter the register of qualified practitioners in the field. Requirements for registration may include the attainment of certain educational qualifications and passing exams. Registration with the relevant body may involve a statutory protection of a title, in that only those who are members of such a body may call themselves by that title (known as protection of title). For example, it is not a requirement to hold a licence to describe oneself or to practise as a surveyor, but to use the title 'Chartered Surveyor' one must be a member of the Royal Institute of Chartered Surveyors. Using a protected title without being registered with the relevant regulatory body is an offence that carries a financial penalty.

Licensing is similar to registration in that the licence to practise depends on the candidate complying with set requirements, most commonly the attainment of certain qualifications and proof of competence through tests. However, it refers to the mandatory requirement to hold a legal permit to practise the range of activities that can be performed by a practitioner (e.g. gas installation). Comparing licensing with registration in the UK context, registration tends to be tied to the protection of a title, whereas licensing refers to the absolute prohibition of the practice of a profession without holding the relevant licence. The use of the term licensing is limited in the United Kingdom, because there are far fewer controlled acts and occupations compared with the United States. However, there is evidence that it is becoming more widespread. In November 2009, for example, the medical profession became the first for which both registration and the requirement to hold a licence is mandatory by UK law, covering some 240,000 professionals. Under the new regulations, anyone practicing any form of medicine such as writing prescriptions and signing death certificates will have to hold a licence.

7.4. **Who is licensed?**

From a political economy perspective, occupational licensing has been a successful labour market institution and has grown as unionization has declined in the United States (Kleiner and Krueger 2009). Figure 7.1 shows trends in the growth of occupational licensing and unionization from 1980 to 2008.[1] Licensing data for the earlier periods shown in the graph are available only at the state/occupational level; the data gathered through the Gallup and Westat surveys for 2006 and 2008 are denoted with a dashed line in the figure (Kleiner and Krueger 2008, 2009). Despite possible problems in both data series, occupational licensing clearly is rising and unionization is declining. By 2008, approximately 29 per cent of workers polled in the Westat survey said they were required to have a government-issued licence to do their job, compared with about 12.4 per cent who said they were union members in the Current Population Survey (CPS) for the same year and less than 10 per cent are covered by the minimum wage. Despite these differences in coverage of the workforce, unionization and the minimum wage have received considerable attention by scholars and policymakers, whereas occupational licensing remains one of the most under-researched labour market institutions.

Aggregate data on occupational regulation in the United Kingdom is not available. To overcome this obstacle, we compiled a break down of qualifications and statutory licensing or registration requirements for exercising each one of the occupational groups outlined in the Standard Occupational Classification (SOC 2000). This exercise enabled us to decide whether the

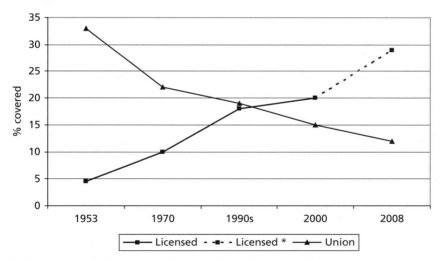

Figure 7.1. Comparisons in the Time-Trends of Two Labour Market Institutions in the United States, 1980–2008: Licensing and Unionization*

* The dashed line from 2000 to 2008 shows the value from state estimates of licensing to the Gallup and PDII Survey results for 2006 and 2008, and the union membership estimates are from the CPS.

occupation was licensed or regulated and subsequently to obtain an estimate of the proportion of workers in licensed jobs. Only those occupations which by law required practitioners to have obtained a specific qualification or to be registered with a professional body were included. Occupations for which registration is voluntary were dropped from the sample. Similarly, occupations for which a licence is legally required to carry out specific activities (protection of function) were also excluded from our sample. This is because there is no way of discriminating between those practitioners that hold a licence and those that do not. However, we recognize that this has resulted in underestimating the proportion of the workforce that is subject to licensing regulations and accept it as a limitation of our study. With these caveats in mind, we estimate that out of the 353 occupational groups included within SOC 2000, 42 occupations can exclusively be performed by someone who is registered or holds a licence.

Using historical data from the Labour Force Survey, we were able to show the growth in occupational licensing from 1997 to 2008 and compare it with aggregate levels of unionization. As it can be seen from Figure 7.2, the proportion of the workforce that is registered or licensed has consistently been rising while levels of unionization have been declining. By 2008, approximately 13.5 per cent of the UK workforce had to be licensed to perform their jobs or some particular aspect of their job. Licensing appears to affect a higher proportion of the workforce than the National Minimum Wage, which after

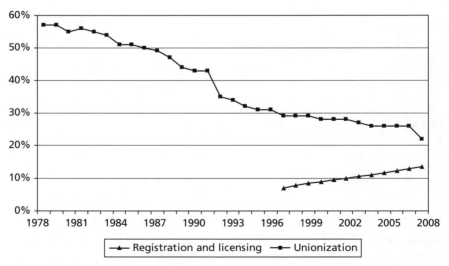

Figure 7.2. Comparisons of Two Labour Market Institutions: Licensing and Unionization in the United Kingdom

Source: Labour Force Survey (2008).

its introduction had a direct impact on an estimated 5 per cent of the UK workforce (Low Pay Commission 2001). Finally, it is evident that although registration and licensing requirements are currently confined to a smaller proportion of the workforce compared with the United States, that figure has consistently been rising the last several years.

7.5. **The effects of occupational licensing**

7.5.1. QUALITY EFFECTS

The arguments in favour of occupational licensing centre around the 'improvement in quality' effect it brings about. Occupational associations screen entrants to professions, barring those whose skills or character suggest propensity to produce low quality output. In addition, performance standards are regularly monitored and deviations can lead to punishments such as financial penalties or being stripped of the licence to practise. Since entry and subsequent performance are monitored in these ways, quality of service should be maintained. However, meaningful policing also requires that job incumbents cannot re-enter the occupation by moving to a new organization or state. To ensure that, strict entry requirements must be enacted which in turn limit labour supply to the occupation and thus increase the price of labour in these occupations. Both the threat of being deprived of the right to exercise a profession and the associated higher earnings provide an incentive for job incumbents first to invest in high levels of training to secure a licence and thereafter to adhere to professional standards. As such, licensing signals to consumers that the service they are receiving meets certain standards and therefore consumer uncertainty is minimized and demand for the service increases (Arrow 1971; Shapiro 1986). Such a reassurance can be particularly useful if the services or products in question pose health and safety risks to consumers. Therefore, a central justification for licensing is that it yields positive externalities to the society with respect to quality and human capital development. Further, that the quality improvements are manifested for those least able to obtain information and with the lowest incomes.

Others have questioned such assumptions. According to Friedman (1962), occupational associations have an incentive to ensure tight restrictions to entry are maintained (as they result in higher fees to practitioners) as well as stifle complaints, innovation, and disciplinary procedures. As such, not only are consumers faced with higher prices but also quality might be compromised as they switch to unlicensed and therefore cheaper practitioners. The difficulty in collecting good quality measures for many licensed occupations often restricts our ability to estimate the impact of licensing on both productivity and service quality. Where such evidence exists, it largely supports Friedman's hypothesis. In their study of mortgage brokers, Kleiner and Todd (2009) find that occupational licensing results in negative outcomes for consumers such as a greater percentage of high interest rate mortgages. Similarly, Wanchek shows that state laws limiting the number of hygienists results in a reduction in consumer's access to dental care. Licensing of dentists was also found to have few effects on malpractise insurance rates or complaints to state licensing boards, but a positive impact on prices for certain dental services (Kleiner and Kudrle 2000). Overall, the evidence so far has failed to demonstrate a link between licensing and better quality services. If anything, consumers appear to be faced with higher prices without a corresponding increase in the productivity of practitioners.

7.5.2. WAGE EFFECTS

Economic theory would predict that occupational licensing would simultaneously restrict the supply of labour to the occupation and enhance consumers' confidence that services are of superior quality. Such an outward shift in demand would lead to an increase in the wages of the licensed. By using the state to monitor entry to the profession and combining this with the legal requirement to hold a licence in order to practise, competition from unlicensed practitioners is eliminated.

Evidence suggests that the supply of practitioners in regulated occupations is indeed restricted by licensing. Kleiner (2006) finds that in states where librarians, respiratory therapists, and dietitians were not licensed, those occupations grew 20 per cent faster compared with states that were licensed. In addition, once an occupation becomes licensed, the corresponding occupational association has the power further to limit supply through various ways. For example, it can upgrade the educational and general requirements for entry and control examination pass rates and residency requirements before one can apply for a licence. Further, they can capture work by unlicensed workers who may have tangential relationships to the licensed occupations, such as hair braiders who were required to obtain a licence because their work was loosely related to the practice of cosmetologists (Kleiner and Krueger 2009). By how much does licensing drive up wages?

To examine whether licensing is associated with higher pay in the United States, we have estimated log wage regressions. We augment a standard earnings equation to include a dummy variable indicating whether a licence is required for the worker's job. We regard these estimates as mainly descriptive, since licensed workers may differ from unlicensed workers in the data in unobserved ways, even after we condition on education and two-digit occupation. If a dummy variable indicating licence status is added to a standard wage equation, having a licence is associated with approximately 18 per cent higher hourly wages (p-value < 0.001).[2] The cross-sectional effect of licensing is similar in magnitude to the estimated effect of belonging to a union (see Lewis 1986), and greater than an additional year of schooling. The regression estimates also include educational attainment, gender, race, age, self-employment, career experience and its square, union status, and no occupation dummy variables in some of the specifications (Kleiner and Krueger 2009).

A further distinguishing characteristic of the Westat survey is that the variable for career experience is the reported *actual* experience of the respondents rather than an estimate based on age and education (Blau and Kahn 2008). Specifically, the question for experience was: 'Since age 18, in how many years altogether have you worked for pay or profit? Please count all years in which you worked either all or part of the year.' The variable tracked well the traditional variable for experience used in human capital analysis.

We also examine if licensed occupations which perform more sophisticated cognitive work tasks, such as doing difficult maths and reading assignments, might be the reason for these wage premiums. If the wage premium is an economic return to higher cognitive abilities and tasks, then the licensing coefficient would decline. Moreover, are licensed or government-certified tasks more education-intensive, which would account for some of the wage premium obtained by regulated workers? In order to address this question using the data from the survey, we examine a question which asks the self-reported use of maths and reading abilities of the practitioners. For example, the reading question asks: 'What (is/was) the longest document that you typically read as part of your job?' And the maths question asks: 'How often (do/did) you solve problems at your jobs using advanced mathematics such as algebra, geometry, trigonometry, probability, or calculus?' We find that the inclusion of these factors is not associated with any change in the association of licensing with wages. On balance, our results lend support for the interpretation that occupational licensing serves as a means to enforce entry barriers to a profession that raise wages (Kleiner and Krueger 2009).

To examine whether licensing is associated with higher pay in the United Kingdom, we use data from the 2008 Labour Force Survey (autumn quarter).[3] In the standard earnings equation, we include a dummy variable indicating whether being licensed or registered is mandatory in order to practise the profession. The OLS regression estimates also include educational attainment, experience and experience-squared, gender, trade union membership, and whether pay setting is determined by a collective agreement as well as sector of employment and is similar though not identical to the model estimated for the United States. Due to the wage premium associated with working in the South East of England, we also control for location of employment. When the licensing dummy is entered to the wage equation, having a licence is associated with approximately 13 per cent higher hourly pay ($p < 0.001$). How does this finding compare with estimates of union membership wage premia? In the 1990s the premium stood at approximately 10 per cent (Blanchflower and Bryson 2003), but has since fallen considerably. According to the most recent estimates, the premium for the period 2000–6 stood at 3 per cent (Blanchflower and Bryson 2009).[4] Therefore, the wage premium associated with working in a regulated occupation in the United Kingdom is greater than the estimated effect of union membership.

Occupational licensing also bears many similarities to the pre-entry closed shop (Kleiner 2000). As with the pre-entry closed shop, only licensed indivi- duals are allowed to practise the profession thus potentially restricting labour supply to the occupation. At its peak, an estimated 5.2 million individuals were covered by closed-shop arrangements, falling to around 2.6 million before its outlawing (Dunn and Gennard 1984; Steward 1995). According to the evidence, the wage premium associated with the pre-entry closed shop was higher than that associated with union recognition (Metcalf and Steward 1992). Steward (1995) finds that in 1984 the pre-entry closed-shop wage differential stood at approximately 17 per cent, only slightly higher than our estimated wage differential for licensing.

Previous research in the United States has demonstrated that the licensing wage differential is higher for occupations that have high educational and training requirements compared with their low wage and low education counterparts (Kleiner 2006). To test whether this is also true in the UK case, we introduce a dummy variable to represent the interaction between licensing and qualifications into our standard log wage regression. We find that the effect of licensing on wages appears to be smaller for low-wage occupations. Whereas the wage differential for unionization is lower for high skill and high education jobs, in the case of licensing it is those occupations that benefit most. As such, licensing contributes to income inequality by raising the wages of individuals who are already above the upper quartile of the income distribution. Similar to the United States, the variance of earnings is not reduced by occupational regulation (Kleiner and Krueger 2009).

7.6. Policy implications for US health care costs

In the United States, one of the major areas of policy discussion and analysis is the rising cost of health care and the reasons for it. Occupational licensing is disproportionately focused on health care, with about 76 per cent of non- physician health care workers being required to have a licence from the government (PDII 2008). One proposal for reducing health care costs is that the federal government no longer pays a premium for health care costs due to licensing, except for physicians. Table 7.1 gives the potential implications for health care costs using a conservative estimate that 15 per cent of the licensing wage effect is increasing costs with little to no increase in productivity (Kleiner and Krueger 2009). Using these assumptions, the impact of reducing the payment due to potential licensing rents to health care workers would reallocate health care costs from providers of the service to consumers by approximately $102 billion in 2008. Further, the lost output or deadweight loss would be between 24 and 30 billion dollars for that same year.

The policy implications within this sector of the US economy of licensing are large in dollar terms but are still less than 1 per cent of overall health care costs. The evidence presented in Table 7.1 suggests that the main influence of licensing for health care workers, who are not physicians, is to raise costs without any measurable effect on the quality of service received by consumers. The implications are a large reallocation effect to relatively high-paid workers and lost output in an economically important and highly politically visible sector of the US economy (Kleiner 2006).

7.7. **Conclusions**

We compare occupational licensing in the United Kingdom and the United States. Although the potential labour market effects of occupational licensing are well documented in the literature, empirical work has often lagged behind, especially in the case of the United Kingdom. To our knowledge, this is the first attempt to map the 'occupational licensing' agenda in the United

Table 7.1. Simulations of the Effects of Licensing on US Health Care Costs

Estimates of US Health Care Expenditures
Health care expenditures are 17% of GDP, approximately $2.4 trillion (Kaiser Foundation 2007).

Labour accounts for 60% of health care spending (Schwieters and Harper 2007).

Therefore, health care labour costs are about $1.44 trillion.

If the US Federal Government were unwilling to pay the licensing wage premium for all health care workers who are not doctors?

Physicians and clinical services account for 21.2% of total health care expenditures. This would mean that physicians account for ($2.4 trillion) × (0.212) = $0.51 trillion.

Thus, total health care labour costs, net of physicians is $1.44 trillion - $0.51 trillion = $0.93 trillion.

Using basic demand analysis, this means that if 76% of health care employees are licensed (using the PDII generated estimates) and the lower range estimate of the wage premium is about 15% (Kleiner and Krueger 2009), then the reallocation effect would be 0.11 × $0.93 trillion = $102 billion, and the dead weight loss should be about $30 billion (e.g. $24 billion if only 80 per cent is deadweight).

Kingdom, estimate its effects at a macro-level, and compare it with the case of the United States, where such data is already available. In the United States, occupational licensing is already a dominant labour market institution affecting approximately 29 per cent of the workforce. Although less common in the United Kingdom, the evidence presented here shows that its importance is increasing. Whereas in the United States, licensing is predominantly a state-level phenomenon, in the United Kingdom it takes place at a national level.

We show that in both countries, occupational licensing has a large impact on wage determination. The wage premium associated with licensing stands at approximately 18 per cent in the United States and 13 per cent in the United Kingdom. For both countries, this is higher than the estimated effect of union membership. Interestingly, in the United Kingdom, licensing has the opposite effect on income inequality compared with unionization. In particular, licensing raises the wages of high-skilled and high-paid individuals thus exacerbating the existing disparity in the distribution of earnings in the United Kingdom. Such a finding confirms previous US estimates, and it is therefore consistent within both contexts.

Our results also validate the view that licensing has a monopoly effect via restricting labour supply to the occupation and thereby increasing wages. In the case of the United States, we show that professional associations exert substantial influence in the regulatory process through intense lobbying and campaigning in the first instance as well as through entry standards, for example changing pass rates for licensing exams. The situation appears to be somewhat different in the United Kingdom. Evidence from dentistry shows that it is government's funding decisions that determine entry to dental schools, whereas entry grades are determined by supply and demand for places at a given time (Jetham 2002). All dental school graduates are eligible to a licence which is granted by the General Dental Council. Although barriers to entry exist in terms of gaining a place in a dental school and getting a licence, they are beyond the control of the relevant professional body.

Finally, the policy implications of occupational licensing extend to many areas. Here we focus on the US health care system. We show that approximately $102 billion would be reallocated from providers to consumers if the licensing rents were reduced. Therefore, licensing increases costs without any evidence of a corresponding increase in the quality of service.

The study of occupational licensing as a labour market intermediary institution has received some attention in the United States. This is the first study to look at its effects in the United Kingdom. Our preliminary findings answer some initial questions, but also raise many others. In particular, how does the licensing premium vary across occupations and industries? Is there a wage premium associated with certification? To what extent does licensing result in better consumer protection and higher quality of services? The answer to such questions will enable us to evaluate more fully the impact of licensing, beyond its wage effects that we develop in our analysis.

Despite this, a number of conclusions can be drawn from this preliminary analysis. The lack of any positive effects of licensing on the quality of services received by the consumers, combined with the higher price paid for such services means that the case for occupational licensing is yet to be made. Governments and regulatory bodies are advised to scrutinize carefully any proposals for occupational licensing given that the evidence demonstrates the existence of a strong element of self-interest behind requests by occupations to be licensed. Consumers are also advised to be cautious when campaigning for the introduction of licensing arrangements for certain occupations (see Fernie, Chapter 8 in this volume).

Second, before embarking on licensing, governments and policymakers should examine the alternatives. Sceptics of occupational licensing have argued that less restrictive approaches can yield the same benefits. For example, certification might be a more efficient way of ensuring that consumers are protected from malpractice. Such a system would reduce information asymmetries between providers and purchasers of services while not interfering with supply and demand of labour to various occupations. It further enables consumers to choose whether they are prepared to pay a premium for someone whose skills have been checked by the government or a professional body.

Thirdly, the effect of occupational licensing on wage disparity highlights another negative by-product that this type of regulation could have. Having an unequal reward weighting across the wage distribution suggests that the wage benefits of occupational licensing are felt by those who are already reaping high returns from education and professional qualifications. As such, a stark warning should go to any government wishing to extend occupational licensing policies to professions typically in the upper quartiles of the income distribution. This is especially the case if these higher incomes are coming at the expense of relatively lower income consumers who now must pay higher price for these services. Moreover, this is an issue for policymakers who are particularly concerned with government exacerbating the currently observed trend of increasing wage inequality in the United Kingdom (see Machin, Ch. 11 in this volume).

☐ NOTES

1. The method used to calculate the percentage licensed prior to 2006 first involved gathering the listing of licensed occupations in each state by Labor Market Information units under a grant from the U.S. Department of Labor (see America's Career InfoNet, http://www.acinet. org/acinet/licensedoccupations/lois_occ.aspx?

stfips=27&by=occ&keyword=&searchType=&). This was matched with occupations in the 2000 census. If no match was obtained, the occupation was dropped. From the census, the number working in the licensed occupation in each state was estimated and used to calculate a weighted average of the percentage of the workforce in the United States that works in a licensed occupation. For 2008, we deleted individuals who were certified from our tally of licensed individuals who were either licensed or certified in the survey conducted by Westat.

2. The estimates in our analysis refer to log points as percentages, with percentages reflecting an intermediate base between the licensed and unlicensed groups (Halvorsen and Palmquist 1980).

3. The Labour Force Survey is a quarterly sample survey of approximately 53,000 private households in the United Kingdom randomly selected from the Postcode Address File (PAF). PAF is prepared by the post office and is stratified geographically. The survey collects information on respondents' personal circumstances and their labour market status. Each respondent is entered into five consecutive surveys, meaning that there is approximately an 80 per cent overlap in surveys for successive quarters. Each respondent is interviewed face to face in their first survey and via telephone interview, where possible, for the rest. The framework of the questionnaire follows that of other big national surveys, whose validity and representation is widely recognized, namely that of the census. The validity and reliability have been previously confirmed through past work.

4. There are variations across different types of workers and workplaces.

☐ REFERENCES

Arrow, K. (1971) *Essays in the Theory of Risk-Bearing*, Chicago, IL: Markham Publishing Co.
Blanchflower, D.G. and Bryson, A. (2003) 'Changes over Time in Union Relative Wage Effects in the UK and the USA Revisited', in J.T. Addison and C. Schnabel (eds.) *International Handbook of Trade Unions*, Cheltenham: Edward Elgar.
————(2009) 'Trade Union Decline and the Economics of the Workplace', in W. Brown, A. Bryson, J. Forth, and K. Whitfield (eds.) *The Evolution of the Modern Workplace*, pp. 48–73, chapter 3, Cambridge: Cambridge University Press.
Blau, F. and Kahn, L. (2008) *The Feasibility and Importance of Adding Measures of Actual Experience to Cross-Sectional Data Collection*. Paper presented at the Cornell-Princeton Conference on the Princeton Data Improvement Initiative, October.
Council of State Governments (1952) *Occupational Licensing Legislation in the States*, Chicago, IL: Council of State Governments.
Dunn, S. and Gennard, J. (1984) *The Closed Shop in British Industry*, London: Macmillan.
Friedman, M. (1962) *Capitalism and Freedom*, Chicago, IL: University of Chicago Press.
Frontier Economics (2003) *Economic Review and Analysis of Occupational Licencing*. Research Report No. 467, London: Department for Education and Skills.
Halvorsen, R. and Palmquist, R. (1980) 'The Interpretation of Dummy Variables in Semilogarithmic Equations', *The American Economic Review*, 70(3), 474–5.
Jetham, S.A. (2002) *The Economics of Occupational Licensing and Dental Practitioners*, MSc Project, London School of Economics.
Kaiser Foundation (2007) Trends in Health Care Costs and Spending (September 2007) The Kaiser Family Foundation, http://www.kff.org/insurance/upload/7692.pdf
Kleiner, M. (2000) 'Occupational Licensing', *Journal of Economic Perspectives*, 14(4), 189–202.

—— (2006) *Licensing Occupations: Ensuring Quality or Restricting Competition?*, Kalamazoo, MI: Upjohn Institute for Employment Research.

—— and Krueger, A.B. (2008) 'The Prevalence and Effects of Occupational Licensing', *NBER Working Paper* No. 14308, September 2008, pp. 1–15.

—— —— (2009) 'Analyzing the Extent and Influence of Occupational Licensing in the Labor Market', *NBER Working Paper* No. 14979 National Bureau of Economic Research.

—— and Kudrle, R. (2000) 'Does Regulation Affect Economic Outcomes? The Case of Dentistry,' *The Journal of Law and Economics*, 43(2), 547–82.

—— and Todd, R.M. (2009) 'Mortgage Broker Regulations that Matter: Analysing Earnings, Employment and Outcomes for Consumers', in Autor, D. (ed.) *Studies of Labor Market Intermediation*, Chicago University of Chicago Press and National Bureau of Economic Research, 183–231.

Lewis, H.G. (1986) *Union Relative Wage Effects: A Survey*, Chicago, IL: University of Chicago Press.

Low Pay Commission (2001) *The National Minimum Wage: Making a Difference*, London: The Stationery Office.

Metcalf, D. and Steward, M. (1992) 'Closed Shops and Relative Pay: Institutional Arrangements or High Density?' *Bulletin*, 54, 503–16.

PDII (2008) Princeton Data Improvement Initiative 2008 Available at http:www.krueger.princeton.edu/PDIIMAIN2.htm.

Schwieters, J. and Harper, D. (2007) 'Seven Steps Toward Gaining Control of your Labor Costs: As Healthcare Organizations Face Shrinking Revenues and Rising Expenses, One Cost-saving Solution could Lie in Addressing your Facility's Labor Costs,' *Healthcare Financial Management*, April, http://www.encyclopedia.com/doc/1G1-162113143.html

Shapiro, C. (1986) 'Investment, Moral Hazard and Occupational Licensing', *Review of Economic Studies*, 53, 843–62.

Smith, A. (1937) *The Wealth of Nations*, New York: Modern Library (originally published in 1776).

Stephenson, E.F. and Wendt, E. (2009) 'Occupational Licensing: Scant Treatment in Labor Texts', *Econ Journal Watch*, 6(2), 181–94.

Steward, M. (1995) 'Union Wage Differentials in an Era of Declining Unionisation', *Oxford Bulletin of Economics and Statistics*, 52(2), 143–66.

Wanchek, T. (2009) 'Dental Hygiene Regulation and Access to Care', *Paper presented at the BJIR Symposium 'Government Regulation of Occupations'*, Centre for Economic Performance, LSE, March.

8 Occupational Licensing in the United Kingdom: The Case of the Private Security Industry

SUE FERNIE

8.1. Background to licensing in the private security industry in the United Kingdom

In July 1996, Paul Steele was seriously assaulted by an unregistered door supervisor outside a club in Cheltenham. Although he was only punched once, he sustained permanent brain damage. The door supervisor concerned had a string of previous criminal convictions for violence, including one for causing grievous bodily harm, one for causing actual bodily harm, and even one for manslaughter, where he killed his 70-year-old landlord. He had apparently already been refused registration by his local council on two previous occasions because of these convictions, but the premises that employed him as a head-doorman were unaware of these refusals. The security company that provided door supervisors to the venue said that they did not know about employees' previous convictions, and that they had no legal way of finding out. During the months of March–June 2003, there were fifteen articles in the national and regional press concerning criminal activity by door supervisors (ranging from murder convictions to drug dealing) and eleven articles about unscrupulous wheel clamping companies. In addition, Home Office Ministers received many letters of concern from Members of Parliament and members of the public about the shady goings-on in the night-time economy.

A second cause for concern, which had been growing since the 1980s and the 1990s, was the increasingly large role played by the private security industry in public life. The wholesale process of contracting out during the 1980s meant that the state was often dependent on a few, large private security firms who would need to demonstrate their integrity. Press stories of private security incompetence blossomed in the 1990s. New Labour was committed to statutory regulation of the private security industry, and, in addition, through its 'partnership approach' to crime control it set down a programme which aimed both to reform and re-legitimize the industry. On 15 July 1997, just a few weeks after the general election, the new Home Secretary Jack Straw emphasized the crucial role that the private security industry would have to play in solving the 'chronic problems of neighbourhood disorder' and that, in order to play this role properly, the industry would have to be properly regulated. He was confident that, by ridding the industry of the cowboy operators, the public would come to realize that the private sector had an important role in the fight against crime: '*That is in the public interest as much as it is in the interests of the industry*' (White, 2008: 196, my italics).

In March 1999, following a lengthy period of public consultation and continued heavy lobbying from security providers and victims of door supervisors' violence, the government published a White Paper entitled *The Government's Proposals for Regulation of the Private Security Industry in England and Wales*. This paper proposed the establishment of a new Authority whose aims would be to help protect the rights and safety of the public by ensuring basic standards of probity within the private security industry, and to maintain and raise standards within the industry for the public benefit. The Private Security Industry Act received the royal assent in May 2001. From March 2006, all individuals working in the contract guarding security sector in England and Wales have required a licence granted by the newly established Security Industry Authority (SIA). The Authority's mission was to transform the industry from a low-pay, low-skill, perceived cowboy operation often infused with criminality to an innovative industry with best practice and which can offer added value to customers, who traditionally have regarded security services as a 'grudge' purchase. [For a thorough account of the background to the legislation, see White (2008)].

To qualify for a licence, an individual must have a criminal record check via the Criminal Records Bureau (CRB), which includes spent convictions, must provide access to at least five years' verifiable data on employment, and must obtain an appropriate qualification (equivalent to NVQ level 2) from a qualified trainer with certification from a QCA-endorsed body. The maximum penalties for working without a licence are six months imprisonment and/or a fine of £5,000. For supplying unlicensed personnel, these same penalties apply if indicted at a magistrates' court; if indicted at a Crown court an unlimited fine and up to five years imprisonment can be handed down. These conditions firmly locate contract security personnel in the most stringent category of Humphris, Kleiner, and Koumenta's typology of occupational regulation (see Chapter 7), but with one major difference: here, a new factor is employment status—in-house security workers (except for door supervisors) are exempt from this legislation.

The rest of this chapter will examine the impact that this Act has had on pay, on levels of employment, and on quality in the private security industry, with particular reference to two sectors: door supervisors and security guards. Some use is made of statistical analysis, but this is an industry which is notorious for lack of data, so reliance is also made on interviews with various stakeholders, participant observation, and examination of official documents. In particular, we shall try to examine the statement posed by Jack Straw, that licensing is *'in the public interest as much as it is in the interests of the industry.*

8.2. **Profile of the private security industry in the United Kingdom**

The private security industry in the United Kingdom is dominated by huge, multinational corporations. G4S, which employs 40,000 in the UK security field alone, has been awarded many large military, police, and public sector contracts. The 550 members of the British Security Industry Association (BSIA), the industry's trade body whose members account for 70 per cent of the total employment in this sector, had a total combined turnover in 2006 of £4.45 billion, £1.7 billion of which was security-guarding turnover. Total member employees were 124,000, of whom 79,500 were employed by security guarding companies. At the other end of the spectrum, there is a host of small, non-BSIA members, often fewer than ten-man businesses, providing security services to smaller and more local clients. The Annual Business Inquiry for 2008 gives 5,683 as the number of enterprises engaged in private security business, with a turnover of £6.3 billion and total employment of 185,000, but it remains almost impossible to estimate the exact numbers of security companies as many are registered as facilities or general management service providers. Table 8.1 gives a flavour of the type of work involved in the industry.

It is also extremely difficult to gauge accurately the numbers of people employed in the UK private security industry from official datasets. The Labour Force Survey (LFS) uses SIC 74.6 which has two subclasses: 'investigation' and 'security and related activities'. According to this, 148,217 people were employed in 2006. But SIC is not always accurate in describing the type of work people do; it describes the employing organization in terms of its main industrial activity and broad classifications are often vague. Skills for Security, the sector skills body, estimates that 500,000 people may be employed in the licensable part of the industry, compared with only 265,000 police officers.

Also according to the LFS, security guards (SOC 9421) and elementary security occupations (SOC 9249) show 188,289 employed in 2006 in both, and 12,135 managers make a total of 200,424. However, there is no data on the size of individual labour markets associated with each job title; so, for

Table 8.1. The Licensed Sector of the Private Security Industry

	Licences held as at November 2009	Remarks
Door supervisors	160,151	The Home Office estimated 95,000 door supervisors were working immediately pre-licensing. 850–900 door companies exist today. Both in-house and contract must be licensed. Staff turnover is very high, with a typical stay of six months or less
Security guarding	111,360	The largest of all sectors, employing an estimated 150,000 people
CCTV	23,103	There are 4.25 million cameras in Britain. £150–300 million a year is spent on the surveillance industry and it is estimated that this spend grows by 20% annually
Cash and valuables in transit	10,434	10,000 operatives across mainly seven companies in United Kingdom. This sector is declining in importance in our cashless society
Vehicle immobilizers	2,128	60 wheel-clamping companies

Source: BSIA and SIA websites.

example, SOC 9249 includes such job titles as lollipop person and many others which actually are unrelated to licensable security duties.

8.3. **Outcomes of licensing**

8.3.1. IMPACT ON JOBS AND PAY

A basic labour market model would suggest that the supply of labour will be restricted by the costs of licensing—for example, the costs of the licence and the entry requirement—and therefore wages will be driven up. Does this hold for the private security industry? First we shall attempt to examine, as far as we can in this area where data is scarce, the impact on jobs.

Over the period 2005–6, when licensing was being rolled out in order to comply with the March 2006 start date, the ONS yearly earnings survey (ASHE) estimates that the number of people employed within the security occupation group increased from 112,000 to 119,000, suggesting there has been no apparent detrimental effect on employment levels. Indeed, in the last decade in the LFS, the percentage of respondents employed within the security occupation group remains consistent at 0.3 per cent: given the size of the data set and its coverage, it is sensible to assume this is reflective of the national levels.

High turnover has always been a problem in this industry. An SIA survey carried out in December 2006 which involved 100 suppliers and 400 door supervisors showed that 45 per cent of suppliers felt that recruitment had been made more difficult post-licensing, mainly because of the lack of candidates who were capable of being licensed. In other words, the criminality criteria, possibly more so than the examination challenge, were responsible for depleting the pool. [Almost one-third of males under the age of 40 in England and Wales have a criminal record (Prime et al. 1998) and this figure is very likely higher for door supervisors, who, by the very nature of their jobs, often attract violent involvement—a sort of catch-22 situation.] However, it must be noted that the newly formed regulatory authority was unable to cope with the processing of licences, leading to short-term shortages of staff. One-third of companies employed more staff, but one-third fewer, than pre-licensing. Half of new recruits were new to the business. Overall, labour turnover for this sample was 53 per cent.

From the door supervisors' perspective, three-fifths had paid for their own training, and three-fourths had paid for the licence. Not surprisingly, 82 per cent of those who had not paid for their licence had not changed employer since licensing—very often there were tie-in clauses. One-fifth of door supervisors came into the business as a second job. Two-thirds felt the availability of work was greater since licensing, and almost half said that their working environment had improved (SIA 2007). Events and pubs/clubs are the most common sectors requiring door supervisors, and since licensing both sectors have been on the increase. Factors such as the continued post-9/11 security concerns, the growth of licensed premises, and the forthcoming Olympics (needing an estimated 15,000 security staff) will also add to the demand for new security personnel.

Various studies (e.g. Anderson et al. 2000; Kleiner and Kudrle 2000) have found that licensed practitioners earn higher wages than their non-licensed counterparts, but Kleiner (2006) notes that this does not hold for occupations with low skill levels. Since the 2001 Act, would-be contract security employees have had to take and pass a course which is deemed to be at NVQ[1] level 2. We are therefore here dealing with an occupation which has more in common with the barbers and cosmetologists studied by Kleiner than those professionals such as dentists which are often the subject of studies on occupational licensing.

We have already discussed the problems in estimating accurately the numbers employed in this industry, and so two sources are used: first, the official data from LFS and ASHE, which, whilst in no way accurate figures, do present us with the opportunity to test the impact of licensing on earnings; and second, data from two surveys carried out by the SIA one year after the Act.

According to interviews held with industry representatives, the split between in-house and contracted workers is approximately 30/70, and therefore if 70 per cent of workers gained a licence after March 2006 one would expect any wage effects to impact on the mean change of the whole industry. Indeed, the annual percentage change in wages for those in category 9241 (security guards and related occupations) in 2007 was 5.1 per cent according to the Annual Survey of Hours and Earnings (ASHE). Yet this effect clearly cannot be attributed simply to licensing as other factors such as an increase in the minimum wage should be considered. Therefore, the behaviour of security guards' pay should be compared with the rest of the 924 category (elementary security occupations), which is a group of occupations requiring roughly the same qualifications, having the same skill levels, and a similar demand and focus. As such it is logical to assume that wages of all occupations in the 924 category will behave similarly. Using ASHE data to carry out a Z-test, we found no evidence to suggest that security guards' mean percentage change in gross hourly earnings was any different from the rest of the 924 group for either 2005–6 or 2006–7.

To further support the idea that licensing has had no significant effect on gross hourly wages, a wage equation was generated using the 2008 LFS October–December quarter, which also allows us to control for variables such as trade union membership. It also means that any short-term effects resulting from the introduction of licensing should have bedded down. As it is impossible to see from the UK data sets whether or not a person is licensed, we used as a proxy for licensing whether or not a person already had or was working towards NVQ level 2, on the grounds that, if one was not obliged to take this qualification, one would not. Twenty-eight per cent of the sample fell into this category. Of course, the results must be treated with extreme caution. Gross hourly pay for a security guard (response rate 26.3 per cent) ranges from £3.98 an hour to £25.98 with a median of £7.69, which is similar to the figure given in ASHE of £7.89. Licensing was observed to have no impact on wages. Indeed, the only significant variable to impact upon pay was being a public sector trade union member, which raised wages by 37p an hour, a not inconsiderable sum in this highly competitive industry. Overall, these results would seem to gel with Humphris et al.'s findings that the effect of licensing on wages in both the United States and the United Kingdom appears to be smaller for low-wage occupations than for highly paid professionals, but we must once again emphasize the data restrictions when dealing with the United Kingdom.

8.3.2. IMPACT ON TRAINING AND QUALITY

If security provision is usually deemed to be a 'grudge purchase' (i.e. consumers seek to find lowest cost provider, with little value placed on quality of service), then theory says that these consumers will be disadvantaged by licensing as all security firms will have to raise their prices somewhat to accommodate the licensing criteria and their employees will be trained to a standard that exceeds consumers' requirements (Shapiro 1986). First of all, most suppliers claim that they have been unable to pass on the cost of licensing to their customers, and second, it is certainly not the case that the standard of training exceeds consumers' requirements.

One door supervisor interviewed in an ethnographic study had this to say of the two-day SITO[2] training course that was popular before licensing:

It's impossible to fail: I could send my dog on it and it would pass (Hobbs et al. 2003: 183)

The old course has been subsumed into a new, thirty hours over four-day course, with two components: roles and responsibilities of door supervisors and communication and conflict management. These are followed by two hours of multiple choice tests. Topics covered include health and safety, drugs awareness, personal qualities of a door supervisor, searching, and equal opportunities.

It is not within the remit of the SIA to approve or vet training providers directly: instead, it defines the skills and knowledge necessary for an individual to work in a particular sector and then endorses awarding bodies, which then approve the providers. In England, the QCA[3] accredits qualifications within the National Qualifications Framework; awarding bodies develop the curriculum in accordance with SIA specifications and approve training bodies; and training providers actually deliver the programmes. Employers in the security industry have commented that skills are lacking in the following areas: communication, customer service, written and oral communication, and problem solving. Generally speaking, occupations with easily assessable skills are more suited to a policy of occupational licensing; those that are subjectively assessed are harder to test for and therefore to include in the licensing requirement (Frontier Economics 2003).

Lister et al. (2001) doubt the relevance of training to the routine experience of door supervisors. They say:

Current provisions are overly generic, do not affect the pragmatics learnt within the workplace and fail to penetrate the tight subcultural norms and values generated by workplace processes of socialization. Research into police training stresses the presence of a profound gap between the taught and lived reality of the role . . . within the context of bouncer training we found less a gap, more an aching chasm. (Lister et al. 2001: 374)

One result of the introduction of licensing has been the ballooning of training courses, some of which have been found to be of dubious (or even illegal) quality. A recent count finds some 130 approved trainers in the London area alone on the SIA web site. If we assume an organization trains five people per week, and that two are paying the going rate of, say £200, and the other three are funded by the government at a cost of around £1,000 per person, then this is not a bad return for a small organization which simply needs to find a room and pay a teacher to deliver training.

In summary, there is a consensus that competency requirements for the courses are too low, and therefore often unsuitable candidates are attracted into the industry. Only in extreme cases does an applicant fail, and this may be why we see no impact on earnings.

With entry to the licensed parts of the security occupations now restricted to those who can pass an exam and show themselves to be of high moral character (Kleiner 2006: 49, and in this case literally true), one would expect that the quality of service provided by those accepted would surpass that of their predecessors or of themselves before training. The licensing authority's definitions of quality lie in two areas: (*a*) the numbers of licences refused or revoked, and (*b*) the new training requirement. On 2 November 2009, 406,869 licences had been granted in total. Twelve per cent of door supervisors and 11 per cent of security guards had their licences either revoked or refused. It was not possible to gain information on the reasons for revocation/refusal, nor to tell if any types of companies were disproportionately represented. By way of comparison, the British Standard 7858, Security Screening of Individuals Employed in a Security Environment, which is used by many security companies, and whose predecessor was used by reputable companies prior to licensing, has a 35 per cent failure rate. This process includes a ten-year employment check as a minimum, compared with the SIA standard of 5, one of the reasons given by some security suppliers in support of their arguments for the dilution of standards brought about by licensing.

The SIA definition of quality emphasizes inputs, not outputs. The applicant is judged fit and proper for the job if s/he passes a test and the relevant criminal record and identity checks. But as Kleiner (2006) points out, licensing tests measure competence, not performance, and we have no way of knowing whether the test will correlate with subsequent performance. The low competency levels have been mentioned earlier.

Reducing the levels of criminality in the business was one of the aims of licensing, and is measured by the SIA in input terms. However, in order to test the outputs of licensing, one would need to analyse a large data set including crimes, occupations, and other variables. Such a data set does not seem to be available. Once again, the only possible approach is a qualitative one. We interviewed the licensing sergeants in two London boroughs with a high proportion of door supervisors to ask for their views on the impact of licensing on bouncers' criminal behaviours.

Both officers concerned had been in the force for more than twenty years. Each had four people in his section to cover approximately 1,000 licensed premises, a number which had almost doubled in the last five years. The premises were mainly clubs but also included petrol stations and late-night shops. No statistics were held by the police on complaints received from public about disorder resulting from relaxed licensing laws, but both said the later into the night the licence, the more complaints received. And, of course, it takes a particularly determined, brave, and sobered-up person to make a complaint about door supervisors.

Both officers felt that the average quality of door staff had improved since licensing. One believed that the incentive to improve behaviour is the threat of losing one's licence but both were disappointed by the SIA's lack of teeth with regard to enforcement. In visits to troubled licensed premises, SIA reps have merely given warnings when faced with non-compliance, for example, not wearing a badge. In the police officers' experience, no door staff have lost their licence or even been fined for any offence—warnings have been the order of the day. So, although the licensing sergeants were in favour of regulation, they were not in favour of a system which has no bite. By contrast, the example was given of a barman selling alcohol to an underage person. The barman would probably get a fixed penalty ticket but the licence holder would get a large fine, for example, £900 first offence. Although in theory such a situation exists with the security industry, in practice large fines are rare.

We asked the officers to try to measure the change in behaviour since licensing of door staff in terms of violence against customers, or of drug-related offences. Both said that there are definitely fewer of these cases—but could offer no statistics to back up their views. However, door staff themselves are now more likely to be threatened by gangs, and alcohol-fuelled attacks on door staff are more frequent. CCTV has helped to identify attacks both by bouncers and on bouncers, and indeed CCTV and not licensing was held by both officers to be the prime reason for improved behaviour.

From the point of view of door supervisors themselves, however, the picture is rather more positive. SIA research carried out with door supervisors in December 2006 shows that 37 per cent thought that the treatment they received from the customers and public had improved and almost half said they were treated better by the police. Sixty-one per cent said that training had improved their ability to do the job, half thought their confidence had increased, and 75 per cent thought their pay and conditions would improve in the long term due to licensing. The licence badge was seen as a symbol of state-sanctioned assurance in the quality of the door supervisor as a profes-sional employee. Indeed, Hobbs et al. (2003) noted the increasing emphasis on professionalism—including attire, demeanour, and an increase in the employment of women bouncers—and it is this aspiration of 'professional-ism' which is most commonly cited by suppliers and security staff themselves when asked for their views on the benefits of licensing.

In the absence of any hard indicators of quality for security guards, we interviewed a representative from the Chartered Association of Loss Adjusters to see if there exists any data on the involvement of security personnel with disasters. Although they could offer no statistical evidence, various anecdotes were related involving moral hazard in security work: apparently, it is not unknown for a bored guard to set a fire, only to recoup the rewards and/or recognition for putting it out. It is difficult to see how such behaviours will be prevented by licensing; reducing hours worked is surely the answer. However, CCTV is the preferred method—all suppliers noted in our interviews the ease of monitoring guards, and indeed of monitoring the monitors, which they stressed was often unavailable to in-house security departments.

To sum up, hard evidence on the quality improvements of licensing in the case of private security is almost impossible to measure given current data limitations. In order to be a useful policy, the benefits of licensing must outweigh the costs of its implementation. In this case, 'benefits' surely mean a better-trained workforce delivering an improved service, and, most importantly, helping to reduce crime, especially in the night-time economy—a stated aim of the legislation. At the moment, we are none the wiser on these matters.

8.4. **Problems with the licensing authority**

The 2001 Act established the SIA to oversee the licensing process and to set up an approved contractor scheme (ACS). According to the National Audit Office (NAO), the police, security suppliers and customers, and the SIA and its constitution have, in many ways, hampered the smooth and effective process of the introduction of licenses and have no 'teeth' in terms of enforcement.

In October 2008, the NAO report *Regulating the Security Industry* (NAO 2008) presented a somewhat critical review of the private security industry regulation process. The pre-licensing estimate of the licensable population was too low (not surprisingly as it was based on dubious data), the time profile of applications was not accurately forecast, and the computer system was just not up to it. NAO also stated that the cost of running the SIA was seriously underestimated. The licence fee was set at £190 from 2004 to 2007. This figure was too low to enable the SIA to break even. The licence fee has been £245 from April 2007. By way of comparison, 200,000 doctors are regulated at a cost of £301 per practitioner, and 660,500 nurses and midwives at £28 each. Many of the smaller security companies we consulted felt that the nurses' registration scheme would have been a better model of regulation to use in this sector.

Despite having a bulk process where companies can apply on behalf of their employees, and an online register of licence holders, SIA does not know which business employs which licensed individuals nor how many private security companies there are today. The NAO estimate that the 100 largest guarding companies account for 75 per cent of turnover, but there are at least 2,000 companies many of which employ ten people or fewer. Such vague information about the industry hampers the SIA in its aim to bring about 100 per cent licensing.

8.5. **Effectiveness of regulation**

It is difficult to estimate the level of compliance with the requirement to be licensed, but SIA research in March 2008 showed that managers and operatives in security and door supervision believe levels of compliance are more than 90 per cent. Spot checks with the SIA and police also put levels of compliance at over 90 per cent.

Eight small compliance teams (fifty-four enforcement staff in total) work with suppliers of security guards and their customers to prevent deployment of unlicensed individuals. The licensing Authority relies on its partners such as the police and the UK Borders Agency to help it carry out enforcement. In 2007, the SIA provided 450 witness statements to the police on licensing offences, and 100 warnings were issued. But the Authority does not receive feedback on such inspections or the results thereof. In 2006, the Better Regulation Executive found that stakeholders thought that insufficient enforcement was being undertaken and that the Authority needed to increase its publicity. All police forces thought that the Authority's problems in processing licences had damaged its credibility. They also felt the organization was not well run and lacked street presence. Local authorities had differing views— some had no contact with SIA, and area teams were described as powerless and under-resourced. As on 29 May 2008, 248,400 valid licences had been issued and 9,033 revoked, including 729 cases where the applicant was found not to have the right to work in the United Kingdom. Very few cases had been taken against individuals—in October 2008, three fines and in one case a fine and a conditional discharge had been levied. Community punishment orders, but no prison sentences, have been handed down. For companies that use unlicensed staff, an Improvement Notice can be given. As on 31 May 2008, the SIA had issued sixty-eight. In addition, twenty companies have had approval for the ACS withdrawn. There are currently 652 approved contractors. The harshest judgement so far was made in November 2008 against Securiplan plc, one of the largest companies. Securiplan continued to employ unlicensed operatives for up to six months after the enforcement date. They were fined £95,000 for nineteen offences of supplying unlicensed operatives, plus £550,000 costs.

The general view from stakeholders in the industry is that the regulation could be much more effective: the SIA lacks teeth and a proper street presence. In its defence, however, the SIA is constrained by the Hampton principles of regulation, meaning that it is unable to put in place a more rigorous enforcement regime.

8.5.1. THE APPROVED CONTRACTOR SCHEME

In February 2008, the SIA carried out a survey of approved contractors, non-approved contractors ($n = 301$), and buyers of security ($n =$ unknown) to try to assess the benefits of the scheme. Fifty-one per cent of approved and 58 per cent of non-approved contractors said that their turnover had increased over the last year. Most of the approved contractors felt that the scheme brought limited or no benefits. Accreditation increased costs, was time consuming, and brought a higher administrative burden. The scheme had not changed the way they operate as they were already maintaining high quality levels. They believed the public were generally unaware of the scheme, and, most importantly, a point which was put to us by all interviewees, most buyers choose on basis of cost. The only advantage of being in the scheme was the ability to deploy security staff whilst their licences are being processed.

With regard to buyers of security, only 25 per cent stated that they always used approved contractors. Large businesses were more likely to use non-approved contractors. Most believed that reputation, skills, honesty, track record, and principally price are more important to them than what they saw as 'government paperwork'. Many felt that, as long as the individual operator is licensed, then the status of the company is immaterial. Thirty-six per cent of buyers review their contract every six months, and 32 per cent every seven to twelve months. (This regularity of contract switch has brought about many TUPE-related problems for the contractors.) Non-approved contractors were seen as no worse than approved, but scheme members were more expensive. Some buyers value relationships built up over years with companies which happen to be non-accredited rather than take notice of the scheme. Most regard it as a waste of time and money (but no figures on responses were provided by the survey). In addition, there were complaints about illegal workers, the slowness of the SIA administration, and complaints that the system which allows accredited contractors to employ security personnel before they are licensed is being abused.

8.5.2. HUMAN RESOURCE MANAGEMENT PRACTICES

One of the aims of licensing was to rid the industry finally of its image as, low-paid, low-skilled, and dominated by criminals and cowboys, to make the job a matter of choice and not desperation, and to educate the buyer of security into the sophisticated world of high-tech, high-quality security provision. It does not appear to have worked very well. However, our interviews with security suppliers show that, instead of licensing, the use of certain human resource practices can lead to gaining custom in a market that is defined by quality, whereas the absence of those practices will be a suitable strategy for those suppliers who still compete on price alone.

Some companies now offer an impressive array of what might be termed 'best practice' human resource tactics: it is now not unusual to see terms such as 'work life balance', 'corporate social responsibility', and 'environmentally friendly', even on the websites of small- and medium-sized companies. Vetting and training are often way above SIA requirements. Some security providers have carved out niche markets for themselves: at least one personal guarding agency employs only Gurkhas, who have become very fashionable as school escorts in expensive areas of Hampstead and as the security guard of choice for Wayne Rooney's mansion. Simon Cowell sacked his personal security guards in favour of ex-commandos. Most companies in the close protection business are staffed by ex-military personnel.

But there is still a large proportion of security buyers who are not interested in this new quality agenda, and who are simply interested in securing the minimum amount of protection for the least possible price. And in a way this is understandable, since the risks of employing 'rogue' companies are not at all clear.

When one attempts to quantify just what these risks might be, one is usually given the example of an officer who cannot speak English attempting to evacuate a building, or the dangers of a cheap officer working his eightieth hour that week falling asleep on the job. But these factors are not overcome by licensing: it may well be possible to pass the (multiple choice) exam with a poor standard of English, and it may well only be the more through companies that routinely give an English or numeracy test to applicants. Falling asleep on the job, likewise, is the result of competing for contracts on price, which also cannot be affected by the licensing of individual workers.

Employment contracts, however, are beginning to be problematic, especially in the close protection sector. All medium-sized companies expressed concern at the 'rogue' companies which they believe have been able to set up since licensing—in fact, one interviewee said he could think of no reputable companies which have set up recently, the estimated £40k start-up fee being seen as impossible for the smaller company. Such 'rogue' companies, which he estimated at as much as 30 per cent of the industry today, tend to make their staff self-employed, which is contrary to the legislation. These self-employed security personnel, unless they are designated as proper businesses, will not be able to obtain adequate insurance. The client, however, does not know this and genuinely believes that they have bought from a company which employs properly licensed and insured people. Close examination of contracts provided by our interviewees shows that suppliers are increasingly looking for indemnities from their customers, which may sound warning bells in this regard.

8.6. **Conclusion**

After many years of lobbying by the industry, MPs, and private individuals, the private security industry, one which had been characterized by poor human resource management practices and infused with criminal elements, became subject to state regulation in the form of licensing of individuals in 2006. The overall impact of this regulation seems to have been bland: the supply of qualified persons did not fall, wages did not rise, and any positive impacts on quality for consumers are extremely hard to gauge. Well-run and good-quality organizations that existed pre-licensing continue to work in the same way, often with standards far above those laid down by the licensing body. What can probably be said with some certainty is that extremely poor-quality operations at the bottom end of the market were forced out, and that in one sector in particular, door supervision, standards overall have probably risen. In the largest sector in the industry, security guarding, it is not clear at all how licensing has solved the problems of alleged market failure: training levels are perceived to be too low, employment practices are still dubious at times, and there is scope for non-compliance with the legislation. There is little evidence that public awareness of the licensing process or its alleged benefits, something essential for licensing to have any bite, has been raised. Problems with the operation of the licensing body have led to huge deficits and a cost per licensed operative being on a par with that for doctors.

On the other hand, what is clear is that the industry is still divided into the high-quality suppliers and the cowboys: but what is not clear is exactly what risk is posed by the 'cowboys'. The simple choice between cost and quality in the provision of security is still present, and the cost minimization approach is still the preferred choice for many buyers. Moral hazard problems are not solved by licensing but by physical monitoring made possible by ever more sophisticated technology.

An answer to the problems posed by licensing individuals may lie in the licensing of companies instead, something that was keenly advocated by interview participants. The NAO in its 2008 report felt that the decision not to regulate companies is out of line with Europe and may be a barrier to effective regulation. This may be about to change: with regard to wheel clampers, primary legislation was announced in November 2009 in the Police,

Crime and Private Security Bill as a result of which the SIA anticipates being asked to operate a compulsory scheme to allay concerns about the activities of some vehicle immobilizers; obscuring signs, imposing excessive fees, and using intimidating behaviour. For the first time, businesses will be licensed in addition to individuals. Ongoing discussions are being held about the feasibility of extending this to other sectors. This comprehensive form of regulation would satisfy the requirements of one of the early champions of regulation in the industry, Bruce George, who states:

Companies should also be subjected to regulation and the Approved Contractors Scheme should be made compulsory. As long as there are firms able to undercut the better firms by avoiding the obligations required of a recognised firm the Dutch auction in standards will continue. (George et al. 2007)

This may well be true, but until we in the United Kingdom have access to extensive data with which to test rigorously the impact of narrow versus comprehensive regulation of the security industry, and especially the impact on quality, it is likely that any putative positive externalities will remain a mystery to the public whose interests are meant to be served.

☐ NOTES

1. National Vocational Qualification—a competence-based qualification with five levels. Level 2 is approximately equivalent to five GCSEs with grades A*–C.
2. Security Industry Training Organization.
3. Qualifications and Curriculum Authority.

☐ REFERENCES

Anderson, G., Halcoussis, D., Johnston, L., and Lowenberg, A. (2000) 'Regulatory Barriers to Entry in the Healthcare Industry: The Case of Alternative Medicine', *The Quarterly Review of Economics and Finance*, 40(4), 485–502.

Better Regulation Executive (2009) *Securing Better Regulation*, London: Department for Business, Innovation and Skills.

Frontier Economics (2003) *An Economic Review and Analysis of the Implications of Occupational Licensing*, Research Report RR 467, London: DFES.

George, B., Button, M., and McGee, A. (2007) 'Applying Best Practice: Lessons from Around the World', *Paper presented to the SIA: Changing the Agenda—Perpetuity Conference*, May.

Hobbs, D., Winslow, S., Lister, S., and Hadfield, P. (2003) *Bouncers*, Oxford: OUP.

——O'Brien, K., and Westmarland, L. (2007) 'Connecting the Gendered Door: Women, Violence, and Doorwork', *British Journal of Sociology*, March.

Home Office (2003) *Private Security Industry: Further Consultation on Proposals to Regulate the Industry*. London: HMSO.

IFF Research (2006) *Door Supervisor Licensing*, London: SIA.

——(2007) *Security Guard Licensing*, London: SIA.

Kleiner, M. (2006). *Licensing Occupations: Ensuring Quality or Restricting Competition*, Kalamazoo, MI: W.E. Upjohn Institute.

——and Kudrle, R. (2000) 'Does Regulation Affect Economic Outcomes? The Case of Dentistry', *The Journal of Law and Economics*, 43(2), 547–83.

Lister, S., Hadfield, P., Hobbs, D., and Winlow, S. (2001). 'Accounting for Bouncers: Occupational Licensing as a Mechanism for Regulation', *Criminal Justice*, 1(4), 363–84.

National Audit Office (2008) *Regulating the Security Industry*, London: The Stationery Office.

Prime, J.S., White, S., Liriano, S., and Wortley, R. (1998) *Criminal Careers of those Born between 1953 and 1978, England and Wales.* Home Office Statistical Bulletin, 4/01, London: HMSO.

Shapiro, C. (1986) 'Investment, Moral Hazard, and Occupational Licensing', *Review of Economic Studies*, 53(5), 843–62.

SIA (2007) *The Impact of Licensing on Door Supervision and Security Guarding*, London: SIA.

——(2008) *Approved Contractor Scheme: Benefits Survey*, London: SIA.

——(2009) *In-house Licensing Review: Outcome Report*, May, London: SIA.

White, A (2008) *The Re-Legitimation of Private Security in Britain, 1945–2001*, PhD thesis, University of Sheffield.

Part III

Low Pay and Minimum Wages

9 The National Minimum Wage after a Decade[1]

MARK B. STEWART

9.1. Introduction

The United Kingdom has now had a National Minimum Wage (NMW) for over a decade. It was introduced in April 1999 with an adult rate of £3.60 per hour and as of October 2010 stands at £5.93. David Metcalf, in whose honour this volume has been written, was a member of the Low Pay Commission (LPC), the body responsible for recommending NMW rates to the government, from its setup in 1997 until 2007. The NMW celebrated its tenth anniversary in very different economic circumstances from those that prevailed when it was first introduced. During most of the NMW's lifetime, the UK economy has exhibited steady economic growth and ever-rising levels of employment. Current economic conditions are very different. Monitoring its impact is as important as ever.

The NMW is widely seen as one of the success stories of the Labour government. It is popular with the public and supported by all three main political parties. However, when it was proposed in the 1992 and 1997 election manifestos, there was huge opposition to it by political commentators, business, and the Conservative government of the time. Dire employment consequences were predicted. The available evidence indicates that these have failed to materialize. The evidence suggests that any adverse effects of both the introduction of the NMW and its subsequent upratings have been small.

Minimum wages and their effects remain highly controversial worldwide. They seem to be less supported by economists than by non-economists and the general public. The debate in the United States in particular over the last twenty years or so has often been acrimonious. The UK experience in general and the research on the effects of the NMW in particular have wider implications for the international debate on minimum wages. Neumark and Wascher (2007) comment that 'the research for the United Kingdom is particularly significant, in our view, because it seems to be widely cited as providing evidence that an increase in the minimum wage does not reduce employment'. Elsewhere, the NMW has been referred to as a 'laboratory', providing data and evidence with wider relevance for the international debate.

This chapter looks at a decade of the NMW in action. It examines how the initial rate was set, how upratings have compared with general wage growth, and asks how many employees have directly benefited from the NMW, and how the rate compares with rates in other countries. It provides an overview of the different approaches that have been used to estimate the employment effects of the NMW and reviews the evidence provided by this research. It asks whether the initial rate was set too low and where the rate should be set now.

9.2. **Setting the initial rates**

When introduced in April 1999, the NMW was set at £3.60 per hour for those aged 22 and over, with a lower rate of £3.00 per hour for those aged 18–21 or still training. (This latter was lower than the £3.20 recommended by the LPC and was applied to those aged under 22 rather than those aged under 21 as also recommended by the LPC.) The 2009 LPC report rightly describes the initial adult rate of £3.60 as being set at a 'conservative' level (LPC 2009: 2). Subsequent changes to the NMW rates are shown in Table 9.1. The upratings in October 2001 and in 2003–6 inclusive increased the NMW faster than average wage growth. In the period since 2007, the LPC has 'adopted a more

Table 9.1. National Minimum Wage—Rates and Comparisons

	Adult NMW (£)	% increase in NMW	% increase in median wage (April)	% increase in AEI	% increase in RPI
	[1]	[2]	[3]	[4]	[5]
April 1999	3.60				
October 2000	3.70	2.8	3.0	4.1	2.6
October 2001	4.10	10.8	5.0	4.1	1.6
October 2002	4.20	2.4	4.0	3.6	2.1
October 2003	4.50	7.1	3.9	3.8	2.6
October 2004	4.85	7.8	3.7	4.8	3.3
October 2005	5.05	4.1	3.4	3.2	2.5
October 2006	5.35	5.9	3.7	4.3	3.7
October 2007	5.52	3.2	3.3	3.6	4.2
October 2008	5.73	3.8	3.7	3.5	4.2
October 2009	5.80	1.2	4.3	1.6	−0.8
October 2010	5.93	2.2	1.1	2.5	4.5

Notes: Column [3]: Median hourly pay excluding overtime, April of each year: ASHE (Table 1.6a). Employees on adult rates whose pay for survey pay-period was not affected by absence. Survey methodology changes occurred in 2004 and 2006: see notes to Table 9.2.
Column [4]: Average Earnings Index, whole economy, SA, including bonuses (July figures for 2010).
Column [5]: Retail Prices Index, all items index.

cautious approach' (LPC 2009: 2). But over the decade as a whole the NMW rates have been increased slightly faster than general wage growth.

The initial LPC recommendation for an adult rate of £3.60 was arrived at by a process that those involved have described as one of triangulation. In addition to the written and oral evidence received, they examined the previous Wage Council rates, international minimum wage rates, and the coverage and cost of various potential NMWs (Metcalf 1999). On the first of these, the LPC's first report (LPC 1998) looked at the last minimum hourly rates set by the largest seven wages councils (which in 1993 accounted for 97 per cent of Wages Council coverage), uprated to March 1998 by the Average Earnings Index (AEI). If we uprate these to April 1999 in the same way, they range from £4.02 (in Retail Food) to £3.44 (in Clothing Manufacture), with an employment weighted average hourly rate of £3.85.

The LPC also compared minimum wage rates across OECD countries in a number of ways. In purchasing power parity (PPP) terms in December 1997, these ranged from £4.56 in Belgium to £1.65 in Portugal. The median of the nine countries in the analysis was the United States with a rate of £3.67 in PPP terms. Uprated to April 1999 using the AEI, this would give an hourly rate of £3.82. There are of course difficulties with conversion of rates using PPPs. In addition, they do not take direct account of prevailing wage rates in the countries concerned. The LPC also looked at minimum wages as a percentage of full-time adult median earnings. For mid-1997, these ranged from 57 per cent (in France) to 31 per cent (in Japan). The recommended NMW rate, deflated to mid-1997, was estimated to be roughly 45 per cent of the UK full-time adult median earnings, putting it near the median of the countries considered.

How many employees were entitled to higher pay as a result of the introduction of the NMW? Answering this question proved difficult for the LPC. They initially predicted that their recommended NMW adult rate would produce coverage of about 8 per cent of adult employees. Overall they expected that slightly over 2 million people (9 per cent of employees aged 18+) would have their pay raised, by, on average, nearly one-third. (On the basis of this they predicted that it would add about 0.6 per cent to the national wage bill.)

However, there were serious problems with the data on which these calculations were based and as a result this figure seriously overstated the number affected. The calculations were based on a combination of two data sources, the New Earnings Survey (NES) and the Labour Force Survey (LFS). Both had problems estimating the number of low-paid workers. The NES was based on pay as you earn (PAYE) records. It therefore missed many low-paid workers, particularly part-timers, who fell below the PAYE threshold. It also had difficulties with those who changed jobs between the sampling date and the reference date. For these and other reasons it under-sampled the low paid.

The LFS is based on interviews with sampled individuals, with resultant potential measurement errors in earnings and hours. In particular, overstatement of hours led to understatement of the derived hourly earnings measure (constructed by dividing weekly earnings by weekly hours) and hence overestimation of the number of low-paid workers. Further errors were caused by the use of proxy interviews in some cases.

Thus, the number below a specified low-pay threshold was viewed as understated by the NES and overstated by the LFS. Adjustments were made to LFS estimates for hours mismeasurement and for proxy interviews. NES estimates were adjusted for employees below the PAYE threshold using the LFS. But the adjusted estimates from the two sources still differed a lot. In the absence of evidence on the magnitudes of the biases remaining in the adjusted estimates, the Office for National Statistics (ONS) provided a 'central estimate' by averaging the estimates from the two sources, a rather unsatisfactory situation for such important statistical information. Metcalf (2002: 570) stated it more strongly: 'such a discrepancy in official earnings statistics beggars belief'. Over the next few years the ONS attempted to implement a number of improvements to the main data sources, meaning that the commissioners were, as Brown (2002: 602) put it, 'sailing with an ever-changing statistical chart'.

As a result of these data improvements, the LPC had to repeatedly revise downwards its estimates of the number directly affected by the initial introduction. The current verdict is that '1.2 million jobs had to have their pay increased to comply with the NMW' (Metcalf 2008: 490). The introduction of the NMW therefore affected the pay of far fewer workers than the LPC had expected and intended at the time that it made its recommendation on the rate.

An interesting question to ask is: what rate would have been required to cover the 8 per cent of adult employees that the LPC thought it was covering with its recommended rate? The required ONS methodological improvements have led to the NES being replaced by the Annual Survey of Hours and Earnings (ASHE). ONS have also applied appropriate weights to earlier NES data to construct a consistent time series back to 1997. Using this reweighted, ASHE-consistent data for April 1999 indicates that an adult NMW rate of £4.12 would have been needed to cover the 8 per cent of adult employees.

It is of course hard to judge the impact that this improved statistical information would have had on the LPC recommendations or the NMW rate implemented. The Confederation of British Industry (CBI) had made strong representations for a rate below that eventually implemented and those involved have suggested that the LPC would have been reluctant to move much above their 'conservative' initial recommendation. However, together with the other elements of the triangulation process described above, an outside perspective might suggest that with better statistical information the initial adult rate could reasonably have been set somewhere between £3.90 and £4.00 per hour.

9.3. **Where are we now?**

Over the subsequent decade, the NMW rate has increased slightly more than the general level of wages. Table 9.2 shows how the adult NMW rate has changed relative to particular points in the wage distribution, based on data from the ASHE. (The numerator of the ratio is the prevailing NMW rate in April of each year—when the ASHE is conducted—and hence for the rows from 2001 onwards the rate introduced at the uprating in the previous October.) The relative NMW rate has risen from about 46 per cent of the median when it was introduced to about 51 per cent in 2007–9. It has also risen relative to the mean and to the other percentiles given in Table 9.2.

Given the increase in the 'bite' of the NMW over the decade, how many employees are now covered by NMW upratings? The 2009 LPC report estimates that in April 2008 some 958,000 jobs held by adults paid at or below the £5.52 rate implemented the previous October, representing about 4 per cent

Table 9.2. National Minimum Wage as a Percentage of Various Points of the Wage Distribution

April	Adult NMW (£)	Adult minimum wage as % of					
		Lowest decile	Lowest quartile	Median	Mean	Upper quartile	Upper decile
1999	3.60	83.9	65.1	45.7	36.6	30.4	21.1
2000	3.60	81.2	64.2	45.4	35.7	29.8	20.6
2001	3.70	80.3	63.0	44.2	34.7	29.0	19.9
2002	4.10	85.2	67.5	47.2	36.5	30.8	21.0
2003	4.20	82.4	65.8	46.5	35.9	30.5	20.8
2004	4.50	85.6	68.3	48.1	37.7	31.6	21.7
2005	4.85	88.0	69.9	49.4	38.5	32.3	22.1
2006	5.05	87.5	70.0	49.7	38.5	32.5	22.3
2007	5.35	89.2	71.7	51.0	39.6	33.6	22.9
2008	5.52	89.7	71.6	50.6	39.2	33.2	22.8
2009	5.73	89.6	71.7	50.7	39.5	33.3	22.9

Source: Low Pay Commission 2010 Report, Table 2.5.

Notes: Wage distribution data from ASHE, April of each year. Employees aged 22 and over whose pay for survey pay-period was not affected by absence. Survey methodology changes occurred in 2004 and 2006; 1999–2004 based on ASHE without supplementary information; 2005–6 uses ASHE with supplementary information; 2006–9 uses ASHE 2007 methodology; standard weights; NMW column gives NMW in April of each year.

of such jobs. It estimates that 5.3 per cent of jobs held by adults paid less than the £5.73 rate that pertained from October 2008. These figures do not tell us the number who directly benefited from each NMW uprating. Some of those paid below the October rate in April would be expected to have been paid above that by October even in the absence of a NMW uprating. Estimating the number of employees who directly benefit from an uprating of the NMW requires an assumption of what would have happened to wages in the absence of the uprating. Under the assumption that in the absence of the uprating wages would have increased in line with median earnings, the LPC estimate that 4.1 per cent of jobs (0.99 million) held by adults were covered by the October 2008 uprating from £5.52 to £5.73. If instead we assume that wages at the bottom of the distribution would have risen in line with prices, the LPC estimates that coverage was between 3.6 per cent (0.86 million) and 4.1 per cent, depending on whether CPI or RPI is used. This type of analysis suggests that probably fewer than a million adult jobs were directly affected by the October 2008 uprating.

When the NMW was introduced, the cross-country evidence suggested that the £3.60 adult rate judged relative to median earnings put the United Kingdom somewhere near the middle of the pack relative to the other countries considered. How do things look following the subsequent upratings over the past decade? Comparing ratios of adult minimum wage rates relative to full-time median earnings in Spring 2008 for the countries in the OECD Earnings Structure Database indicates that the UK rate is still roughly at the median judged in these terms.

Over the decade the adult NMW rate has risen from £3.60 in April 1999 to £5.93 at the most recent uprating in October 2010. This represents an average annual increase of 4.4 per cent. Over an equivalent period, the AEI has shown an average annual increase of 3.7 per cent.[2] Thus, the NMW has risen relative to the AEI at an average annual rate of 0.7 per cent. If the initial April 1999 rate had simply been increased in line with the AEI, it would have reached £5.49 in October 2010 on this basis. Viewed the other way round, £5.93 in October 2010 deflated by the AEI is equivalent to £3.89 in April 1999. As pointed out in Section 2, the initial setting of the NMW rate was hampered by problems with the statistical information on the wage distribution at the time. At the end of Section 2, it was suggested that with the aid of better statistical information on the wage distribution at the time the initial rate might reasonably have been set somewhere in the range £3.90–£4.00. If uprated in line with AEI, this range is equivalent to £5.95–£6.10 in October 2010.

As seen in Section 2, to cover the 8 per cent of adult employees that the LPC thought it was covering with its recommended rate, the initial rate would have needed to have been set at £4.12. If this had then been uprated in line with the AEI, it would have resulted in a rate of £6.28 in October 2010. Viewed from this perspective the higher average increase over the decade than that in the

AEI has not yet been enough to make up for the low level initially set due to the inadequate statistical information on the wage distribution at the time.

9.4. **What effects has the NMW had on employment?**

The investigation of the impact of the NMW on employment has used three main broad approaches. The first of these uses individual-level data to compare directly affected workers with a group whose wages were already slightly above the new minimum. The second uses the geographical variation in the impact of a change in the minimum on wages. It compares areas of the country where the change in the minimum directly affected a relatively high proportion of employees with areas where only a relatively low proportion were affected. The third broad approach uses firm-level data and compares firms with a high proportion of directly affected workers with firms with a lower proportion. This categorization distinguishes studies on the basis of the core comparison being made and the type of data used. Another important distinction is between studies that examine the economy as a whole and those that focus on a single low-paying sector. Stewart (2009) reviews the evidence in more detail than space allows here (see also Metcalf 2008).

The first approach, used by a number of chapters, focuses on employees directly affected by the introduction of, or an increase in, the NMW, namely those paid below the new rate whose wages needed to be raised to comply. A 'difference-in-differences' estimator is used. One would expect employees with wages below the new minimum to be more affected than a group from higher up the wage distribution. However, a direct comparison of the two groups would not be appropriate to identify any causal effect since, even in the absence of a minimum wage change, those at the bottom of the wage distribution have lower subsequent employment probabilities. This makes the difference-in-differences approach a natural one to take. The difference between the two groups in a period in which the minimum wage changed can be compared with the equivalent difference in a period in which it did not.

We want to ask what the employment position of those directly affected by the introduction of, or an increase in, the NMW would have been if the minimum had not changed. We cannot observe this alternative state of the world. So the aim is to find a suitable comparison to enable us to address this counterfactual question. This is done by using a comparison group in conjunction with a comparison between change and no-change periods. If after suitable adjustment those in the comparison group are similar enough to those directly affected, the employment effect of the NMW can be estimated by a ceteris paribus comparison of the employment experiences of the two groups.

This approach was used to estimate the impact of the 1999 NMW introduction on employment probabilities by Stewart (2004). The subsequent upratings have been examined in a number of other chapters. Most recently, Dickens et al. (2009) have applied the approach to each of the upratings between 2001 and 2006 inclusive. These studies have used various contrasting datasets, particularly the LFS and the NES/ASHE. In the LFS, they have examined various constructions of the wage measure. They have checked the robustness of the results by examining various modifications to the simple estimator. They have used a 'regression-adjusted' difference-in-differences estimator, adding a vector of individual characteristics to the equivalent regression equation to sweep up any differences in observable characteristics between the 'directly affected' and 'comparison' groups that are not picked up by the additive group and time effects. They have used a 'wage gap' variable as well as a binary group variable. They have extended the specification to multiple wage groups covering the rest of the wage distribution to improve the estimation of the effects of the individual characteristics without changing the comparison. They have used multiple time periods, with additional time effects. They have used a suitable nonlinear model for the employment transition probability as an alternative to a linear one. No significant adverse employment effects are found for any of the demographic groups considered for any of these specifications or in any of the data sets examined. The conclusion on the evidence from the direct individual-level comparison studies is fairly clear and unambiguous.

The second approach uses geographical wage variation to estimate the effect on employment. It can still be viewed as a 'differential impact' approach, but in this case we use the fact that the impact varies geographically. Once again it is based on a simple idea. The fact that the UK minimum wage is the same in all parts of the country while wage levels generally vary geographically means that the 'bite', or extent of the impact on wages, varies geographically. In some areas of the country, a change in the NMW rate has relatively little impact since few employees are paid below the new rate, while in others many more need their wages raised to comply with the new rate. The NMW reaches far further up the wage distribution in Redcar than in Reading, in Middlesborough than in Milton Keynes. This variation in bite can be exploited to estimate the effect of the NMW introduction, or subsequent NMW increases, on employment. The competitive labour market model then predicts that, other things equal, we should see a relative decline in employment in low-wage areas where the NMW bites more deeply into the wage distribution than in higher wage areas where relatively few employees are paid below the new NMW rate. The chapters using this approach test this prediction in various ways.

This approach was used by Stewart (2002) to estimate the effect of the 1999 NMW introduction on employment. The analysis divides Great Britain into 140 'local areas'. This division is used in a variety of estimation methods. The analysis is conducted at both the area level and the individual level; estimates are presented based on both cross-sectional changes and individual-level panel data; both estimates based on comparing groups of low-wage and high-wage areas of the country, and estimates using the proportion of employees in an area initially below the NMW as a continuous measure are used; and employment rates and probabilities using LFS data, using Annual Business Inquiry (ABI) data, and using NES data are all examined. In all cases the estimated effects on employment are not significantly different from zero. In addition, consistent with the hypothesis of no effect, the estimates are positive as often as negative. Overall the chapter finds that employment growth after the NMW introduction was not significantly different in areas of the country with a high proportion of low-wage workers, whose wages needed to be raised to comply, from that in areas with a low proportion of such workers.

With this method too an extensive range of data sources and specifications has been used in several studies. Some of these studies have been hampered by difficulties with the data used and variable constructions, which cause problems of interpretation (see Stewart 2009). The others do not find there to have been worse employment performance in areas where the NMW and its increases bite more than in areas where wages are less affected.

The third approach uses firm-level comparisons. In an innovative paper, Machin et al. (2003) investigate the impact of the introduction of the NMW on the UK residential care homes sector. They conducted their own postal surveys of employers in this sector before and after the introduction of the NMW. They use the data they collected to examine the relationship between changes in employment and the fraction of workers at the home initially paid below the incoming NMW. Before the introduction of the NMW about one in three workers in this sector were paid less than the level at which it was introduced. In April 1999, after its introduction, they find a spike of about 30 per cent of employees paid exactly at the NMW. They find little evidence of non-compliance. The introduction of the NMW caused a major shift in the wage structure in this sector. It is clearly a sector in which the NMW introduction 'bit hard'.

The product market side of the sector is important and unusual and needs to be stressed. A significant proportion of the residents in the homes have their fees paid by local authorities or social services. The level of local authority/social security funding was not increased to meet the NMW, making it hard for homes to pass on their increased wage costs. Prices were to a large degree capped. In addition to having a large proportion of low-wage workers and price caps, the sector also consists of large numbers of small firms doing a very homogeneous activity in geographically concentrated markets and is not unionized. For all these reasons we might expect this sector to be particularly vulnerable to the introduction of a NMW. If disemployment effects are going to be found anywhere, this sector would seem to be a prime candidate. However, an important corollary of these features is, as Machin et al. (2003: 156) caution, that 'one must be careful not to extrapolate from studies of one sector (especially the kind of sector we study) to conclusions about the economy as a whole'.

They find a sizeable impact on wages and a moderate employment reduction following the NMW introduction. However, as they point out, the estimated employment effect is 'not sizeable given how heavily the wage structure was affected' (Machin et al. 2003: 154). My conclusion about the Machin et al. (2003) estimates is that there is evidence of a disemployment effect in this sector, but that it is of moderate size and that we might label it 'fragile'. First, finding such an effect requires the inclusion of the set of control variables in the model to produce the effect—it is not evident in the raw data. Second, this disemployment effect is not found when data on changes in an earlier period (when there was no minimum wage in this sector) are additionally used to capture the counterfactual, suggesting that the simpler estimates may not be due to the effect of the minimum wage. Third, the survey response and matching rates that produce the balanced panels used to estimate these effects are worryingly low and cause for concern about how representative these data are.

To sum up, most of the empirical evidence on the impact of the NMW on employment points to an absence of significant negative effects of either the introduction of the NMW or its subsequent upratings. This is particularly true when data on individual employees is used. The only convincing exception to this is the research analysing the residential care homes sector. Thus, the empirical case for adverse employment effects of the NMW rests on the studies of this sector. Its product market side is unusual and one must be careful not to make inferences to other sectors or the economy as a whole. In fact, the estimated employment effects for this sector are rather small given how heavily the wage structure was affected and there are a number of reservations about the strength of the evidence. Outside this very particular sector, the bulk of the evidence indicates that the NMW has had little or no adverse impact on employment.

9.5. How can this be?

It is sometimes suggested that evidence of no negative employment effects, and even possible positive effects, because they are counter to economic theory, must be the result of defective empirical methodology. It is important to remember that this is not the case. While the simplest economic model predicts that an increase in the minimum wage will reduce employment, more sophisticated and realistic models do not. In the simplest neoclassical model of a competitive labour market, all workers are paid their marginal product. The introduction of a minimum wage above the market clearing wage will induce firms to lay off workers and reduce employment. There is a clear prediction that employment will fall.

When the labour market is not fully competitive, the picture is more complicated. In the neoclassical model, each firm takes the wage as given and can hire as many workers as it wants at that wage. In monopsony-type models, individual firms have some degree of power in the setting of their wages. In these models an increase in the minimum wage can, up to a point, lead to a rise in employment. More generally, if the firm has some degree of monopsonistic power in wage setting, there is no longer a clear prediction of the sign of the impact of a minimum wage on employment.

The various models that have been proposed differ in the source of this employer power in the wage-setting process. An employer may have some degree of monopsony power if, for example, there are search frictions or mobility costs which make it costly for a worker to change jobs. There can also be this type of effect when there are differing valuations of the non-pecuniary aspects of jobs. There may be 'efficiency wage' effects where firms by paying employees more raise their productivity, for example, by raising employee morale or motivation, or increasing the cost of job loss to the employee, or reducing the quit rate. As a result of these and other potential influences of this type, the effect of an increase in the minimum wage on employment cannot be predicted unambiguously in more complex situations.

Firms may have used other routes to adjust to the introduction of, or an increase in, the NMW (see e.g. Metcalf 2008). Some firms may be able to adapt by reorganizing their operations so as to increase the productivity of the affected workers in line with their increase in wages. Some firms may adjust at the hours margin rather than the number of workers. Some firms may be able to pass on the increase in wage costs by raising prices, depending on the degree of competitiveness of the product market in which they operate and the wage structures of their competitors. Some firms may be able to absorb the extra wage costs as a reduction in profits without threatening their survival, depending on the economic rents in the sector and how profitable they were before the change.

9.6. **Conclusions and looking forward**

Outside the very unusual residential care homes sector, the evidence indicates that the NMW has not had an adverse effect on employment. Alongside this, it was pointed out in Section 2 that to cover the 8 per cent of adult employees that the LPC thought it was covering with its recommended rate for the introduction of the NMW, the initial rate would have needed to have been set at £4.12, and in Section 3 that if this rate had then been uprated purely in line with the AEI, it would have resulted in a rate of £6.28 in October 2010.

In combination, these features (the too low initial rate and the lack of employment effects) suggest that the LPC should recommend, and the government of the day implement, NMW increases above those in the AEI to continue the catch up with the initially intended rate of coverage, while continuing to monitor the impact on employment. This line of argument suggests an increase in October 2011 to £6.28 plus annual AEI growth at the time of the LPC recommendation, which might perhaps take it to around £6.40.

☐ NOTES

1. This chapter is based on a paper presented at the conference in honour of David Metcalf, at LSE, on 14 December 2009. The author thanks David Marsden, David Metcalf, and other participants at the conference for helpful comments.
2. The AEI adjustments in this paragraph and the next are based on seasonally adjusted AEI with a six-month lag. Thus, the April 1999–October 2010 comparison uses (seasonally adjusted) AEI growth from October 1998 to April 2010.

☐ REFERENCES

Brown, William (2002) 'The operation of the Low Pay Commission', *Employee Relations*, 24, 595–605.

Dickens, R., Riley, R. and Wilkinson D. (2009) 'The Employment and Hours of Work Effects of the Changing National Minimum Wage', Report to the LPC.

LPC Low Pay Commission (1998) *The National Minimum Wage*, First Report, Cm. 3976, London: The Stationery Office.

——(2009) *National Minimum Wage*, LPC Report 2009, Cm. 7611, London: The Stationery Office.

Machin, S., Manning, A. and Rahman L. (2003) 'Where the Minimum Wage Bites Hard: Introduction of Minimum Wages to a Low Wage Sector', *Journal of the European Economic Association*, 1, 154–80.

Metcalf, D. (1999) 'The Low Pay Commission and the National Minimum Wage', *Economic Journal*, 109, F44–66.

——(2002) 'The National Minimum Wage: Coverage, Impact and Future', *Oxford Bulletin of Economics and Statistics*, 64, 567–82.

——(2008) 'Why has the British National Minimum Wage had Little or No Impact on Employment?', *Journal of Industrial Relations*, 50, 489–572.

Neumark, D. and Wascher W. (2007) 'Minimum Wages and Employment', *Foundations and Trends in Microeconomics*, 3, 1–182.

Stewart, M.B. (2002) 'Estimating the Impact of the Minimum Wage Using Geographical Wage Variation', *Oxford Bulletin of Economics and Statistics*, 64, 583–605.

——(2004) 'The Impact of the Introduction of the UK Minimum Wage on the Employment Probabilities of Low-Wage Workers', *Journal of the European Economic Association*, 2, 67–97.

——(2009) 'The National Minimum Wage after a Decade: An Examination of the Evidence on Employment Effects', *Paper presented at Labour Market Policy in the 21st Century: A conference in honour of David Metcalf*, LSE, 14 December 2009.

10 Minimum Wages and Wage Inequality

ALAN MANNING

10.1. Introduction

From its establishment in 1997 until 2007, David Metcalf was a member of the Low Pay Commission (LPC) that effectively sets the level and form of the National Minimum Wage (NMW). Formally, the LPC makes recommendations to the government which then decides whether or not to accept them, but in practice its recommendations have been wholly accepted.

A very important reason why the recommendations of the LPC have carried such authority is because of the way in which the LPC set about its work. Crucially, its recommendations are strongly based on evidence so that, for example, the claim that the NMW would cost millions of jobs could be shown to be demonstrably false. This evidence-based approach of the LPC was in line with wider government commitments to 'evidence-based policymaking', though this probably had more staying-power in the LPC than in government more generally. As the member of the LPC with the greatest background in economics, I suspect that David played a very important role in establishing the credibility of the LPC.

The initial minimum wage was set at a modest level of £3.60 per hour, reflecting a feeling that it was best to start low and evaluate its effects rather than run the risk of setting it too high. Employers and their lobbying organization, the Confederation of British Industry (CBI), were very concerned about job losses, and the Bank of England was worried about the potential effect on inflation. The research indicated these fears were exaggerated, and in subsequent years, the rate was raised faster than average earnings, and coverage was extended to younger workers. In the more uncertain economic times of recent years, the LPC has again recommended only modest increases in the minimum wage. Metcalf (2007) and Brown (2009) provide excellent overviews of the research.

But, although the minimum wage is here to stay, there is considerable modesty about the effects it is thought to have on the economy. For example, the LPC estimates that at most 5 per cent of workers are beneficiaries of it and that there are fairly modest if any spillovers. As a result one could be forgiven for drawing the conclusion that the minimum wage is largely irrelevant for the most commonly used measures of wage inequality among lower earnings, such as the ratio of the median to the tenth percentile, the 50–10 ratio. As a result accounts of the evolution of wage inequality, for example, Machin (chapter 11 in this volume), often make almost no mention of the minimum wage. The minimum wage is seen as being of considerable value to a small number of people and is worthwhile for that reason. But, although there are sometimes claims by politicians to the contrary, it is no big deal for the economy as a whole.

Here, I will argue that this view is mistaken, that the minimum wage has a larger effect on the wage distribution than commonly believed. To make this case I will discuss both British and American evidence. The outline of this chapter is as follows. The next section provides a brief overview of the history of the NMW and some evidence on its impact. I then discuss evidence for spillovers for the United Kingdom and the United States. I then discuss why there might be spillovers and, finally, what are the implications of recognizing the existence of spillovers for the setting of the NMW.

10.2. **A brief history of the NMW**

Going into the 1997 general election, the United Kingdom was the only major economy with no explicit or implicit minimum wage, the Wages Councils (that had set minimum wages in certain sectors) having been abolished in 1993. In the 1997 election, one of the main issues dividing the parties was the NMW—the Labour Party wanted to introduce one, the Conservative party to retain the status quo. At the time the NMW was regarded as very controversial, the Conservative Party was claiming that such a policy would cost millions of jobs, an estimate kindly provided by Patrick Minford.

Following the Labour Party's landslide victory in the 1997 election, the introduction of the NMW became government policy. But rather than legislate directly, the new government set up an independent LPC in July 1997 to make recommendations on the appropriate form and level that the minimum wage should take.

David Metcalf was one of the founding members of the LPC, which first reported in June 1998, recommending a single minimum wage for all adults aged 22 and over and a lower rate for those aged 18–21. Initially, no minimum wage was set for those aged 16–17. Over time the adult minimum has been uprated and a minimum wage extended to those aged 16–17.

10.3. **The minimum wage and wage inequality in the United Kingdom**

What has been the effect of the NMW on UK wage inequality? I start with some background on the evolution of UK wage inequality. Figure 10.1 presents some commonly quoted statistics on the evolution of UK wage inequality in hourly earnings for the period 1975–2009 inclusive using data from the New Earnings Survey (NES) and its successor, the Annual Survey of Hours and Earnings (ASHE). The basic facts are well known but will be summarized here.

At the top of the earnings distribution, represented here by the 90/50 ratio, the figure shows an almost uninterrupted increase from 1977 to 2009. There is perhaps some indication of a slowdown in the rate of growth after about 2005. Nevertheless, it is still more or less accurate to say the past thirty-five years have seen the high-paid pulling ever further away from the average. The picture for the bottom part of the earnings distribution, summarized by the 50/10 ratio, shows a rather different picture. From 1977 to the mid-1990s, there was a rise in lower tail wage inequality that more or less mirrors the rise in upper tail wage inequality. But after the mid-1990s, something different seemed to happen—there has been a fall in lower tail wage inequality with most of the change after 1997. This fall has not reversed all of the earlier rise— lower tail wage inequality is now at about 1990 levels but has not reversed

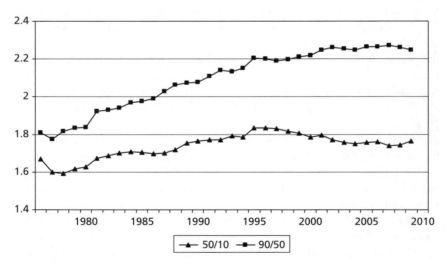

Figure 10.1. UK Wage Inequality, 1975–2009

Source: NES/ASHE. Data relate to hourly earnings excluding overtime for all workers.

the rise seen in the 1980s. The seemingly inexorable rise in upper tail pay inequality has not occurred at the lower tail.

I will not provide here a complete explanation of these changes in wage inequality—see chapter 11 by Stephen Machin for that. What I want to focus on is the role—if any—of the NMW in explaining the fall in wage inequality since the mid-1990s. It is tempting to think that the NMW has something to do with the fall in lower tail wage inequality since the 1990s but does such a claim stand up to scrutiny?

There are a number of potential problems with arguing that the NMW can explain an important part of the fall in lower tail wage inequality. First, the timing does not seem to be quite right with the peak in lower tail wage inequality occurring before the introduction of the NMW. However, most of the fall in lower tail wage inequality occurred after the introduction in 1999, so this criticism is not fatal.[1]

To investigate this a little further, Figure 10.2 plots the change in the log 50/10 ratio against the change in the log NMW for each year after 2000. Logs are used to show proportional changes in the ratio and the NMW—these are approximately equal to percentage changes. Each data point is marked with the year in which the minimum is raised—which is always in October. If the minimum wage affects the 50/10 ratio, we would expect years with a big

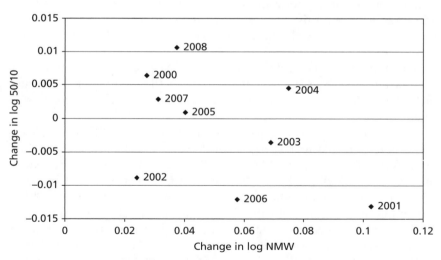

Figure 10.2. The Relationship between Changes in Lower Tail Wage Inequality and Changes in the Minimum Wage

Notes: Data from NES/ASHE. Labelling refers to the year of increase of minimum wage so that '2006' is the change in log 50/10 from April 2006 to April 2007.

increase in the minimum wage to be associated with smaller than average changes in the ratio, that is, to see a negative relationship in Figure 10.2. A regression shows the relationship is negative but the coefficient only has a t-statistic of 1.35, so is not significantly different from zero at conventional levels. The problem is that some years—2002 and 2006—have large falls in lower tail wage inequality but relatively small increases in the minimum wage. However, the number of observations is relatively small so this is also hardly conclusive.

Another problem with believing that the NMW has had a large impact on the 50/10 ratio is that the best estimates of the number of workers directly affected by the minimum wage never get to 10 per cent. When the minimum wages was first being introduced, estimates of how many workers would be directly affected were around 7–8 per cent but it subsequently became clear that this was an overestimate, the product of the problems with the earnings statistics in the Labour Force Survey (LFS)[2] (see the chapter by Stewart). Since then, the LPC has produced estimates of the numbers affected which are generally no higher than 5 per cent. For example, the 2009 report of the LPC (Low Pay Commission 2009, Figure 2.10) estimated that in April 2008 only 3.4 per cent of workers aged 22 and above were paid at or below the minimum wage and that 5.3 per cent would be affected by the increase that had already been accepted for October 2008. Because earnings grow over time, that estimate of the numbers directly affected in October 2008 is almost certainly an overestimate. And the LPC expressed the view that this was the highest number of workers directly affected that had been seen to date—this can also be seen in Figure 10.3.

What this means is that if the NMW is to have affected the 50/10 ratio, it must be affecting the earnings of the 10th percentile, who the LPC estimated in 2008 were paid 10 per cent above the minimum wage, that is, there must be spillovers.

One might think it possible that spillovers extend to the 10th percentile but the compression in lower tail wage inequality does not stop there. Figure 10.4, taken from an LPC report (LPC 2009, Figure 2.12), shows the percentage increase in earnings relative to the median for all percentiles of the adult hourly pay distribution. One can see that, for the period up to 1998, a monotonic relationship with inequality widening at all points. But, since 1998, all percentiles up to about the 25th have risen faster than the median. If one thought this was explained by the NMW, one would have to argue that the NMW has an effect up to the 25th percentile. The 2009 LPC report suggests that the NMW is responsible for this but not much in the way of hard evidence is provided to support this claim.

What formal evidence we have on the existence of spillovers relates to the period just after the introduction of the NMW and essentially none was found. Dickens and Manning (2004a) looked at evidence from the LFS (using a better

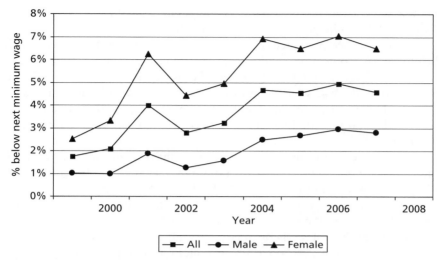

Figure 10.3. The Percentage of Workers Affected by the NMW
Source: Butcher et al. (2010).

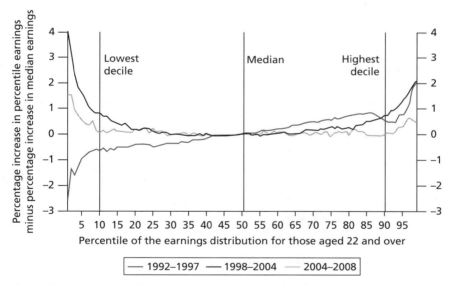

Figure 10.4. Percentage Changes in Earnings by Percentile of the Earnings Distribution
Source: Low Pay Commission (2009).

methodology than that initially used by the ONS) and found essentially no impact above the 5th percentile. And Dickens and Manning (2004b) examined data from the residential care homes sector (a sector greatly affected by the NMW) and, again, concluded there were little or no spillovers. However, both of these studies were of a period immediately after the first introduction of the NMW and it is quite possible that things are different now.

All the evidence presented so far is circumstantial and it would be very helpful to have some more solid evidence for a link between various measures of wage inequality and the NMW. At the aggregate level this is difficult because the NMW is what it says on the tin—a *national* minimum wage. One would like to have variation in the minimum wage across areas and then see whether areas with high minimum wages have lower levels of wage inequality.

Although we do not have area variation in the level of the NMW, we do have area variation in the bite of the minimum wage because the general level of earnings varies quite a lot across the United Kingdom while the minimum wage does not. So, we would expect the NMW to have little effect on the wage distribution in London where wages are generally rather high but a much bigger impact in Wales where wages are generally rather low. If this was the case, we would expect to see a bigger fall in lower tail wage inequality in low-wage areas of the country than in high-wage areas. Figure 10.5—taken from Butcher et al. (2010)—plots the change in the 50/10 ratio for the period

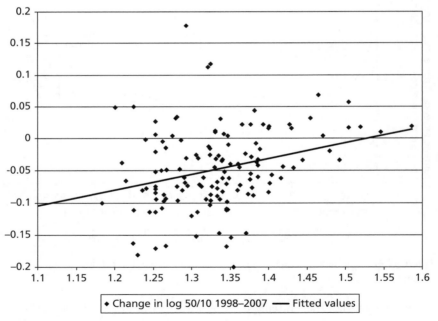

Figure 10.5. Changes in Regional Wage Inequality

Source: Butcher et al. (2010).

1998–2007 against the proportion low paid in 1997 where each data point is a local authority. One does indeed see the negative relationship one would expect if the NMW affects the 50/10 ratio.

Of course, there are perhaps other factors that can account for the variation across local authorities in the fall in lower tail wage inequality. It may be that differential changes in unemployment or changes in the skill mix or changes in the number of immigrants can account for this. All of these factors are investigated by Butcher et al. (2010) but no factor, other than the initial level of wages, is found to be significant. There is, of course, a leap in going from assuming that one can equate the initial level of wages with the bite of the NMW, so this evidence is, once again, suggestive rather than conclusive. The NMW would have to stop being national and to have regional variation for the evidence to be stronger. It is for this reason that I now turn to a discussion of the United States where there is some subnational variation in the minimum wage.

10.4. The minimum wage and wage inequality in the United States

The United States introduced a federal minimum wage in 1938. Although coverage is not universal (it has been extended over time), this can broadly be thought of as a floor below which no wage rates can go. However, individual states can enact higher minimum wages if they so desire. Historically the federal minimum has been raised only occasionally but by large amounts when it was. The number of states with minima above the federal minimum tends to be largest in the periods when the federal minimum has not been raised for many years. This can be seen in Figure 10.6 that presents the real value of the federal minimum and the effective minimum (computed as a weighted average of the maximum of the state and federal minima). The federal minimum wage remained constant in nominal terms over the nine-year period between 1981 and 1990. Similarly, the federal minimum wage remained at $5.15 between September 1997 and July 2007, and by July 2007, the real value of the federal minimum was lower than it had been at any point in the past fifty years. In the late 1980s, only fifteen states' minimum wages exceeded the federal minimum wage; by 2007, thirty states' minimum wages did. As a result, the average real value of the minimum wage applicable to workers in 2007 was not much lower than it was in 1997, and was significantly higher than if states had not enacted their own minimum wages.

Figures 10.7a and 10.7b—taken from Autor et al. (2009)—plot the evolution of the 90/50 ratio and 50/10 ratio for US hourly earnings. As in the United Kingdom, upper tail wage inequality shows an inexorable rise but

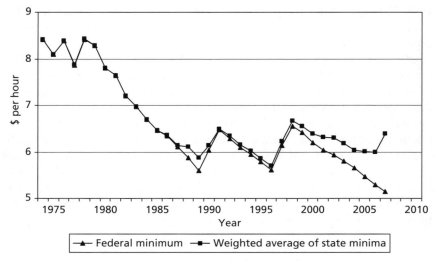

Figure 10.6. Federal and State Minima in the United States (2007$)

Source: Autor et al. (2009).

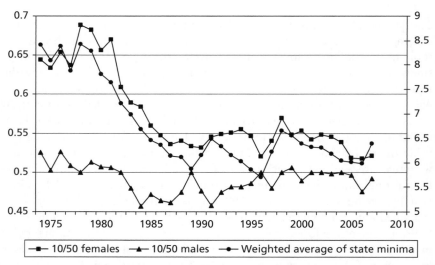

Figure 10.7a. Lower Tail Wage Inequality and the Minimum Wage in the United States

Note: The scale on the minimum wage variable is chosen to best show the correlation.

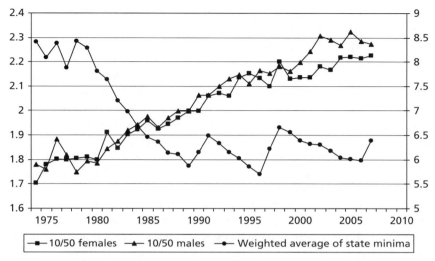

Figure 10.7b. Upper Tail Wage Inequality and the Minimum Wage in the United States

Note: Same note as for Figure 10.7a

lower tail wage inequality shows a more complicated pattern with rises in the 1980s and then a modest fall. By the end of the period, lower tail wage inequality is not very different from the beginning of the period.

As in the United Kingdom, it is very tempting to make a link between changes in the minimum wage and lower tail wage inequality, particularly in the 1980s. That there is such a link (especially for women) has been shown by DiNardo et al. (1996). Perhaps the best-known study is by Lee (1999), who essentially argued that all of the rise in lower tail wage inequality in the 1980s could be explained by the fall in the real value of the minimum wage.

He investigated this using a regression of the form:

$$w_{st}(p) - w_{st}(50) = \alpha_t + \beta_1^p(w_{st}^m - \mu_{st}) + \beta_2^p(w_{st}^m - \mu_{st})^2 + \epsilon_{st}$$

where $w_{st}(p)$ is the log hourly wage at percentile p in state s in year t, $w_{st}(50)$ is the median log hourly wage, w_{st}^m is the log minimum wage in force in state s in year t, and μ_{st} is a measure of the average hourly wage in state s in year t. The basic idea behind this regression is that the left-hand side is a measure of inequality and the right-hand side is a measure of the bite of the minimum wage, measured by the minimum relative to average wages in the state. The quadratic specification is used to capture the sensible idea that the impact of the minimum wage depends on how high it is set.

Using this specification, Lee (1999) finds powerful effects of the minimum wage on wage inequality. As in the United Kingdom, this runs into the problem that this implies the minimum wage is affecting percentiles of the wage distribution far above where it actually seems to bite. Figure 10.8—again taken from Autor et al. (2009)—shows the proportion of hours paid at or below the minimum.

Autor et al. (2009) argue there are problems with the Lee methodology which lead to an overestimate of the importance of the minimum wage. The Lee specification makes an assumption that the degree of inequality in a state is uncorrelated with the average level of wages, a claim that is not supported by the data. If one alters his specification to include state fixed effects to capture the idea that some states have intrinsically more inequality than others, a different problem emerges. This is caused by the fact that a measure of average wages appears on both the left-hand side (the median) and the right-hand side of the estimating equation. This causes a correlation that is spurious between wage inequality and the minimum wage.

Autor et al. (2009) propose a method for dealing with this problem and show that the estimates of the impact of the minimum wage on inequality are substantially lower than those proposed by Lee. However, this study still finds that the minimum wage has an apparent effect on the wage distribution considerably above those who are directly paid the minimum. This still leaves the minimum wage as of non-trivial importance for the evolution of observed lower tail wage inequality—as in the United Kingdom. So there does seem to be evidence for spillovers in both countries—we now turn to a discussion of why they might exist.

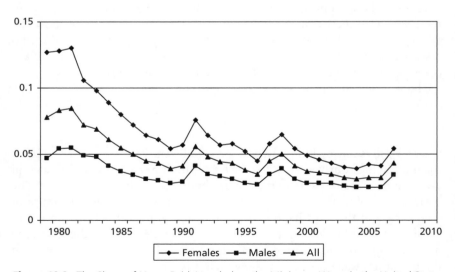

Figure 10.8. The Share of Hours Paid At or below the Minimum Wage in the United States
Source: Autor et al. (2009).

10.5. **Explaining spillovers**

The evidence presented so far suggests that the minimum wage in both the United States and the United Kingdom has more pervasive effects on observed wage inequality than one would expect given the numbers of workers who seem to be paid the minimum. This raises the question as to why we observe these apparent spillovers though perhaps the best answer to that question is 'why not' as we will not lack for potential explanations.

The first possible explanation is measurement issues. On this view the minimum wage does not affect the wages of anyone who is really paid above the minimum but appears to do so because the wage data we use is measured with error. Such measurement errors are very likely to occur when, for example, hourly earnings are derived by dividing a measure of weekly earnings by a measure of weekly hours. Indeed, it was exactly because this was the only information on hourly earnings available in the UK LFS prior to 1999 that the initial ONS estimates of the proportion of workers paid the minimum wage were substantial overestimates. The reason measurement error leads to apparent spillovers in the observed wage distribution is that some of those observed with wages above the minimum are actually paid the minimum and consequently receive any rise in it. As a result, a rise in the minimum appears to raise the earnings of those above the minimum.

For the US studies, this might be a serious issue. Autor et al. (2009) investigate whether all the observed spillovers can be caused by measurement problems and fail to reject this hypothesis. In the US data there are also sizeable proportions of workers observed to be paid below the minimum, something one might also expect if the measure of wages has sizeable measurement errors.

However, this explanation for the spillovers is less plausible for the United Kingdom as there is good reason to believe that the NES/ASHE data is of high quality. For example, trivial proportions are observed to be paid below the minimum. So, one is left with the conclusion that, most likely, there are real spillovers.

In the competitive model, the 'puzzle' arises because labour economists often have in mind a model in which the marginal product of a worker is simply a given, uninfluenced by anything else happening in the economy. If this were the case, then a minimum wage would simply truncate the wage distribution at the minimum as all those previously paid below it would lose their jobs. There would be truncation, but there would be no spike. This model is a simple one and convenient to work with, but there is no particular reason to believe it to be true and plausible generalizations can readily explain the existence of spillovers.

Although claims are sometimes made to the contrary, it is actually relatively straightforward to construct theoretical models of the labour market in which there are spillovers. If the labour market is competitive, one would expect workers who are paid similar wages to be close substitutes. One cannot then raise the wages of some workers to the minimum without affecting the demand for labour of workers paid higher than the minimum. This change in demand will then also affect the market-clearing wage. Teulings (2000, 2003) works through a model with this property fully and uses it to conclude that virtually all of the rise in US lower tail wage inequality in the 1980s could be explained by the fall in the real value of the federal minimum wage.

If the labour market is not competitive but has some monopsonistic element to it then, again, one would expect the minimum wage to have spillovers with the effect this time working through an effect on the supply of labour to individual firms. The discussion that follows is largely drawn from Manning (2003).

Providing a theoretical model in which there are spillovers is not difficult. For example, the very popular Burdett-Mortensen model (Burdett and Mortensen 1998) predicts that a binding minimum wage affects wages at every point in the wage distribution although the effect is weaker as one moves up the percentiles. But, this theoretical model does not make it very clear why we might expect spillovers.

A simple-minded approach to firm wage setting might conclude that the only effect of the minimum wage on the wage chosen by an employer will be if it is a binding constraint but that an employer who pays strictly above the minimum will be unaffected by changes in it, that is, there will be no spillovers. Another way to put this is to say that there can only be spillovers to the extent that the minimum wage affects the productivity of workers or the labour supply curve facing the firm.

An effect on productivity is most likely to occur if there are changes in employment as a result of the minimum wage that affect the output of the product and hence, through an industry demand curve, the price. Such an effect is likely to be similar at all points in the wage distribution: the evidence discussed above does not support this view.

So, the most likely route for spillovers is through the labour supply curve to an employer. Why might labour supply to an employer depend on the minimum wage? Consider an employer who initially pays just above what is going to be the minimum wage. When a minimum wage is introduced, the gap narrows between this employer's wage and the wages paid by lower wage employers. As a result it is less likely that workers of those employers will come to work for this one if they get a job offer and more likely that this firm's workers will leave to go to work in those firms (though they will still be taking a wage cut, it is smaller than before). Hence the labour supply to this employer is likely to fall. As one moves up the wage distribution, the impact of what happens in minimum wage employers is likely to have less and less impact on an employer. Hence, the minimum wage will reduce labour supply to employers who pay above the minimum wage but proportionately more in low-wage employers.

This implies that an increase in the minimum wage raises the elasticity of the labour supply curve facing an employer: this, through the usual mechanism in monopsony, leads firms to choose higher wages. But, it is likely that this change in the elasticity is smaller in higher wage firms as they are less-influenced by the minimum wage so this effect declines as wages increase. Hence, there will be spillover effects that decline as one moves up the wage distribution.

A final reason why spillovers might occur is if workers are concerned not just about their own wages but 'relativities'. Wage rises for the lowest paid as a result of the minimum wage will reduce relativities unless those workers paid above the minimum get some pay increase, that is, unless there are spillovers. In addition, firms that want to provide some incentive for the lowest paid workers to get pay rises or promotions may also want to maintain relativities.

So, the problem is not really to explain why there might be spillovers but an embarrassment of potential explanations for why they might be there. Our existing studies cannot distinguish between these competing theories and that is a potentially interesting line for future research.

Once one acknowledges the existence of spillovers, how does this affect the appropriate level of the minimum wage, that is, how should the LPC conduct its business? That is the subject of the next section.

10.6. **Spillovers and the level of the minimum wage**

If we believe the minimum wage has spillovers, how does this affect the level at which it should be set? We will consider two aspects to this question—the effect on wage inequality and the effect on employment.

If the minimum wage has spillovers, then the effect on the wage distribution reaches further up than one might have expected. To give an example, suppose one is thinking of setting the minimum wage at a level such that 10 per cent of workers are directly affected. If one suddenly realizes there is a spillover, does this become more or less attractive? The answer is that it depends. Suppose the spillover reaches to the 25th percentile. If one wants to raise the wages of workers in the bottom half relative to the top half of the wage distribution, this makes the minimum wage more effective in reducing wage inequality so one is likely to favour it more. However, if the spillovers are very large this may not be the case. Suppose, for the sake of argument, that spillovers were so strong that everybody got the same percentage increase in wages (which was the assumption made by Patrick Minford when he estimated in the 1990s that the NMW would cost millions of jobs). Then an increase in the minimum wages has no effect on wage inequality—it simply raises all wages. If one is interested solely in wage inequality, this makes a minimum wage rather unattractive.

All of this discussion has neglected the fact that the minimum wage may also have some effect on employment. If such employment effects exist, how does this affect the optimal minimum wage when there are spillovers? The answer depends on what one thinks is the effect of the minimum wage on employment, a controversial topic. If one thinks the minimum wage costs jobs then anything—like spillovers—that increases the effect of the minimum wage on the wage distribution makes the minimum wage a less appealing policy. However, if—as some studies suggest—the minimum wage may, over the range set in the United States and the United Kingdom, raise employment then anything that increases the effect of the minimum wage on the wage distribution makes the minimum wage a more appealing policy.

It is also worth noting that the existence of spillovers affects how one might investigate the effect of the minimum wage on employment. In the United Kingdom, an influential methodology (Stewart 2004a, 2004b) has been to compare the employment rates of workers paid below the minimum wage with workers paid just above. The justification has been that the first group is affected by the minimum, the second not. But the existence of spillovers casts doubt on this assumption. If spillovers exist then the rise in wages may be very similar for the two groups and so the expected employment effects would also be similar, which is the conclusion drawn by these studies.

10.7. **Conclusion**

Since its origin in 1997, the NMW has gone from being a highly controversial policy to one commanding universal support from all the main political parties. Although the Conservative Party abolished the wages councils and fought the introduction of the minimum wage, they no longer propose to remove the National Minimum Wage. In an interview in the *Guardian* in 2005, David Cameron, then the new leader of the Conservative Party, said 'I think the minimum wage has been a success' and 'it turned out much better than many people expected, including the CBI'. And, in a 2008 lecture, the then shadow chancellor, George Osborne, said that 'modern Conservatives acknowledge the fairness of a minimum wage'. And the Conservative Mayor of London, Boris Johnson has supported a 'living wage' for London, essentially a higher minimum wage to take account of higher living costs in London. The bottom line is that the UK's NMW is here to stay—it may be that the Conservatives do not increase it as much as the Labour Party would have done but these are relatively small differences.

David Metcalf has played a very important role in this remarkable transformation that has seen the NMW become an established part of the UK labour market landscape for the foreseeable future. However, while the NMW is here to stay it is widely believed to have had rather limited effects on the labour market. In this chapter I have argued that David's work has been of rather more substance, that the minimum wage has had a more pervasive effect on wage inequality than previously thought, and has played an important role in the decline of lower tail wage inequality that we have seen over the past ten to fifteen years. There is a lot for David's successors to live up to.

☐ NOTES

1. It should be noted that NES/ASHE collects its data for one week in April each year. As the NMW was introduced in April 1999, it is widely believed that it is not entirely clear whether the 1999 data is better thought of as before or after the NMW was in place—it is probably a mixture of both.
2. The initial estimate was an average of 10 per cent that came from the LFS and 5 per cent from the NES. It subsequently became clear that the LFS estimate was an overestimate caused by measurement problems in the construction of hourly earnings in the LFS.

☐ REFERENCES

Autor, D., Manning, A., and Smith, C. (2009) 'The Contribution of the Minimum Wage to U.S. Wage Inequality over Three Decades: A Re-Assessment', *MIT Working Paper* 3279, Massachusetts Institute of Technology, Massachusetts.

Brown, W. (2009) 'The Process of Fixing the British National Minimum Wage, 1997–2007', *British Journal of Industrial Relations*, 47, 429–43.

Burdett, K. and Mortensen, D.T. (1998) 'Wage Differentials, Employer Size, and Unemployment', *International Economic Review*, 39(2), May, 257–73.

Butcher, T., Dickens, R., and Manning, A. (2010) 'The Impact of the National Minimum Wage on the Wage Distribution', *Low Pay Commission Research Project*.

Dickens, R. and Manning, A. (2004a) 'Has The National Minimum Wage Reduced UK Wage Inequality?', *Journal of the Royal Statistical Society Series A*, 167, 613–26.

————(2004b) 'Spikes and Spill-overs: The Impact of the National Minimum Wage on the Wage Distribution in a Low-Wage Sector', *Economic Journal Conference Papers*, 114, C95–101.

DiNardo, J., Fortin, N.M., and Lemieux, T. (1996) 'Labor Market Institutions and the Distribution of Wages, 1973–1992: A Semiparametric Approach', *Econometrica*, 64(5), September, 1001–44.

Lee, D. 1999. 'Wage Inequality in the United States During the 1980s: Rising Dispersion or Falling Minimum Wage?', *Quarterly Journal of Economics*, 114(3), August, 977–1023.

Low Pay Commission (1998) *The National Minimum Wage. First Report of the Low Pay Commission*, June 1998.

——(2009) *The National Minimum Wage. Low Pay Commission Report 2009*, May 2009.

Machin, S. (2011) This volume, chapter 11.

Manning, A. (2003) *Monopsony in Motion: Imperfect Competition in Labor Markets*, Princeton, NJ: Princeton University Press.

Metcalf, D. (2007) 'Why Has the British National Minimum Wage Had Little or No Impact on Employment?' *CEP Discussion Paper*, No. 781, April 2007.

Stewart, M. (2004a) 'The Impact of the Introduction of the UK Minimum Wage on the Employment Probabilities of Low Wage Workers', *Journal of the European Economic Association*, 2, 67–97.

——(2004b) 'The Employment Effects of the National Minimum Wage', *Economic Journal*, 114, C110–6.

Teulings, Coen N. (2000) 'Aggregation Bias in Elasticities of Substitution and the Minimum Wage Paradox', *International Economic Review*, 41, 359–98.

——(2003) 'The Contribution of Minimum Wages to Increasing Inequality', *Economic Journal*, 113, October, 801–3.

11 Changing Wage Structures: Trends and Explanations

STEPHEN MACHIN

11.1. Introduction

Studying changes in the inequality of labour market earnings has been a major focus of economists and other social scientists for a long time, but this research area has experienced a significant resurgence in the recent past as wage structures have altered significantly in many countries. Labour economists, in particular, have invested a lot of time and effort in learning more about trends in wage inequality and in developing and implementing tests of competing explanations of what factors underpin the observed changes (see the surveys of Katz and Autor 1999; Machin 2008; Machin and Van Reenen 2008).

This chapter offers a contemporary review of what we have learned from this work in the context of providing an up-to-date picture of what has happened to wage inequality in the United Kingdom. I first focus upon documenting the patterns of change and trends in wage structures, and then on explaining why these changes have occurred.

The chapter highlights that there have been different episodes of changes in wage inequalities. In the 1970s, there were reduced inequalities but, in terms of what followed, these narrowings were small in magnitude. The 1980s saw very rapidly rising wage inequalities, with wage gaps widening out at all parts of the wage distribution. In the 1990s, changes were more muted but wage gaps continued to rise. In the 2000s, a rather different picture emerged, with upper tail inequality continuing to rise, but lower tail inequality stagnating. Throughout this time period skilled workers have improved their position relative to less-skilled workers and there is some evidence that labour market polarization has caused a hollowing out of middle-paying jobs.

Turning to explanations, I argue that the standard supply–demand model of the labour market is successful in picking up some, but not all, of these observed changes. A key long-run driver has been skill-biased technology change (SBTC), which has been developed further in work that links closely to the polarization phenomenon from the observation that many jobs that have been lost have been through technology substituting for jobs that mainly involve routine tasks (task-biased technical change, TBTC). The impact of labour market institutions dovetails well with these technology-based explanations of changing wage structures.

The rest of the chapter is structured as follows. Section 2 spends some time describing the basic facts in terms of what has happened to wage inequality over the last four decades. Section 3 considers explanations of the observed patterns of change. Section 4 ends with some general observations and concluding remarks.

11.2. Laying out the facts on changes in UK wage inequality

This section lays out the basic facts on changes in UK wage inequality. There are five subsections, respectively looking at overall changes in wage inequality, changes in educational wage differentials, patterns of labour market polarization, labour market polarization, decadal differences, and how the UK experience compares internationally.

11.2.1. OVERALL CHANGES IN WAGE INEQUALITY SINCE 1970

Figure 11.1 displays the evolution of the differential between the 90th and the 10th percentile of the earnings distribution (the 90/10 ratio) for full-time men and women since 1970, based upon New Earnings Survey (NES) and Annual Survey of Hours and Earnings (ASHE) data.[1] The figure reveals what by now has become a well-known pattern. From the late 1970s onwards, the 90/10 ratio significantly increased and inequality is now a lot higher than it used to be. This is the case for men and women, though the increase in the 90/10 ratio for women tends to taper off from the late 1990s.

Figure 11.2 separately considers the upper and lower halves of the distribution. For men, upper tail wage inequality (measured by the 90/50 wage ratio) rises sharply from the late 1970s and consistently throughout the entire period up until 2009. Male lower tail wage inequality (measured by the 50/10 wage ratio) also shows a significant increase, but with most of its increase concentrated in the 1980s and early to mid-1990s. Following that it flattens out. For women, the story is similar, though there are some subtle differences. Most notable is the halting of the increase in lower tail inequality from the mid-1990s.

Overall, however, what is very clear from Figures 11.1 and 11.2 is that wage inequality is significantly higher now than it was some thirty or forty years ago. This is true for men and women, and is the case in both the upper and lower halves of the distribution.

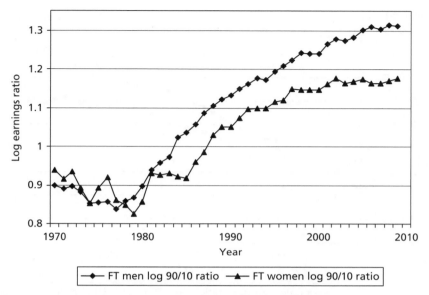

Figure 11.1. 90/10 Log Weekly Earnings Ratios, Full-Time Men and Women, 1970–2009

Source: National Equality Panel Analysis; 1968–96 New Earnings Survey (NES); and 1997–2009 Annual Survey of Hours and Earnings (ASHE).

11.2.2. CHANGES IN EDUCATIONAL WAGE DIFFERENTIALS

Rising wage inequality has been accompanied by increasing gaps within and between different groups of workers. The wage premium received by graduates as compared to non-graduates is a between-group wage differential that has received considerable attention in the literature. Figure 11.3 shows the wage gap between graduates and non-graduates from 1980 to 2004. The premium rises sharply from 1.48 in 1980 to 1.60 by 1990 and continues to rise, albeit at a more modest pace, up until 2004. This is in line with the idea, recognized in various places in the literature, that education has become more highly valued in the labour market and that this is one of the key features of rising wage inequality.

11.2.3. LABOUR MARKET POLARIZATION

In terms of employment, another key feature of rising labour market inequality has been the polarization of jobs growth (Goos and Manning 2008). Figure 11.4 (taken from Mieske 2009) shows this very clearly, with there being very rapid growth over time in the top two deciles of job quality (as measured by median occupational wages from 1979). Employment actually fell from deciles 2 through 8, showing a hollowing out of the distribution, but there is positive growth for the bottom decile.

(a) Men

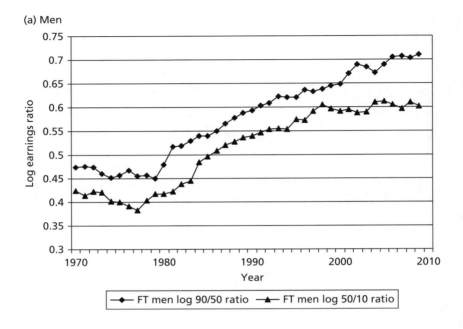

(b) Women

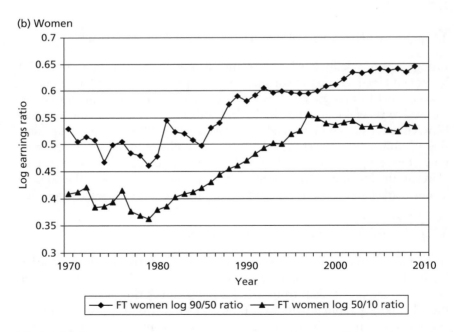

Figure 11.2. Upper Tail (90/50 Log Earnings Ratio) and Lower Tail (50/10 Log Earnings Ratio) Inequality, Full-Time Men and Women, 1970–2009: (a) Men, (b) Women

Source: As for Figure 11.1.

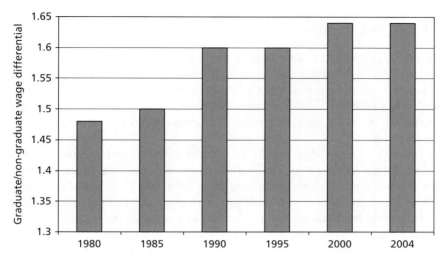

Figure 11.3. Graduate/Non-Graduate Earnings Differentials, 1980–2004

Source: Graduate/non-graduate earnings differentials derived from General Household Survey (GHS) and Labour Force Survey (LFS) data. Updated from Machin and Vignoles (2005).

Notes: Wages are for full-time workers. The relative wage ratios are derived from coefficient estimates on a graduate dummy variable in semi-log earnings equations controlling for age, age squared, and gender (they are the exponent of the coefficient on the graduate dummy).

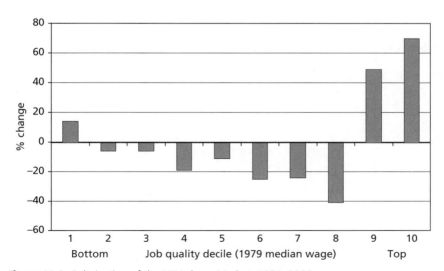

Figure 11.4. Polarization of the UK Labour Market, 1979–2008

Source: Taken from Mieske (2009). Percentage changes are for the entire period.

11.2.4. DECADE-BY-DECADE DIFFERENCES

The results presented to date make it very clear that wage inequalities are now significantly higher than they were forty years ago. However, looking more closely reveals different episodes of changes in wage inequalities. Table 11.1 looks at decade-by-decade changes in overall upper and lower tail wage inequality. It reveals some different evolutions across the four decades covered by the analysis.

Table 11.1 shows that the 1970s actually saw reduced inequalities (for women) but, in terms of what followed, these narrowings were relatively small in magnitude. The 1980s were very different. They saw very rapidly rising wage inequalities, with wage gaps widening out at all parts of the wage distribution, for both men and women. The scale of these changes kick-started the now large literature on changes in wage inequality (in the United States, see Bound and Johnson 1992 or Katz and Murphy 1992; and in the United Kingdom, see Nickell and Bell 1995; Schmitt 1995; Machin 1996*a*).

In the 1990s, changes were more muted but wage gaps continued to rise, at approximately half the pace of the 1980s, and still being characterized by rising upper and lower tail inequality. In the 2000s, a rather different picture emerged, with upper tail inequality continuing to rise (albeit at a more modest rate, especially for women), but with lower tail inequality no longer increasing.

The stagnancy of the 50/10 differential in the 2000s based upon the ASHE data requires comment because it has been stated in some places that lower tail inequality has fallen in the current decade. Other data sources suggest there may

Table 11.1. Trends in UK Earnings Inequality Indices

	Trends in UK full-time weekly earnings inequality indices (annualized percentage points)			
	1970–80	1980–90	1990–2000	2000–9
Men				
90–10 ratio	0.0	2.4	1.1	0.7
90–50 ratio	0.1	1.2	0.6	0.6
50–10 ratio	−0.1	1.2	0.5	0.1
25–10 ratio	0.0	0.6	0.2	0.0
Women				
90–10 ratio	−0.8	1.9	1.0	0.3
90–50 ratio	−0.5	1.0	0.3	0.3
50–10 ratio	−0.3	0.9	0.7	0.0
25–10 ratio	−0.1	0.3	0.4	−0.2

Source: National Equality Panel Analysis; 1968–96 New Earnings Survey; and 1997–2009 Annual Survey of Hours and Earnings.

have been a modest reduction in the 50/10 ratio. In Brewer et al.'s (2009) analysis of Family Resources Survey data, the 50/10 differential is constant for full-time men and falls by 0.3 percentage points a year (up to 2008) for full-time women. In the ASHE data the 25/10 differential for full-time women falls slightly (by 0.2 percentage points a year). Probably the key observation is that lower tail inequality is no longer rising in the 2000s, and may be falling in its lower regions.

Overall, Table 11.1 makes it evident that the period where wage inequalities rose significantly and fastest was the 1980s. Considering different parts of the distribution in more detail makes this even clearer. Figure 11.5 shows real earnings growth at the 10th, 25th, 50th, 75th, and 90th percentiles of the distribution by decade. The faster growth at the top that occurred in the 1980s is very clear. The 1990s looks rather like a toned-down version of this, but the other decades show a more mixed pattern.

The polarization story also alters when one considers decadal differences. Figure 11.6 shows polarization from 1979 to 1999 and from 1999 to 2008

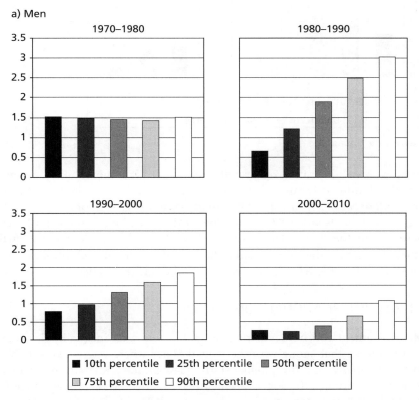

Figure 11.5. Real Weekly Earnings Growth at Different Percentiles by Decade: (a) Men, (b) Women

b) Women

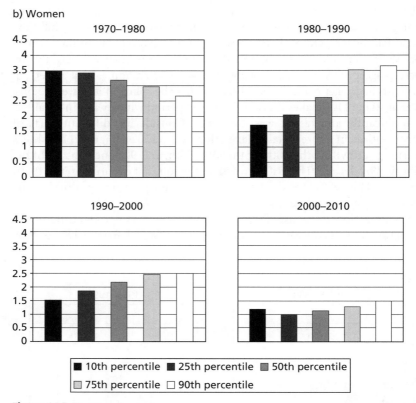

Figure 11.5. Continued

(now expressed in annualized growth rates to permit comparability). Far and way the dominant feature of this figure is growth at the top end (in the 9th and 10th deciles). The much smaller increases in the growth of low-wage jobs seen in the 1980s and 1990s in the lowest decile is, interestingly, no longer observed in the 2000s. However, the J-shape of the employment growth schedule remains the same, despite the lack of growth at the bottom decile, thus preserving the relative pattern seen in the earlier decades.

11.2.5. INTERNATIONAL COMPARISON

Many commentators have remarked upon the rapid wage inequality rise in the 1980s arguing that, along with the United States where wage inequality also rose very rapidly (and from higher starting levels), the UK labour market was pinpointed as one of the few places that then experienced rising wage inequality. Table 11.2 picks up on this by showing OECD data on male 90/10 wage ratios in 1970, 1980, 1990, 2000, and 2008 (or the closest year to that) for twelve countries.

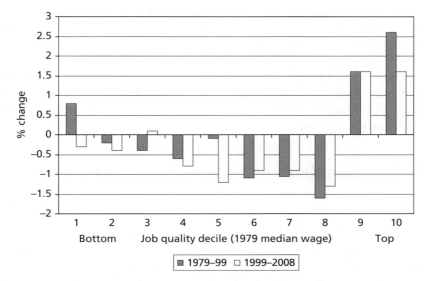

Figure 11.6. Polarization in the 2000s Compared to the 1980s and 1990s

Source: Taken from Mieske (2009). Percentage changes are now annualized to permit comparability across the sub-periods.

Table 11.2. Male 90/10 Wage Ratios across Countries, 1970–2008

	1970	1980	1990	2000	2008
Australia	2.4[a]	2.7	2.7	3.1	3.5
Denmark		2.1	2.2	2.5	2.7[e]
Finland	—	2.5	2.5	2.4	2.6[e]
France	3.7	3.3	3.3	3.0	2.9[d]
Germany	—	2.5[b]	2.5	2.8	2.9[d]
Japan	2.6[a]	2.6	2.8	2.8	2.9
Korea	—	4.1[b]	3.2	3.7	4.7
The Netherlands	—	2.3[b]	2.5	2.9	2.9[d]
New Zealand	—	2.2	2.5	2.7	3.1
Sweden	2.2[a]	2.1	2.1	2.4	2.4[c]
The United Kingdom	2.7	2.7	3.3	3.4	3.7
The United States	3.4	3.6	4.4	4.8	5.0

Source: Taken from OECD Stat Extracts web site (http://stats.oecd.org/index.aspx).

Notes: Data is from different years to the column header for some countries as denoted by the following superscripts: a—1975; b—1984; c—2004; d—2005; e—2007.

Table 11.2 confirms the 1980s increases in the 90/10 for the United Kingdom and the United States, with relative stability elsewhere. However, when one moves to the 1990s and 2000s the picture is not so clear. In the 1990s, wage inequality starts to rise in some countries like Australia, Germany (see Dustmann et al. 2009 for much more detail on this), Korea, the Netherlands, and Sweden. In the 2000s, rising wage inequality appears to be the norm, even in the Nordic countries where rises are small but there are increases, leaving only France having a stable wage structure over time.

11.3. Explanations of changing wage structures

In this section, I consider explanations of changing wage structures in more detail. I begin by considering the usefulness of a simple supply–demand model of the labour market in accounting for the observed changes, then move on to discuss possible drivers of these shifts in relative demand and supply that have been considered in the wage inequality literature.

11.3.1. THE ORTHODOX SUPPLY–DEMAND MODEL

In the orthodox supply-and-demand model, wage inequality increases come about because of an increase in the relative for skilled workers. Katz and Murphy (1992) first formalized the issue of changing wage gaps between different workers at different points in the wage distribution in a simple model of relative demand and supply of skills. They specified a production function where output is produced with two labour inputs, skilled and unskilled workers, and where these two sorts of workers are substitutes.

The basic logic of their argument is that the relative wage of the two worker types varies with their relative demand and supply. If demand outstrips supply, the relative wage will increase (and will fall if demand lags behind supply). This is, in essence, Tinbergen's race (1974) between supply and demand. Katz and Murphy argue that the recent patterns of change have seen relative demand for skilled workers outstrip relative supply and so wage gaps between skilled and unskilled workers have increased.

They test this notion through a simple time series model that relates the relative wage of college-educated versus high-school-educated workers to shifts in relative demand and supply. To do so they estimate a relative wage equation of the form:

$$\ln(W_s/W_u)_t = \gamma_0 + \gamma_1 \text{trend} + \gamma_2 \ln(N_s/N_u)_t + v_t \tag{1}$$

where $(W_s / W_u)_t$ is the log of the skilled to unskilled wage, relative supply is measured by the log of the ratio of the number of skilled to unskilled workers $(N_s / N_u)_t$, and v_t is an error term. They proxy relative demand by a trend arguing,

Table 11.3. Estimates of the Relative Supply and Demand Model for the United Kingdom

	Estimates of relative wage equation (dependent variable: $\ln(W_s / W_u)_t$)			
	Amior (2008)			This chapter
	(1)	(2)	(3)	(4)
	GHS, LFS earnings, GHS, LFS supply	GHS, LFS earnings, GHS supply	GHS, LFS earnings, LFS supply	GHS, LFS earnings, GHS, LFS supply
Coefficients on:				
Time trend	0.007 (0.001)	0.008 (0.002)	0.008 (0.003)	0.012 (0.002)
ln(Relative Supply), in$(N_s / N_u)_t$	−0.168 (0.032)	−0.174 (0.044)	−0.200 (0.079)	−0.220 (0.058)
R-squared	0.48	0.37	0.28	0.50
Sample size	33	30	22	39

Source: Estimates in (1)–(3) taken from Amior (2008). The earnings sources are General Household Survey (GHS) for 1974–91, Labour Force Survey (LFS) for 1993–2007; 1992 is omitted. The combined supply series are GHS for 1974–83 and 1986, LFS for 1984–5 and 1987–2007; the GHS supply series covers 1974–2006 (excluding 1997 and 1999) and the LFS series runs from 1984 to 2007 (excluding 1986).

Notes: The preferred sample has thirty-three observations, and includes all years between 1974 and 2007 (inclusive), with the exception of 1992. Estimates in (4) are my own calculations from 1972 to 2010 based upon GHS data from 1972 to 1996 spliced to LFS data from 1997 to 2010.

for example, that new technologies that drive the relative demand for skilled workers up have been trending up through time. Using US time series data from 1963 to 1987, they found $\hat{\gamma}_2$ to be significantly negative (equal to −0.7), showing that relative supply increases depress the relative wage, and a significant trend increase in the college premium of 3.3 per cent per annum ($\hat{\gamma}_1$=0.033).[2]

Estimates of this model for UK data from 1974 to 2007 (taken from Amior 2008) are reported in Table 11.3, together with updated estimates from 1972 to 2010. The model seems to fit the data well in the United Kingdom also. The estimated coefficient on the supply variable is (as predicted) negative and significant and in the range of −0.17 to −0.22.[3] However, the positive coefficient on the trend variable shows that, despite the very sharp increase in the relative supply of graduates, there must have been an even faster growth in relative demand for graduates. Depending on specification, this trend growth was of the order of around 1 per cent per year over and above the supply changes.

11.3.2. SKILL-BIASED TECHNICAL CHANGE

The estimates of the Katz–Murphy model for the United Kingdom make it evident that relative demand has shifted in favour of more educated workers, and that this has been a key feature of rising wage inequality. In the research on rising wage inequality and shifts in relative demand for skills, a strong focus has been placed upon what are the key drivers of change. A lot of the literature has concluded that skill-biased technical change (SBTC) has been the key driver of such change.[4]

Stated in its simplest form, the SBTC hypothesis says that new technologies lead to higher productivity, but only some (more skilled) workers possess the necessary skills to operate them. Therefore, in response to introducing these kinds of technologies into their workplace, employers raise demand and/or wages for highly skilled workers who are complements with the new technologies. Lower wages, or lay offs, occur for less-skilled workers who do not possess the skills to use the new technologies.

A typical approach adopted to test this (first used in the pioneering paper by Berman et al. 1994) comes from estimating statistical models relating the skilled wage bill share (to model relative demand shifts that occur through rising relative wages and/or relative employment) to observable measures of technical change. These kinds of models have been estimated in a large number of studies, usually using data on workplaces or industries, to ask whether more technologically advanced workplaces or industries experienced faster skill demand shifts. There is now an abundance of empirical research that suggests that SBTC is an important and international phenomenon. Table 11.4 shows some selected UK studies showing this, for a range of different technology indicators, time periods, and data sources.[5]

It is worth noting that the studies reaching this conclusion for the United Kingdom (Machin 1996b; Machin and Van Reenen 1998) use data from the period where wage inequality rose fastest. A natural question to ask, given the decade differences in changing patterns of wage inequality noted in Section 2, is whether such effects still operate. The new analysis described in the first row of Table 11.4 confirms that they do. Even in the 2000s, the industries experiencing faster increases in skill demand are those with higher R&D intensities.

11.3.3. TASK-BIASED TECHNICAL CHANGE

In an important recent paper, Autor et al. (2003) have recast the SBTC hypothesis, especially the impact of computerization, in a fresh light. They argue that the nature of jobs and the tasks done by workers in their jobs are key to thinking about the way in which technological changes impact on the wage distribution. They argue that computers raise the demand for jobs where non-routine tasks are required of more skilled and educated workers, but they substitute for jobs with routine tasks done by middle-educated workers (like manufacturing production, or secretarial jobs). Thus, routine non-manual tasks may be replaced by computers, whilst some non-routine tasks done by manual workers (like cleaning) are largely unaffected by ICT. This area of work has become know as task-biased technical change (TBTC).

Table 11.4. Summary of UK Evidence on SBTC

Study	Unit of analysis	Time period	Skill demand measure	Technology measure	Coefficient estimate on technology variable (standard error)	Controls
This chapter	17 manufacturing industries	2000–8[a]	Graduate wage bill share	R&D/value added (Y)	0.176 (0.081)	$\Delta\log K_{jt}$, $\Delta\log Y_{jt}$
Machin and Van Reenen (1998)	15 UK manufacturing industries	1973–89	Non-production wage bill share	R&D/value added (Y)	0.026 (0.009)	$\Delta\log K_{jt}$, $\Delta\log Y_{jt}$, year dummies
Machin (1996b)	16 UK manufacturing industries	1982–9[a]	Non-production wage bill share	R&D/sales (S)	0.065 (0.026)	$\Delta\log K_{jt}$, $\Delta\log S_{jt}$, one-digit industry dummies
	16 UK manufacturing industries	1980–5[a]		Innovation count from 1970s	0.092 (.053)	
	398 British workplaces	1984–90[a]	Managers, senior technical and professional employment share	Micro computers introduced	0.044 (0.022)	Dummy for employment decline, one-digit industry dummies

Notes: A subscript denotes that models are long differenced (i.e. treated as a single cross section in changes) and so no year dummies need to be included as controls.

Autor, Levy, and Murnane present empirical evidence in favour of the TBTC hypothesis by presenting evidence of non-monotone impacts of computers on the demand for jobs, with a strong complementarity existing between computerization and the demand for non-routine jobs and a strong substitutability with the relative demand for jobs involving routine tasks. Autor and Dorn (2009) have further studied TBTC, showing evidence that there has been an increased demand for service sector jobs in places where larger numbers of routine jobs have been lost to technical change. The argument they offer is that people displaced from jobs with routine tasks are more likely to find employment in the new kinds of service sector jobs available in modern labour markets.

Mieske (2009) has estimated variants of the Autor-Dorn TBTC models for ninety-eight UK counties in the 1990s and 2000s. The key hypothesis she tests is that having more routine task jobs initially causes the hollowing out of middle of the distribution jobs and that this polarization results in an increased demand for low-wage service sector jobs. Evidence for this idea is reported in Table 11.5 (taken from Mieske 2009). It is indeed the case that

Table 11.5. Some UK Evidence on Task-Biased Technical Change (Mieske 2009)

	Changes in the non-graduate service share of employment and initial share of jobs with routine tasks (across ninety-eight counties)					
	1992–2008		1992–2000		2000–8	
Coefficient on:						
Initial routine employment share	0.038	0.029	0.032	0.030	0.044	0.026
	(0.015)	(0.016)	(0.012)	(0.013)	(0.024)	(0.025)
Controls	No	Yes	No	Yes	No	Yes
R-squared	0.15	0.21	0.22	0.25	0.10	0.20
Sample size	392	392	196	196	196	196

Source: Taken from Mieske (2009).

Notes: Four-year differenced models based on ninety-eight UK counties. Coefficient estimates reported with standard errors in parentheses. The control variables included are (all in changes): graduate share, working student share, non-graduate migrant share, female employment share, elderly share, inactivity, and unemployment.

there seems to have been faster cross-county growth in the non-graduate service share in places where there were initially more routine tasks that could be substituted for by new technologies. Moreover the finding remains robust both for the 1990s and 2000s, providing some evidence that TBTC matters for the changing nature of the UK labour market.

11.3.4. AN ASIDE ON INTERNATIONAL TRADE

In the earlier literature on wage inequality there were (sometimes heated) debates about whether technology or trade matters most for explaining changes in labour market inequality. This is probably because many people's 'first guess' was that it was the opening up to international trade that had caused the labour market position of less-skilled workers to deteriorate and that this was likely to be a prime mover in raising wage inequality.

Even writing now, little evidence can be marshalled to support this viewpoint. Direct effects of international trade have proven very hard to identify (Desjonqueres et al. 1999). In the skill demand regressions trade measures rarely correlate well and the explanatory power of technology variables strongly dominates.

Of course, current ongoing research looking at the very rapid increase in trade flows with countries like India and China is likely to result in new evidence on this, but even here it is secondary and indirect effects of trade that form the main focus of interest (e.g. Bloom et al.'s (2009) study of trade-induced technical change). I shall leave this aside with what has become the usual comment that surely trade will matter for labour market inequality at some point, whilst noting that good evidence supporting this conjecture does not yet exist.

11.3.5. LABOUR MARKET INSTITUTIONS

The final issue I consider in this chapter is the other possible driver that has received attention in the wage inequality literature, namely the role of labour market institutions. The argument usually posed here is that in places where there has been a change in the strength of labour market institutions, this can affect wage inequality. Where institutions have weakened (like union decline, or falling values of real minimum wages), this removes protection for low-wage workers, so their relative wages fall, and wage inequality rises. In the case of strengthening institutions (e.g. equal pay legislation), then it is hypothesized that this can curb inequality.

Card and DiNardo (2002) report time series evidence of a strong (negative) connection between US 90/10 log hourly wage gap and the real minimum wage. Evidence in Machin (2010) shows a time series regression of the UK 90/10 log weekly wage differential on union density and a time trend also produces a strong association between rising inequality and falling unionization. In both cases, however, if one looks at 90/50 regressions, there is a significant upper tail wage inequality impact, which seems odd. Similarly, adding the union density to the time series models of relative demand–supply given in Table 11.3 makes no difference and the estimated coefficient on the union variable is insignificant.

Micro-data estimates do show the effects of falling unionization on wage inequality in the United Kingdom for the 1980s (see the decompositions in Bell and Pitt 1998; Gosling and Machin 1995; Machin 1997, which show about 20 per cent of rising UK wage inequality can be attributed to union decline). However, there is no more recent evidence on the issue. It seems sensible to conclude that union decline and minimum wages may help to explain some part of the changes in wage inequality, but that their effect is probably fairly modest.

11.4. **Conclusion**

This chapter has studied changes in the structure of wages in the United Kingdom over the last four decades. Wage inequality is significantly higher now than it was in the past. This is the case for upper and lower tail wage inequality. There are decade-to-decade differences in the patterns of change and it seems clear that the 1980s was the period where wage inequalities seemed to open out at all parts of the distribution. After that the picture has become more complex.

In terms of explanations, it seems reasonable to conclude that the evidence shows the wage distribution has been characterized by long-run growth in the relative demand for skills driven by technology change (rather than trade) and that changes in skill supply and institutional changes have affected the timing of how skill- and task-biased technical change impact upon the wage structure in different contexts. The importance of skills, and how education policy links to them, is discussed in chapter 12 by Vignoles (2011); and given the role of skill- and task-biased technical change in shaping the evolution of wage inequality, it is evident that this is a key aspect of where labour market inequality is likely to go in the future.

☐ NOTES

1. The NES data runs up to 1996 and the ASHE data from 1997 to 2009.
2. Autor et al. (2008) present more up-to-date estimates, reporting that the same kind of pattern continues into the 1990s and 2000s.
3. For the particular form of the production function used to derive (3), the inverse of this coefficient is the elasticity of substitution between skilled and unskilled workers. The estimates in Table 11.3 suggest a substitution elasticity of about 5, which is a line with the magnitude of the elasticity of 5.8 reported in Manacorda et al. (2006).
4. For straightforward descriptions of the SBTC hypothesis, see Machin (2003, 2004). The assertion that SBTC is the key driver is by no means without controversy. See Card and DiNardo (2002) for a very sceptical position.
5. Further international studies are surveyed in a more detailed table in Machin (2008).

☐ REFERENCES

Amior, M. (2008) *The Skill Divide and the North–South Graduate Exodus: How have Changes in the Supply and Demand for Graduate Workers Affected Britain's Regional Labour Markets?*, Unpublished MSc dissertation, University College London.

Autor, D. and Dorn, D. (2009) 'Inequality and Specialization: The Growth of Low-Skill Service Jobs in the United States', *National Bureau of Economic Research Working Paper* 15150.

——Levy, F., and Murnane, R. (2003) 'The Skill Content of Recent Technological Change: An Empirical Investigation', *Quarterly Journal of Economics*, 118, 1279–333.

——Katz, L., and Kearney, M. (2008) 'Trends in U.S. Wage Inequality: Re-Assessing the Revisionists', *Review of Economics and Statistics*, 90, 300–23.

Bell, B. and Pitt, M. (1998) 'Trade Union Decline and the Distribution of Wages in the UK: Evidence from Kernal Density Estimation', *Oxford Bulletin of Economics and Statistics*, 60, 509–28.

Berman, E., Bound, J., and Griliches, Z. (1994) 'Changes in the Demand for Skilled Labor within U.S. Manufacturing Industries: Evidence from the Annual Survey of Manufacturing', *Quarterly Journal of Economics*, 109, 367–98.

Bloom, N., Draca, M., and Van Reenen, J. (2009) *Trade Induced Technical Change? The Impact of Chinese Imports on Technology, Jobs and Plant Survival*, Centre for Economic Performance, London School of Economics, *mimeo*.

Bound, J. and Johnson, G. (1992) 'Changes in the Structure of Wages in the 1980s: An Evaluation of Alternative Explanations', *American Economic Review*, 83, 371–92.

Brewer, M., Muriel, A., and Wren-Lewis, L. (2009) *Accounting for Changes in Inequality Since 1968: Decomposition Analysis for Great Britain*, Institute for Fiscal Studies Report for National Equality Panel, London.

Card, D. and DiNardo, J. (2002) 'Skill-Biased Technological Change and Rising Wage Inequality: Some Problems and Puzzles', *Journal of Labor Economics*, 20, 733–83.

Desjonqueres, T., Machin, S., and Van Reenen, J. (1999) 'Another Nail in the Coffin? Or can the Trade Based Explanation of Changing Skill Structures be Resurrected?', *Scandinavian Journal of Economics*, 101, 533–54.

Dustmann, C., Ludsteck, J., and Schoenberg, U. (2007) 'Revisiting the German Wage Structure', *IZA Discussion Paper* 2685.

Goos, M. and Manning, A. (2007) 'Lousy and Lovely Jobs: The Rising Polarization of Work in Britain', *Review of Economics and Statistics*, 89, 118–33.

Gosling, A. and Machin, S. (1995) 'Trade Unions and the Dispersion of Earnings in British Establishments, 1980–90', *Oxford Bulletin of Economics and Statistics*, 57, 167–84.

Katz, L. and Autor, D. (1999) 'Changes in the Wage Structure and Earnings Inequality', in O. Ashenfelter and D. Card (eds.) *Handbook of Labor Economics*, Vol. 3, Amsterdam: North-Holland.

——and Murphy, K. (1992) 'Changes in Relative Wages, 1963–87: Supply and Demand Factors', *Quarterly Journal of Economics*, 107, 35–78.

Machin, S. (1996a) 'Wage Inequality in the UK', *Oxford Review of Economic Policy*, 7, 49–62.

——(1996b) 'Changes in the Relative Demand for Skills in the UK Labour Market', in Alison Booth and Dennis Snower (eds.) *Acquiring Skills: Market Failures, Their Symptoms and Policy Responses*, Cambridge: Cambridge University Press.

——(1997) 'The Decline of Labour Market Institutions and the Rise in Wage Inequality in Britain', *European Economic Review*, 41, 647–58.

——(2003) 'Skill-Biased Technical Change in the New Economy', in D. Jones (ed.) *New Economy Handbook*, London: Academic Press.

——(2004) 'Skill Biased Technology Change and Educational Outcomes', in G. Johnes and J. Johnes (eds.) *International Handbook of the Economics of Education*, Cheltenham: Edward Elgar.

——(2008) 'An Appraisal of Economic Research on Changes in Wage Inequality', *Labour*, 22, 7–26.

——(2010) 'Changes in Wage Inequality in the Last Forty Years', forthcoming in P. Gregg and J. Wadsworth (eds.) *The Labour Market in Winter: The State of Working Britain*, Oxford: Oxford University Press.

——and Van Reenen, J. (1998) 'Technology and Changes in Skill Structure: Evidence From Seven OECD Countries', *Quarterly Journal of Economics*, 113, 1215–44.

————(2008) 'Changes in Wage Inequality', in *New Palgrave Dictionary of Economics*, Basingstoke: Palgrave Macmillan.

——and Vignoles, A. (eds.) (2005) *What's the Good of Education? The Economics of Education in the United Kingdom*, Princeton, NJ: Princeton University Press.

Manacorda, M., Manning, A., and Wadsworth, J. (2006) 'The Impact of Immigration on the Structure of Wages and Employment: Theory and Evidence From Britain', *CEP Discussion Paper* 754.

Mieske, K. (2009) *Low-Skill Service Jobs and Technical Change*, Unpublished MSc dissertation, University College London.

Nickell, S. and Bell, B. (1995) 'The Collapse in Demand for the Unskilled and Unemployment Across the OECD', *Oxford Review of Economic Policy*, 11, 40–62.

Schmitt, J. (1995) 'The Changing Structure of Male Earnings in Britain, 1974–88', in R. Freeman and L. Katz (eds.) *Differences and Changes in Wage Structures*, Chicago: University of Chicago Press.

Tinbergen, J. (1974) 'Substitution of Graduate by Other Labour', *Kyklos*, 27, 217–26.

Vignoles, A. (2011) 'Education, Training, Skills and an International Perspective', Chapter 12 in this volume.

12 Education, Training, Skills, and an International Perspective

ANNA VIGNOLES

12.1. Introduction

Education, training, and skills were at the heart of the New Labour agenda and continue to be a high priority for the new government of the United Kingdom. Certainly, there has been a genuine expansion of education opportunities and a substantial increase in the resources dedicated to early years, primary, and secondary school since the mid-1990s. However, two long-term problems remain. The first is both a social and an economic issue, namely the persistent underachievement of pupils from lower socio-economic backgrounds, despite some recent improvements in the situation. So one of the major issues facing this current government is the same as that faced by Labour in 1997, namely how do we improve the educational performance of the poorest in our society? The other economic issue is the inability of the education and training system to supply the quantity and types of skills required by the labour market. This chapter focuses on both these persistent problems. Whilst the ability of the education and training system to meet the needs of the labour market relates more immediately to the economic success of the United Kingdom, social inequities clearly also have a longer run economic and non-economic impact. Further, as we move forward through challenging economic times, we are facing even more pressure on the system, as unskilled or low-skilled young people leave education and attempt to enter a very difficult labour market. This pressure will mean that growing social inequities are likely to become an increasingly important policy issue in the near future.

This chapter starts with a brief overview of recent trends in education achievement and compares the UK situation to that in some other countries. It asks whether the United Kingdom suffers from specific policy problems in the educational arena: for example, does the United Kingdom have a particularly high proportion of unskilled workers as received wisdom has it? The chapter then considers recent policy developments in the UK education and training system and gives suggestions for possible policy solutions.

12.2. **Trends in education achievement and skills**

The previous Labour government increased the share of resources spent on education since 1997. The proportion of GDP spent on education rose from 5.2 to 5.9 per cent between 1995 and 2006 though it fell back to 5.2 per cent in 2007.[1] Per capita expenditure on primary and secondary education increased from 3.6 per cent of GDP to 4.3 per cent in 2006, again falling back to 3.9 per cent in 2007.[2] Certainly, the Labour government did much to live up to their claim that education was a top priority. So with this additional investment, what has happened to education and skills in the United Kingdom during this past decade?

Firstly, there has been a large increase in post-compulsory (post-16) education participation in the United Kingdom since 1997, though this is a trend which dates back forty years rather than just over the past fifteen years. The proportion of young people remaining on in full-time education beyond the age of 16 stood at 80 per cent in 2009, up from 70 per cent in 1997 and up from just under half the age group in 1985.[3] Furthermore, the proportion of young people participating in higher education has also risen dramatically since the 1980s, although it has remained stubbornly at just below 40 per cent since 2000 (OECD Factbook 2010). However, just as the United Kingdom has expanded its education provision so too have other countries, leaving the United Kingdom chasing a moving target.

Despite this increase in education participation, there are some signs that all is not well across the entire system. The proportion of young people (16–18-year olds) who are not in education, employment, or training (known as the NEET group) has remained at approximately one in ten since the early 1990s.[4] Since the 2008–9 financial crisis, the proportion of young people who are NEET has started to rise. Given economic conditions, the rise in youth unemployment is perhaps unsurprising. However, what must be remembered is that a persistent one in ten young people have, throughout the boom years of the late 1990s and 2000s, found it difficult to enter the labour market and that this is a structural not a cyclical problem.

Conventional wisdom has it that the problem with our NEET group is that too high a proportion of each cohort drops out of the education system at age 16 with few or no qualifications. In fact, the proportion of each cohort not achieving a pass in the national examinations taken at age 16 (General Certificates of Secondary Education or GCSEs) has reduced from 8 per cent in 1997 to 5 per cent in 2007, whilst the proportion achieving less than five pass grades in these age 16 exams[5] reduced from 13.6 per cent in 1997 to 10.1 per cent in 2007.[6] That is the good news. However, despite this improvement in school achievement, in comparison with other countries, the United Kingdom still has a relatively low proportion of young people participating in full- or part-time post-compulsory schooling (Figure 12.1). In 2007, 71 per cent of young people aged 15–19 in the United Kingdom were in full-time or part-time education, as compared to 81 per cent for the OECD as a whole, and 84 per cent for the nineteen EU countries. These international comparisons may explain the political momentum behind the legislation introduced by the previous Labour government to increase the compulsory education and training participation age to 18 by 2015.

Obviously how long young people stay in school is just one measure of the success of an education system. The skills produced matter too. Focusing on cognitive skills specifically, data from the OECD Programme for International Student Assessment (PISA)[7] suggest that UK pupils are above average in science, and average in mathematics and reading at the age of 15. Whilst we might have some concerns about the robustness of these international tests, it is puzzling that the United Kingdom does relatively well in terms of the skills

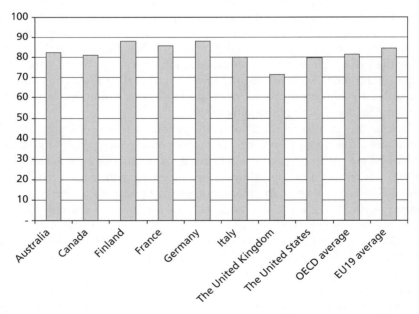

Figure 12.1. OECD Full-Time and Part-Time Participation in Education at Age-Range 15–19 in 2007

Source: OECD.

of its 15-year olds because other data clearly indicate that the UK working age population has a deficit of basic skills. This latter point is also obvious from the fact that firms in the United Kingdom are prepared to pay a higher wage premium for workers with quite basic levels of skill compared to many other OECD countries, suggesting a skill shortage (Denny et al. 2003; Hansen and Vignoles 2005). How do we reconcile the low level of skill of a sizeable proportion of UK adults with the PISA result that suggests that UK 15-year olds perform at a similar level to 15-year olds in other countries?

We might think that this apparent anomaly is because the flow of young people into the labour market is more skilled, at least as measured by PISA, whilst the stock of older less-skilled workers remains a problem. In other countries it is certainly true that older workers are less skilled. In the United Kingdom, older workers are less qualified but evidence from other international tests, such as the International Adult Literacy Survey, suggests that older workers are not significantly less skilled than younger UK workers (Hansen and Vignoles 2005). Rather, the reason why we do relatively well in PISA international tests when students are aged 15 and yet poorly when we compare adult skill levels is that in other countries more basic skills are acquired post-age 15 than in the United Kingdom. As discussed earlier, this is partly because in many other OECD countries a larger proportion of young people continue in full-time education beyond this age. The high drop-out rate at 16 is a major problem of the UK system.

Qualifications are another common metric to measure the skill (and by implication the productivity) of our work force. Equating qualifications across countries is notoriously difficult. It is evident however, from Figure 12.2, that the proportion of the UK population which is unqualified, and by implication lower skilled, is higher than in many other major competitor countries. The United Kingdom also has a lower proportion of its population with intermediate qualification levels.

Thus whether we look at education participation rates, cognitive skill levels, or qualification levels, we come to the conclusion that the United Kingdom does indeed have a higher proportion of low-skilled workers than many other countries.

The United Kingdom therefore has a contradiction: in terms of our average performance, we compare well to other countries, whereas in the low skill group we have a higher proportion of our population leaving the education system relatively early and achieving very little in terms of qualifications and skills. It is this inequality in the UK education system that most worried the previous Labour government over the last decade or so, for two reasons: social equity, as those leaving the education system with few skills tend to come from socially disadvantaged backgrounds; and economic, as unskilled workers have great difficulty in finding and sustaining employment at great economic cost to the state.

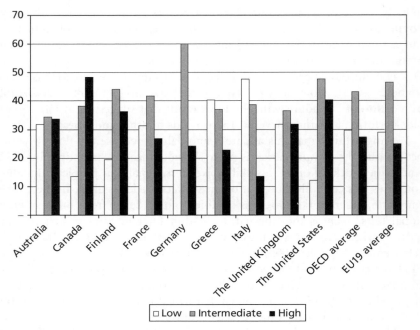

Figure 12.2. Proportion of the Working-Age Population with Different Levels of Qualification by Country

Source: Leitch Interim Report, 2006. Data for working-age population.

12.3. **Social divisions**

So how great are the social divisions within the UK education and training system? Gaps in educational achievement between socio-economically advantaged and disadvantaged individuals emerge early in the United Kingdom (see Goodman and Gregg 2009 and work cited therein) and remain entrenched. The United Kingdom also has higher than average socio-economic education achievement gaps.[8] In UK data, deprived children are identified by whether or not they receive free school meals (FSM), which is an indicator of whether their family is in receipt of welfare benefits. One-fifth of deprived children (defined as those in receipt of FSM) achieved five A*–C grade GCSEs in 2007, compared to around 50 per cent of less-deprived pupils. Nevertheless, the gap between advantaged and deprived students has reduced somewhat since 2003 (DCSF 2008).[9] The socio-economic gap, although narrowing in very recent years (see Figure 12.3), remains large when you look at university participation. Indeed, much of the increase in participation over time in higher education has been amongst more advantaged groups of students (Blanden and Machin 2008).

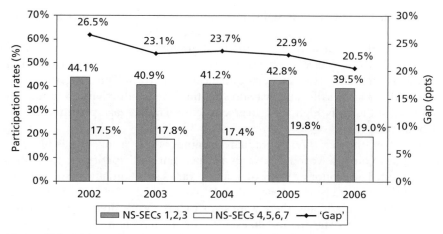

Figure 12.3. Higher Education Participation Rates by Socio-economic Class for Young People Aged 18–20

Source: Department for Innovation, Universities and Skills (2008).

Notes: NS-SECs categories 1, 2, and 3 include Professional, Managerial, and Intermediate Occupations, respectively. NS-SECs categories 4–7 include small employers and own account workers, lower supervisory and technical occupations, semi-routine occupations, and routine occupations, respectively.

The socio-economic gap in university enrolment in the United Kingdom largely reflects the fact that disadvantaged students have much lower educational achievement at school, rather than any specific barriers that prevent their entry to higher education (Chowdry et al. 2008). The underlying problem is diverging academic achievement between rich and poor students at the very earliest stages of their development. The emergence of early gaps in education achievement between socially advantaged and disadvantaged children was a key justification for another major New Labour policy, namely shifting additional education investment to the earlier years of a child's life.

12.4. The value of education and training

It is of course the interaction between the supply of skilled labour and the demand for skills that really matters, and this can be measured by what employers are prepared to pay for skilled workers in the UK labour market. We have already noted that the price paid for basic literacy and numeracy is high in the United Kingdom compared with other countries, suggesting a relative deficiency of these skills. Here we consider what the market tells us about the supply and demand for higher level skills.

Despite the expansion in the supply of graduates, UK degrees and higher level qualifications have, on average, held their economic value, measured in terms of the wage premium such qualifications attract. This suggests strong demand for such skills and reassures us that the productivity of graduates remains sufficiently high for a degree to command a wage premium in the labour market.

However, the *variation* in graduate earnings is increasing, and is likely to continue to do so if we move towards a 50 per cent participation rate in higher education. The economic value of a degree varies substantially by subject and institution (Sloane and O'Leary 2004; Walker and Zhu 2005). Furthermore, for the newest graduates, there were signs that the wage premium associated with a degree was starting to fall, even before the recession. The new government will need to monitor this situation since for some types of graduates rising unemployment and falling relative wages are likely to occur. This situation may be exacerbated if the cuts in public expenditure also reduce the public sector demand for more skilled workers.

Any fall in demand for some types of graduates will have major implications for both the government and universities, particularly if such changes in the labour market need to be accompanied by cuts in public expenditure on higher education (HE). How we fund HE will be a challenge if the value of some degrees is falling, reducing their demand, and if public sector investment in HE is to be reduced. From an efficiency perspective, we obviously want to invest less in degrees that have little economic value in the labour market. However, HE is not a free market and state subsidy continues to be high, so whilst the government can potentially shift the burden of some costs from the state to students, HE will remain costly to the Treasury as increases in tuition fees and accompanying student loans are costs that are borne by the state now and only paid back later at a subsidized rate of interest. If the state continues to invest heavily in HE in this way, we need to ensure that such investment is in higher education that has good economic or social value. Whilst market signals should encourage students to invest in more valuable degrees, the government will need to take additional precautions to protect students by ensuring universities provide sufficient information on likely graduate outcomes from different institutions and for different subjects. We also need to be concerned that if the size of the HE sector contracts, it is likely that the most disadvantaged students will be the ones who do not get to go to university, with significant implications for social mobility.

So even if generally there is a high demand for skills in the labour market, the type of skills being produced by the education and training system matters. Currently, not all the qualifications produced by the system have high value in the market. For example, the economic value of lower level qualifications, particularly some vocational qualifications like NVQ1[10] and NVQ2, is minimal (Blundell et al. 2005). This contrasts with the relatively high value of apprenticeships (McIntosh 2007). Recent curricular changes have introduced a raft of new qualifications, many of them at GCSE level or below and with a vocational orientation. The new government will need to determine whether this continual curricular reform is really providing students with productivity-enhancing qualifications that are valued highly in the labour market. Before attempting to invent yet more qualifications aimed at the least skilled workers, policymakers need to also acknowledge that continual reform of the vocational qualification system by the state has come at a price. Firstly, employers struggle to identify the worth of the myriad qualifications now available, and secondly, the school system has to spend considerable resources adapting to constant changes in curricula. Letting the system bed down and enabling existing qualifications to be modified slowly may be the only way to allow the system to gain some stability and to improve incrementally the content of lower level vocational qualifications.

12.5. **Policy solutions**

So looking both backward at what has worked since 1997 and forward to the policy problems the new coalition government faces, what are the likely policy solutions? We argue in this section that the new government should be doing two key things with regard to education, to improve UK's economic performance and tackle social inequities. Firstly, the government needs to recognize that the skills being demanded by the labour market do not always match the supply of skills available. Secondly, it should continue to intervene early, using both family and school based interventions, to improve the cognitive and non-cognitive development of more socially disadvantaged and vulnerable children. This will, in addition to addressing social inequity, also tend to reduce the proportion of unskilled workers in the work force. We make the case for these approaches below. However, there are also a number of things the government should avoid, which we also spell out.

12.6. **Boosting the supply of skilled workers**

One way in which the previous Labour government hoped to boost the supply of skilled workers was to raise the education and training participation age. As mentioned earlier, it is not clear what real impact this legislative change might have. However, policymakers can potentially learn from the experience of a robustly evaluated programme, namely the Education Maintenance Allowance (EMA). The objective of the EMA was to raise post-compulsory educational participation of young people from low-income families. EMA is a means-tested allowance paid weekly in term time to students aged 16–19 who stay on in full-time education. One unique feature of the EMA is that it was evaluated prior to national implementation.[11] Whilst Dearden et al. (2009) found a small significant impact from EMA on participation (2–3 percentage points), they found no significant impact from EMA on female qualification rates and only small effects for males. In other words, although paying poorer students to remain on in full-time education may have induced them to do so, the impact on their educational achievement (and potentially their productivity) in the long run is not proven. By corollary, the decision to extend compulsory education and training to age 18 may encourage more young people to stay on in education and training but will not necessarily lead to genuine increases in young people's qualification and skill levels.

Indeed, the challenge of teaching young people who would otherwise have left the school system in a way that both engages them and boosts their skill should not be understated. The system singularly fails to achieve this for around one in ten young people who currently leave the education system at 16 with insufficient skills to enable them to find work. Engaging in economically valuable vocational training, such as apprenticeships, is seen as the answer. However, just as schools struggle to engage these disadvantaged young people, so firms do not want to employ or train them. Providing these youngsters with sufficient cognitive and non-cognitive skills to enable them to access work, further education or training will continue to be a critical challenge facing the current government. This is one reason why we argue for the new government to continue to focus on interventions in the early years of childhood as a means of boosting the supply of skilled workers. Early intervention is essential if we are to prevent a disproportionately high number of our young people leaving the school system with insufficient skills and qualifications.

And what about adults who have passed through the system and are currently languishing in low skill jobs or unemployment? There is only weak evidence that interventions to improve adult cognitive skills can be successful. When the state intervenes to encourage adults to up skill (or at least get qualifications), often it has little impact on their productivity and wages (Blundell et al. 2005). Evidence from neuroscience also suggests that cognitive skills are less able to be improved later in life (Cunha and Heckman 2008) and policy focus might therefore be better placed on improving adults' non-cognitive skills, such as their attitudes and communication skills. This evidence also supports our view that early intervention is essential.

12.7. **Invest early**

Recent evidence from a large Joseph Rowntree funded project confirms the importance of early intervention and the intergenerational persistence of attitudes and aspirations that lead to the lower achievement of poorer children (Goodman and Gregg 2009). The Labour government recognized the importance of early investments in education. For example, there was a 40 per cent increase in education expenditure in primary schools (between 1997 and 2006) and this had a positive impact on educational achievement (Machin et al. 2007). By contrast, the previous Labour government's initiatives to improve adult skills have not proved as effective. For example, the pilot phase of the *Train to Gain* programme which subsidizes firms to provide training to low-skilled adults was found to be relatively ineffective as it subsidized a large amount of training that would have taken place anyway (Abramovsky et al. 2008). Whilst we do not claim that effective adult interventions are impossible, the evidence base clearly supports the view that earlier interventions are more likely to be successful.

There is also a strong intergenerational component to educational achievement and family environment is crucial in determining pupil outcomes (Goodman and Gregg 2009). Policymakers need to continue to develop family-based interventions. The evidence on parenting programmes is substantial, with a number of effective programmes that have been used in the United States and the United Kingdom, such as the Family Nursing Partnership, the Incredible Years Programme, and SureStart. This therefore is a fruitful avenue of intervention to pursue.

12.8. **Market forces—a cautionary tale**

Another question for any new government to consider is whether to further develop the quasi-market that now exists in the school system. All major parties are now committed, to a lesser or greater extent, to markets and competition in education. In 1988, parents were first given the power to choose their child's school, with the idea that schools would become more accountable as a consequence and that this would tend to improve educational standards. Yet recent empirical evidence suggests that competition between schools has had only a limited impact on mean education achievement (Burgess and Slater 2006; Gibbons et al. 2008). Equally, marketization has not led to big increases in social segregation across schools as was once feared (Gorard et al. 2003; Allen and Vignoles 2007). So there has been a lack of a competition effect (for good or bad). This is partly because market forces are constrained in the United Kingdom and the introduction of parental choice has not radically altered the pre-existing system of allocation to schools according to residential location. Any policy change that frees up the market further, for example, by allowing more schools to enter and exit the market, will need to be monitored both for its impact on mean achievement in surrounding schools and its impact on social segregation across schools.

Although competition may not have had a measurable causal impact on achievement, school league tables have certainly increased the emphasis on the metrics of education, and the key thresholds that pupils are expected to achieve (e.g. five A*–C GCSEs). There is a danger that this diverts attention from broader educational goals and away from pupils who are not near particular thresholds. It may also encourage schools to meet government targets, for example, five A*–C GCSEs via easier routes, by encouraging pupils to take easier equivalent qualifications. The Labour government's response to this problem was to include mathematics and English in the key metric of five A*–C GCSE grades to ensure that schools also focus on these core academic subjects. This is only a partial solution. Generally, the previous Labour government grappled with the tension between setting targets for accountability reasons, and avoiding schools' subsequent efforts to meet these targets in less than optimal ways. The current Coalition government will no doubt continue to face this problem. The metrics need to provide sufficient information to guide parents, yet be broad enough to avoid an overly narrow focus and relevant, so that schools can genuinely be held accountable for the outcomes. The latter point is crucial. Holding schools accountable for outcomes that are currently outside their control is problematic. For example, setting minimum targets for schools in areas which are extremely disadvantaged and in which students have extremely low prior achievement may reduce the motivation of the teachers and hence the effectiveness of the schools.

12.9. Policy overload and cost-effectiveness

We have already made the point that the education and training system may be close to policy overload. Further, in an era of financial conservatism, the coalition government needs to think about only adopting cost-effective policies and ceasing policies which cannot be shown to be cost-effective. Some apparently attractive interventions, such as reductions in the pupil–teacher ratio, are in fact relatively costly in terms of the benefits they produce. By contrast, the evidence suggests that improving teacher effectiveness is likely to be more successful, although we are some way from knowing how best to do this (Slater et al. 2009). In general, we make a plea for robust evaluation of each and every major policy adopted by the current government and for there to be more concerted attempts by policymakers and academics alike to undertake rigorous cost–benefit analyses of different policy options. If funding for education does need to be reduced, we urge the current government to use this as an opportunity to cut policy that is burdensome on schools and for which there is no robust evidence on its effectiveness.

12.10. Conclusion

So in summary, the Coalition government has a full agenda on education, training, and skills. The main messages are that we should continue to intervene early rather than late. Although little consolation for the current generation of low-skilled adults, in the long run, interventions that improve the skills of young people will resolve our current problem of low-skilled adults. Equally, we need to be mindful that simply increasing participation post-16 will not automatically mean rising skill levels. Instead, specific (and early) family-focused interventions are needed to genuinely improve the skill levels of deprived young people. However, after more than a decade of constant policy reform under the Labour government, politicians might do well to remember also that the system needs time to respond to change and less may be more in this particular policy domain.

☐ NOTES

1. Country Statistical Profiles, 2010, OECD.
2. Country Statistical Profiles, 2010, OECD.
3. http://www.dcsf.gov.uk/rsgateway/DB/SFR/s000849/SFR12_2009v2.pdf
4. NEET statistics—Quarterly Brief, 2009, Department for Schools and Families, http://www.dcsf.gov.uk/rsgateway/DB/STR/d000870/NEETQuarterlyBriefQ22009.pdf
5. The UK education system has a non-compulsory examination taken by most students at age 16 called a General Certificate of Secondary Education. Students can take different numbers of these examinations and by decree five passes in these examinations at grades A*–C (i.e. grades A*, A, B, or C) is considered a minimum school-leaving level of skill. Most students who stay in school to take an academic examination at age 18 (A levels) and go on to higher education achieve more than this minimum level at GCSE. Many students who do stay on past age 16 do so in Further Education Colleges where they study vocational qualifications as an alternative (or alongside) A levels.
6. Derived from information provided to the Houses of Parliament in response to a Parliamentary Question. See Hansard 21 July 2008 Column 936W and http://www.publications.parliament.uk/pa/cm200708/cmhansrd/cm080107/text/80107w0045.htm
7. http://www.oecd.org/dataoecd/60/1/39727764.ppt#2417

8. http://www.oecd.org/dataoecd/60/1/39727764.ppt#2390,21,Slide 21
9. The FSM rate has dropped during this period, so this narrowing of the gap is not caused by selection bias.
10. National Vocational Qualifications level 1 and 2, low-level vocational qualifications generally acquired post-school.
11. The evaluation design was based on a longitudinal cohort study of random samples of young people living in EMA pilot areas and control areas.

⬚ REFERENCES

Abramovsky, L., Battistin, E., Fitzsimons, E., Goodman, A., and Simpson, H. (2010) 'Providing Employers with Incentives to Train Low-Skilled Workers: Evidence From the UK Employer Training Pilots', *Journal of Labour Economics*, 29(1), 153–93.

Allen, R. and Vignoles, A. (2007) 'What Should an Index of School Segregation Measure?', *Oxford Review of Education*, 33(4), 643–68.

Blanden, J. and Machin, S. (2008) 'Up and Down the Generational Income Ladder in Britain: Past Changes and Future Prospects', *National Institute Economic Review*, 205(1 July), 101–16.

Blundell, R., Dearden, L., and Sianesi, B. (2005) 'Evaluating the Impact of Education on Earnings: Models, Methods and Results from the NCDS', *Journal of the Royal Statistical Society Series A*, 168(3), 473–512.

Burgess, S. and Slater, H. (2006) 'Using Boundary Changes to Estimate the Impact of School Competition on Test Scores', *CMPO Working Paper* 158.

Chowdry, H., Crawford, C., Dearden, L., Goodman, A., and Vignoles, A. (2008) 'Widening Participation in Higher Education: Analysis Using Linked Administrative Data', *Institute for Fiscal Studies Report* No. R69, mimeo.

Cunha, F. and Heckman, J. (2008) 'Formulating, Identifying, and Estimating the Technology of Cognitive and Noncognitive Skill Formation', *Journal of Human Resources*, 43(4), 738–82.

DCSF (2008) Department for Children, Schools and Families Annual Performance Report 2008: Progress against Public Service Agreements, CM 7507, London: HMSO.

Dearden, L., Emmerson, C., Frayne, C., and Meghir, C. (2009) 'Conditional Cash Transfers and School Dropout Rates', *Journal of Human Resources*, 44(4), 827–57.

Denny, K.J., Harmon, C.P., and O'Sullivan, V. (2003) 'Education, Earnings and Skills: A Multi-country Comparison', *Institute for Fiscal Studies Working Paper* W04/08.

Department for Innovation, Universities and Skills (2008) *Full-time Young Participation by Socio-economic Class (FYPSEC)*, 2008 update, 25 June 2008. http://www.bis.gov.uk/assets/biscore/corporate/migratedd/publications/f/fypsec-paper-2008.pdf

Gibbons, S., Machin, S., and Silva, O. (2008) 'Choice, Competition and Pupil Achievement', *Journal of the European Economic Association*, 6(4): 912–47.

Goodman, A. and Gregg, P. (eds.) (2009) 'Children's Educational Outcomes: The Role of Attitudes and Behaviours, from Early Childhood to Late Adolescence'. Final Report for the Joseph Rowntree Foundation.

Gorard, S., Taylor, C., and Fitz, J. (2003) *Schools, Markets and Choice Policies*, London: RoutledgeFalmer.

Hansen, K. and Vignoles, A. (2005) 'The United Kingdom Education System in Comparative Context', in S. Machin and A. Vignoles (eds.) *What's the Good of Education?: The Economics of Education in the UK*, Princeton and Oxford: Princeton University Press.

Leitch Review of Skills (2006) 'Prosperity for All in the Global Economy—World Class Skills', Final Report, December, HMSO.

Machin, S., McNally, S., and Meghir, C. (2007) 'Resources and Standards in Urban Schools', *Centre for the Economics of Education Discussion Paper* 79, London School of Economics, http://cee.lse.ac.uk/cee%20dps/ceedp76.pdf

McIntosh, S. (2007) 'A Cost-Benefit Analysis of Social Returns to Apprenticeship and Other Vocational Qualifications', *DfES Research Report* 834.

OECD (2009) *Education at a Glance*, Paris: OECD.

—— (2010) OECD Factbook 2010: Economic, Environmental and Social Statistics, Paris: OECD.

Slater, H., Davies, N., and Burgess, S. (2009) 'Do Teachers Matter? Measuring the Variation in Teacher Effectiveness in England', *CMPO Discussion Paper* 09/212.

Sloane, P.J. and O'Leary, N.C. (2004) 'The Return to a University Education in Great Britain', *IZA Discussion Paper*, IZA DP No. 1199, Bonn, Germany.

Walker, I. and Zhu, Y. (2005) 'The College Wage Premium, Over Education and the Expansion of Higher Education in the UK', University of Warwick, mimeo.

Part IV

Pay and Incentives in the Public and Private Sectors

13 Weak Incentives: When and Why

JOHN ROBERTS

13.1. Introduction

Traditionally, matters of compensation per se have not been a central focus of public policy in the English-speaking economies, except for the case of the minimum wage. Redistributive taxation and various benefits programmes addressed income differentials, but the nature and levels of the pay leading to these differentials were largely left to private contracting. In the last months of 2009, however, this may have been changed.

The Obama Administration's 'pay czar', Kenneth Feinberg, slashed the pay of the top executives in the companies that have not repaid the government bailouts they received in 2008 and 2009, and the British government instituted a one-off 50 per cent tax on bonuses in the financial services industry broadly, although the announced targets were bankers. Both these moves seem to have been largely responsive to the public outrage about the high pay of the bankers, who were blamed for the 2008 financial crisis and the Great Recession that followed.

Moreover, the way people are paid is also being subjected to policy scrutiny. Feinberg directed that much more of total compensation in the companies he oversees take the form of restricted company stock that must be held for a long period, and the US Federal Reserve has proposed that it should have the power to review compensation for bankers (including ones quite far down the banks' hierarchies) and reject pay packages that are seen to encourage excessive risk-taking.

Strikingly, in recent years the general refrain from observers of businesses has been that pay should involve much sharper, stronger incentives than firms have typically offered: 'Bring the market inside the firm.' The idea is that rewarding performance will induce people to work harder and smarter. At the most senior levels (which are the best documented), there has been considerable movement in that direction. Twenty years ago, Michael C. Jensen and Kevin J. Murphy (1990) documented that CEOs' earnings in large US corporations were only minimally affected by changes in their companies' performance. In the intervening years, this has changed considerably, mostly through the addition of large amounts of stock- and option-based compensation for top executives (Holmström and Kaplan 2001). This has made top executives' earnings much more sensitive to their companies' performance. It has also increased their overall compensation immensely, especially compared to average employee earnings, which have been largely flat.

This divergence between the earnings of top executives and the average worker underlies much of the public's current antipathy to fat cats' pay. At least in the United States and the United Kingdom, the growing gap was not too much of an issue until recently, because the public accepted the idea that people who could be credited with making huge amounts of money for their shareholders deserved to be well paid. But the poor performance of business in the recent past, and the speed with which bankers in particular have been prepared to pay themselves immense bonuses months after receiving government bailouts, has ignited rage.

The divergence between top executives' pay in the public and quasi-public sectors and average earnings in the United Kingdom has also provoked policy interest. A parliamentary select commission has called for a 'Top Pay Commission' to investigate pay in these organizations and to name and shame ones that were adjudged too generous (*Guardian* 2009). Meanwhile, some commentators are arguing that high pay in these bodies is driven by the pay levels in the private sector and they are calling for control of private sector pay (Toynbee 2009).

Public outrage and envy may be very attractive basis for public policy to some opportunistic politicians, but they ought not to be so appealing to those actually concerned with public welfare. The design of compensation and reward systems is in fact a very complex problem, and heightened emotions are not particularly useful in dealing with this task. However, cold-blooded economic theory has given some very useful insights about how to pay, and some important empirical work has supported the theorizing. Notably, David Metcalf did some of the earliest and most interesting empirical work in this area (Fernie and Metcalf 1998, 1999).

In this brief essay, I will highlight some of the lessons of this theorizing. The bulk of these lessons concern the way pay should respond to performance, rather than its total amount, because most of the theory assumes that the magnitude of the total pay package will be determined by competitive pressures—what is required to attract and retain the person in question. (The extent to which this is a valid assumption is very much open to debate, especially at the director level.)

The theoretical framework on which we draw is principal–agent theory. In its starkest form, it envisions two parties: the Principal (conventionally 'she') and the Agent ('he'). The Agent is able to make decisions or take actions that benefit the Principal, but the two have a divergence of interests: What the Agent is intrinsically motivated to do is not completely in the Principal's interest. For example, the Principal might want the Agent to work longer or harder than he would choose to do on his own. So her problem is to find ways to motivate him to act more in her interest. This is complicated by the assumption that she cannot perfectly observe his actions, or that she does not have the information to evaluate whether his decisions are really in her best interest, while the available performance measures are not accurately reflective of his choices.

In attempting to motivate the Agent, the Principal may use the design of the pay system, but she also may have access to other rewards, like job design, giving him personal autonomy, promotions or (in a multi-agent context) status, or peer pressure. She may also seek to get the Agent to identify with her objectives, so the underlying conflict of interests is reduced. We will, however, focus largely on the use of pay to motivate, and, in particular, on how much pay should vary with observed performance.

We identify a number of situations where, in contrast to the position expounded in recent years by many management consultants, the ideal pay scheme should be quite insensitive to measured individual performance, that is, where weak incentives are best. Some of these results are derived from very standard models of the sort that have been used for years, and the conclusions are familiar. Others stem from newer work and are quite novel.

13.2. **Basic agency theory**

The most widely used principal–agent modelling is due to Bengt Holmström and Paul Milgrom (1991).[1] Like most of agency theory, it treats the Agent as taking an action (called 'effort', although other interpretations are possible) which has value to the Principal but is costly for the Agent. It further assumes particular preferences for the Agent over risky income and costly effort,[2] that the Agent's effort choice e determines the outcome x for the Principal only up to the impact of (normally distributed) randomness[3] and that the pay contract is linear in the Agent's realized performance: $w = a + bx$.[4] The term a here is the part of pay that is guaranteed and does not vary with performance, while b indicates the fraction of measured output that goes to the Agent as a reward. Note that b measures the strength of incentives, because an increase in b increases the returns to the Agent for supplying extra effort, which raises expected output. However, increasing b also means that the Agent's income will vary more with the random component of realized performance.

The model yields a specific formula for b^*, the optimal strength of incentives.[5] This formula follows from balancing the gains in expected performance that result from inducing more effort by raising the strength of incentives against the costs to the Agent of the extra effort that is induced and the extra income risk that he faces with stronger incentives.[6]

From this formula follow a number of implications for the strength of incentives. None is surprising, but it is useful that they exist. First, and most significantly for applications, if the noise in the performance measure is large, then any individual incentives should be quite muted: bad measures ideally lead to weak incentives. For example, the Agent could be a middle-level manager in a large corporation, with the only measure of performance being aggregate firm profits. The Agent's actions do have an influence on overall profitability, but many other factors intervene, so the connection between the two is largely random. With so much noise in the measure, profits are virtually useless to evaluate the manager's contribution, and his pay ought not to depend on this measure.[7] Second, if the Agent is especially risk averse, it is too costly to have his pay be very dependent on random realized performance. To the extent that one expects that risk aversion declines with wealth, this argues against making low-wage workers' pay depend very much on their realized performance, even if top executives might get performance pay. If the Agent cannot respond easily to strengthened incentives by increasing his effort choice, then he again should face weak incentives, since the extra income risk he faces with stronger incentives does not yield much return in extra effort and output. Finally, if extra effort from the single Agent is not worth much, again the incentives to work harder should be weak. For example, if the Agent is but one person on an assembly line, then getting him alone to work faster has little value (although it might be worthwhile to increase the incentives for all the workers together).

13.3. **Multitasking**

A natural and realistic extension of the basic agency model allows that there could be multiple activities that the Agent might undertake for the Principal (Holmström and Milgrom 1991). A striking conclusion in this context is that it may be best to give very weak incentives for activities that, on their own, could get very strong incentives, so long as there are other activities that the Agent is supposed to undertake that are poorly measured.

In particular, suppose there are two tasks that the Agent might undertake. Suppose the Agent has no intrinsic preference between the two tasks. Instead, his cost of effort depends only on the total amount he exerts, not on how he splits his time between tasks.[8] Suppose the noise (variance) affecting the performance measure for task 1 is small, but that on task 2 is large. Then if the Agent is to undertake only task 1, he should receive relatively strong incentives, and if only task 2 is to be undertaken, then the incentives offered should be weak. But with the assumed cost structure, if both sorts of effort are to be induced via a linear contract of the form $w = a + b_1 x_1 + b_2 x_2$, they must be rewarded equally ($b_1 = b_2$) or else the Agent will spend all his time on the better rewarded task. This is because reducing effort on the one task and increasing it on the other by the same amount leaves the costs he experiences unchanged but increases his expected income.

Moreover, the optimal common level of incentives for the two tasks is not simply some average of the two intensities that would be obtained in isolation, even though this already would mean giving relatively weak incentives for task 1. Indeed, one can show that the optimal common value of b in the multitasking context may be strictly less than the optimal value of b_2 in the case where the Agent is responsible only for task 2. So bad measures for one task lead to very weak incentives for other tasks for which the measures are good.

A prime example of this point involves merit pay for teachers. Usually, proposals for merit pay involve using student results on standardized tests as the performance measure for the teacher. These are relatively direct measures of the teacher's efforts in teaching the examined subjects, and if that were all we wanted the teacher to do, quite strong incentives would be appropriate. But if the teacher also has responsibilities where his efforts are not well measured, like inculcating civic values or promoting ethical behaviour, or simply teaching subjects that are not covered on the tests, then these tasks will be ignored if rewards based on the tests are strong. Even if the teachers care a lot about these unmeasured and unrewarded tasks, they will tend to shift their efforts away from them in a way that may be socially undesirable.

The rewards to publishing in research universities are quite strong, even after tenure is granted, because they often come in the form of outside job offers with higher pay and perks. Meanwhile, in many of these institutions, the rewards to teaching are much more muted, perhaps because the quality of teaching is not well measured. Consequently, complaints about the quality of teaching, even (or especially) by the 'star' faculty, are to be expected. Interestingly, in graduate business schools, where students are older, are typically paying their own way, and are not dependent on faculty recommendations for jobs, the pressures from students to teach well are much stronger. Thus, it is common in these business schools for faculty to devote much more effort to teaching than seems to be the case in undergraduate programmes.

Luis Garicano and Richard A. Posner (2005) have pointed out a multitasking incentive problem at the organizational level. The U.S. Federal Bureau of Investigation is charged both with law enforcement (its traditional task) and, post-9/11, with counterterrorism. Arrests and convictions are clear measures of performance on the former, but no comparable measures exist for counterterrorism, where success often just means that nothing untoward happened.

The reward systems inside the bureau are geared towards law enforcement, which appears to have led to less than ideal performance in fighting terrorism.

13.4. **Biased and manipulable measures**

More recent research in the agency context has downplayed the role of uncertainty in the relationship between the Agent's choices and the performance measures that drives the standard model. Instead, this work has looked at situations where the available measures are biased, not reflecting—even in expectation—the value created by the Agent's choices (Baker 1992). In this case, the Agent may be led to adopt behaviours that improve his measured performance while not improving—or even actually decreasing—the value created, that is, he is led to manipulate the measures.

A particularly pertinent set of examples of the impact of basing rewards on biased measures concerns several different aspects of banking in the period leading up to the financial crisis that began in 2008. Each involves measures used in compensation that reflected only some of the risk and return that the Agent's choices generated. Immediate returns were measured and rewarded, but the longer term impacts of the Agent's choices were not figured into their rewards. Consequently, the bankers focused on the short term, even to the extent of taking overall risks that were value-destroying.

The American retail bankers who wrote sub-prime mortgages in huge numbers, even for 'NINA borrowers' (those with 'no income and no assets'), were rewarded just for the volume of loans they made, with no adjustment for the risk involved if local housing prices should ever fail to keep rising. Presumably, this reward structure was put in place because the relevant bank executives expected to be able to sell the mortgages and avoid the risks of default and also because they too may have fallen subject to the wishful belief that there was not a bubble in housing prices. The result was that hundreds of billions of dollars were lent to people who had no hope of paying if they could not refinance based on appreciation of the property and, even more, to people who would never be able to make their payments once the 'starter' interest rates they were initially charged rose to market levels.

Investment bankers took large numbers of mortgages (including lots of sub-prime ones), packaged them together to aggregate the cash flows that owning them would generate, and then created 'derivative' Collateralized Debt Obligation (CDO) assets from them. These CDOs involved taking the package of mortgages and creating a collection of new financial assets that were claims on the aggregate stream of payments from the package of mortgages. These new assets differed in their priority to get repaid. Holders of the highest ranked asset would get paid before the holders of any lower ranked asset. Then, if there was any money left over, the holders of the second-ranked asset would be paid, and so on down the line. The idea was that the highly ranked assets would involve little risk, but low-ranked ones might be quite risky.

In fact, many very risky 'tranches' of these CDOs were rated as almost risk-free by the ratings agencies that are charged with evaluating the risk in financial assets. This appears to have been the result of another instance of badly designed incentives, which motivated the ratings agencies not to exp-lore very thoroughly what the actual risks were and to rate the assets higher than they deserved. Apparently, the long-term effects that such misestima-tions and misstatements might have on the rating agencies were not ac-counted for in the incentive plans they used.[9]

Billions of dollars of these assets were then bought by bankers and other investors. The bankers making the actual purchase decisions also did not face the full impacts of their choices, because their bonuses were based on current returns to their investments, and there was no provision to 'claw back' the rewards if the investments turned bad. Of course, the inaccurate ratings from the agencies made these investments seem safer than they were, at least in part justifying the investments. And there would seem also to have been a sub-stantial failure of the risk management function in the banks, whose moni-toring was supposed to prevent excessive risk-taking.

Finally, the people in AIG's financial products group who sold astronomical amounts of Credit Default Swaps (CDSs) were again motivated by biased measures that did not reflect the risks they were incurring. These CDSs were, in essence, insurance contracts that promised to compensate the holder if a financial asset were to default. Unlike most insurance contracts, however, these were not subject to any regulatory oversight. Trillions of dollars of these contracts were written, a huge fraction of which were not actual insurance sold to holders of risky assets, but simply bets on which firms might get in trouble. But the first-order contracts often involved CDOs based on the sub-prime mortgages. When these mortgages started failing, immense claims were suddenly made on AIG to pay off on its CDSs. AIG was primarily an insurance company—the CDS business was a sideline. The possibility that AIG would fail threatened thousands of business contracts around the world that required one or both parties to carry insurance. This would have caused chaos in the financial and other markets, so the US government stepped in and gave AIG $180 billion, which was quickly passed on to the holders of its CDSs. This amount equalled fully one dollar in every ten raised by the corporate and individual income taxes in the United States in 2008.

The simple lesson here is that it is unwise to give strong incentives based on only some aspects of the overall risks and returns that the Agent's actions generate.

To model manipulation, consider again the multitasking framework.[10] Suppose the value created by the Agent's efforts is some weighted average of the two effort levels, but the actual value created is not directly observed in any fashion that would permit a contract on it. However, there is some other measure, with different weights on the two sorts of effort, that is observed and which could be the basis for evaluating and rewarding the Agent. This measure does carry some information about the Agent's choices and so it is potentially useful. However, using this measure leads the Agent to distort his choices towards those that increase measured performance, not value creation. He will also exert extra effort to the extent that it increases the biased performance measures, not to the extent that it increases value.

Examples abound. If rewards are based on accounting measures of earnings (rather than, say, cash flow), managers will be inclined to adopt accounting rules that generate better reported earnings, even if they lower actual economic returns (e.g. through tax effects). If salespeople are given a bonus for meeting a target in a certain time period, they will delay making further sales once the target is reached (saving the sales for the next period) and they will tend to slacken off if the end of the period is close and there is little chance of meeting the target. If a health services organization is measured by costs and waiting times for treatment, it will focus on these measures rather than on the well-being of the people served.

The solution here again involves a formula. It indicates that the strength of incentives given on the basis of a biased measure should be smaller the greater is the bias in the measure, that is, the greater is the difference between the effect of increasing efforts on the performance measure and the effect on actual value created. If paying on the measure does not distort behaviour much from what would be value-maximizing, then strong incentives are appropriate. But if rewarding on the measure induces behaviour that is far from optimal, then the measure should get little weight. Really biased measures are of little value and should not be used at all.

13.5. **Cooperation**

Another case in which weak incentives are appropriate is when various forms of cooperation are desired. 'Cooperation' here means actions or decisions that promote the interests of other parties or groups in the organization or those of the overall organization itself, as opposed to the direct responsibilities of the Agent in question. Cooperation in this sense is crucial within organizations. Managed organizations exist when there are important interdependencies between parties that are not easily solved by contracts between the separate parties. Then hierarchy and authority replace market contracting. Still, it is necessary to get Agents (as employees) to take actions that respond to the spillovers.

Often, cooperation can be treated simply as a hard-to-measure activity. For example, it might consist of sharing information and helping: telling whether Agents have cooperated honestly and fully in this context is difficult. In this contest, the multitasking results apply (Holmström and Milgrom 1991; Roberts 2004: 141).

For example, BP plc, the energy company, developed a highly decentralized organizational design for its 'upstream', exploration and production arm in the 1990s (Roberts 2004, 182–90). Functional experts who had previously been located at corporate headquarters in London were dispersed to the various business units around the world. This meant that a unit manager who had a problem could not just call headquarters for help. Instead, BP developed 'peer groups' consisting of business units that were apt to face similar technological problems. Strong norms were established within the peer groups that if one had a problem, one asked one's peers for help and that, if asked, one gave help. This sharing of knowledge was a pure form of cooperation. There were no explicit rewards for cooperating, but those who did not cooperate were regarded badly by their peers and were probably known to top management. These weak incentives were appropriate, given the problems of measurement. At the same time, the incentives for individual performance, while stronger than they had been previously, were not so intense as to crowd out the sharing. This mix worked well— often 30 per cent of the technical staff were at other units on 'peer assists' at any given time.

Cooperation in another context may simply involve avoiding bad behaviour. For example, the firm might want managers to develop investment proposals, and to do so it might reward investments that are implemented successfully. This means, however, that the managers have an interest in having their proposals developed, not necessarily in having the best ones carried out, because if their projects are not adopted, they get nothing. Then, if the managers alone know how good their projects are, paying them for having a project adopted and succeed will lead them to exaggerate the attractiveness of their projects. This will undermine allocating capital efficiently. One solution is to tie managers' pay to overall corporate results, so they care about efficient capital usage. Doing so then typically leads to lowering the incentives for developing projects (e.g. because competition for capital provides alternative incentives for project development). A model along these lines is due to Michael Raith and Guido Friebel (2010).[11]

13.6. **Experimentation**

Another situation calling for weak incentives is one where the Principal wants to motivate experimentation. While much of the concern around the financial crisis has been that bankers were motivated to take excessive risks (because they were paid a lot for short-term results and not charged for longer run losses), in many situations the Agent may need to be induced to take the risks involved in trying something new.

This idea is modelled by Gustavo Manso (2009). Suppose there are two possible ways to try to accomplish a particular task. One, the standard approach, is well understood and has a known probability of success. The other is new and untried, and the probability it will succeed is uncertain. Without additional information, the tried and true method is the better bet—it is more likely to succeed. However, the new method might be better.

In particular, suppose that if the new method were tried and generated a successful outcome, then updating beliefs on the basis of that information would make the new method appear more likely to succeed in the future than the old method. This means it may be worthwhile to get the Agent to experiment with the new method. If it succeeds, then it will be used henceforth. If it fails, then he will revert to the established method.

Crucially, the Principal cannot tell which method the Agent has adopted. Then her problem is to decide whether she wants to induce experimentation or to get the Agent to do the tried and true thing, and then to provide incentives for him to do what she wants. In each case, however, the activity is costly for the Agent, so he must also be induced not to slacken off and blame lack of success on bad luck.

The details of the analysis are complex, and the results depend on whether the Agent finds the old way or the new less taxing. But some key insights emerge. If the Principal wants to induce the tried and true way, then the optimal contract is exactly as from standard agency theory: The Principal offers significant rewards for success in each period. This leads the Agent to exert effort and to apply it to the old way of doing things, because it is more likely to succeed and generate the reward for success.[12]

If the Principal is trying to get the Agent to experiment, on the other hand, then a success in the first period is bad news about the Agent's action choice, because success is more likely to occur when the Agent is disobeying and using the old way. So if the Agent would rather use the old way, the Principal may need to give extremely weak first-period incentives: she may even need to reward early failures! At a minimum, she should not reward early success. At the same time, she will have to give substantial rewards for success in the second period to induce effort at all.

These sorts of incentives are perhaps to be found in highly innovative organizations such as 3M (Roberts 2004, 258–60, 276–8). There, projects that seemed interesting but do not work out do not adversely affect the evaluation of the engineers and scientists involved. At the same time, the strong incentives given for success are not monetary, but rather, as in universities, in the form of peer respect and status. Silicon Valley accords even more with this model. Entrepreneurs who fail do not suffer a stigma. Indeed, venture capitalists are said to be attracted to proposals from entrepreneurs who have learned through failure using other people's money. But the returns to ultimate success are huge.

13.7. **Divergent beliefs**

The final context calling for weak incentives that we will consider has been identified and modelled by Eric Van den Steen (2010). It is one where people fundamentally disagree about the likelihood that alternative ways of approaching a problem will succeed. For example, one party may believe in focusing on increased marketing as the best way to increase sales and the other on improving product quality. Or one person may believe in engagement with a foreign power to bring about change and another may advocate confrontation. It is not that the two are working on the basis of different information that leads to their different views. Rather, they just disagree about the probabilities of various events and perhaps about the mechanisms that bring them about. So knowing that another party disagrees does not make one want to reconsider what one believes.

In this case, if the Principal and Agent disagree about the right way to do things, then giving the Agent strong performance incentives encourages him to do what he thinks right, rather than what the Principal wants done. Assume the parties cannot contract over what course of action the Agent will take, even though both will observe his choice, because it is just too hard to describe things to a third party who could enforce an agreement. Then the solution is for the Principal to hire the Agent under a contract that pays him a fixed wage, independent of the realized performance, where the wage is more than he can earn elsewhere. This will make him want to keep his job. The Principal then tells the Agent which alternative to pursue, and the Agent decides what he will actually do. If the Agent obeys, he receives the fixed wage (no performance pay); if he disobeys, the Principal is supposed to fire him.

In this context, Van den Steen argues that the Principal should own all the assets involved in the organization. Then, if the Agent does disobey and is to be fired, his position is weak and that of the Principal is strong. This makes both the Agent less likely to disobey and the Principal more ready to carry out the threat of firing should he nevertheless transgress. Both these forces tend to induce the desired obedience. Thus, several of the features that have frequently been seen as characteristic of firms—weak performance incentives, the firm owning the assets, and the employee being subject to the boss's orders—all emerge together from one model. Even if there is an issue of motivating the Agent to exert effort, the incentives that this analysis indicates are significantly weaker than they would be absent the disagreement on the best alternative.

13.8. **Lessons for policy**

This chapter has identified a number of circumstances where weak incentives are appropriate, including situations of fundamental disagreement about the best course of action and the desire to encourage cooperation, experimentation, or multitasking. Still, the clearest lesson is that strong incentives based on bad measures (whether noisy or biased) are a very bad idea.

The interesting issue is why organizations would put such bad incentives in place. After all, the incentives are labelled 'bad' precisely when they lead the Agent to act in ways that are bad for the Principal. So why would she adopt such measures? Why, for example, did the executives in the banks adopt reward schemes that led to short-run rewards for their traders that threatened the very survival of the institutions they led?

One answer is that the executives setting the pay did not understand the dangers that they faced. This may indeed have been the case with some of the retail bankers who thought the danger of a housing price collapse was small. And the insurance executives at AIG may not have realized that the financial products group was writing derivative contracts carrying potential liabilities of more than twice the market value of the entire firm. Mistakes do happen.

But a more appealing explanation is that the people we have treated here as Principals were not real Principals. The ultimate Principals in whose interests actions and decisions are supposed to be taken are the shareholders of the firm. The executives of the firm are the Agents of the shareholders, not real Principals as they would be if they owned the firm they managed. So we have to look to the incentives these executives faced to set compensation systems that were in the interests of the shareholders. This is an important, complex topic for future work. It may also cast some light on the issue of whether pay levels, and not just the forms of compensation, are appropriate and competitively justified.

□ NOTES

1. For an elementary exposition, see Milgrom and Roberts (1992: ch. 7).
2. Namely, that utility for income w and effort e is $-\exp(-r(w - c(e)))$, where r is a measure of risk aversion and $c(e)$ is the cost of effort in monetary terms.
3. That is, $x = e + z$, where z is a normal random variable with mean zero and variance v that is independent of the effort choice. Thus, the Agent's choice determines the expected level of realized, measured performance.
4. Linear pay schemes are common (e.g. a salary plus commission for a sales person), but the assumption of linearity here is formally justified by earlier work by Holmström and Milgrom (1987) that showed that this model with linear contracts can be viewed as a reduced form representation of a dynamic agency problem.
5. The formula is $b^* = P'(e)/(1 + vrc''(e))$ where $P'(e)$ is the marginal product of effort in increasing the expected value of x, v is the variance in the realized value of output x, r measures the Agent's risk-aversion, and $c''(e)$, the second derivative of the cost of effort function, is an inverse measure of how readily the Agent's choice of e responds to increased incentives.
6. If there were no issue of imperfect measurement, the solution would simply be that the optimal strength of incentives should be given by $b^* = P'(e)$. The Agent on his own will select an effort level such that the marginal cost to him of more effort is equal to its expected return, b. Thus, this value for b^* leads to the marginal value of extra effort equalling its marginal cost.
7. If pay based on group performance induces Agents to 'think like owners', changing their attitudes to work, or to monitor one another against slackening off, then it might be worthwhile.
8. Then, if e_i, $i = 1, 2$ is the effort exerted on each task, the overall cost of effort is $c(e_1 + e_2)$.
9. The likelihood of housing prices across the whole United States falling together (as they did) was also underestimated.
10. See Gibbons (2005) for a simple exposition of these ideas.
11. An earlier but less complete analysis along these lines is Athey and Roberts (2001).
12. If the Agent would rather experiment, then these incentives may need to be stronger than if the option to try the new way was not there.

□ REFERENCES

Athey, S. and Roberts, J. (2001) 'Organizational Design: Decision Rights and Incentive Contracts', *American Economic Review*, 91(2), 200–5.

Baker, G. (1992) 'Incentive Contracts and Performance Measurement', *Journal of Political Economy*, 100(2), 598–614.

Fernie, S. and Metcalf, D. (1998) '(Not) Hanging on the Telephone: Payment Systems in the New Sweatshops', CEPDP 390, Centre for Economic Performance, London School of Economics and Political Science, London, UK.

—— —— (1999) 'It's Not What You Pay it's the Way That You Pay it and That's What Gets Results: Jockeys' Pay and Performance', *Labour*, 13(2), 385–411.

Friebel, G., and Raith, M. (2010) 'Resource Allocation and Organizational Form', *American Economic Journal: Microeconomics*, 2(2), 1–33.

Garicano, L. and Posner, R.A. (2005) 'Intelligence Failures: An Organizational Economics Perspective', *Journal of Economic Perspectives*, 19(4), 151–70.

Gibbons, R. (2005) 'Incentives Between Firms (and Within)', *Management Science*, 51(1), 2–17.

Guardian (2009) 'Pay Commission should Investigate Top Public Sector Salaries, MPs Say', 21 December 2009, Accessed at http://www.guardian.co.uk/politics/2009/dec/21/pay-commission-public-sector-salaries, 17 January 2010.

Holmström, B. and Kaplan, S.N. (2001) 'Corporate Governance and Merger Activity in the United States: Making Sense of the 1980s and 1990s', *Journal of Economic Perspectives*, 15(2), 121–44.

—— and Milgrom, P. (1987) 'Linearity and Aggregation in the Provision of Intertemporal Incentives', *Econometrica*, 55(2), 303–28.

—— —— (1991) 'Multitask Principal–Agent Analyses: Incentive Contracts, Asset Ownership and Job Design', *Journal of Law, Economics and Organization*, 7(special issue), 24–52.

Jensen, M.C. and Murphy, K.J. (1990) 'Performance Pay and Top Management Incentives', *Journal of Political Economy*, 98(2), 225–64.

Manso, G. (2009) 'Motivating Innovation', *Working Paper*, MIT Sloan School of Management.

Milgrom, P. and Roberts, J. (1992) *Economics, Organization and Management*, Englewood Cliffs, NJ: Prentice-Hall.

Roberts, J. (2004) *The Modern Firm: Organizational Design for Performance and Growth*, Oxford: Oxford University Press.

Toynbee, P. (2009) 'Justice in Pay Packets Starts at the Top. Across the Board', *Guardian*, 22 December 2009, Accessed at http://www.guardian.co.uk/commentisfree/2009/dec/22/public-sector-pay-politics-craven, 17 January 2010.

Van den Steen, E. (2010) 'Interpersonal Authority in a Theory of the Firm', *American Economic Review*, 100(1), 469–90.

14 Modernization, Privatization, and the Public Service Ethos in the United Kingdom

MARIA KOUMENTA

14.1. Introduction

Throughout the last few decades the public sector has been bombarded by restructuring initiatives. In a context of dissatisfaction with bureaucratic approaches to public administration, New Public Management has emerged as a response to calls for a more efficient and customer-focused model for organizing the internal workings of the government. The United Kingdom was quick to adopt such principles and translate them to policy initiatives. The advent of the Conservative government in 1979 signalled the contraction of the public sector via privatization and contracting out, whereas public sector managers were encouraged to emulate their private sector counterparts with regard to their personnel practices. This approach did not radically change after New Labour was elected in 1997. Performance management and audit systems such as performance-related pay, key performance indicators, and league tables were extended to cover a wider range of public sector employees and agencies, and the policy of involving the private sector in the provision of public services was preserved. Indeed, some commentators have argued that New Labour has gone even further with private sector involvement than its predecessors with the wholehearted adoption of the Private Finance Initiative (PFI) being characteristic of such intentions (Bach 2002).

Such exposure to market-based initiatives and the resultant changes in sectoral composition of the public service have raised concerns with regard to their impact on the long-established set of ethical standards that have traditionally characterized employment in the public sector. The PFI is considered to be a major force in that direction. As Bach and Givan (2004) suggest, PFI schemes have more long-term consequences than previous market-oriented initiatives because contracts are signed for twenty-five to thirty-five years compared to, for example, three years under compulsory competitive tendering. As a result, any workforce implications of the current public sector policies are likely to be more widespread and have a more lasting impact.

The 'public service ethos' has been part of the UK public sector culture for a number of decades. Its roots can be traced back to the 1854 Northcote and Trevelyan report into the Organization of the Permanent Civil Service which laid the principles that have come to shape the notion in the UK public service. It refers to 'an individual's predisposition to respond to motives grounded primarily or uniquely in public institutions' (Perry and Wise 1990: 368). Following this definition, studies have examined the construct as an attitude towards which certain individuals are predisposed and which guides their decision to seek employment in public organizations as well as their behaviour within these organizations thereafter. Historically, its study has rested on the crossing point of diverse academic disciplines such as organizational psychology, public administration, and economics. This partly explains the different terminology often used by various scholars and commentators (e.g. public sector ethos, public service motivation, pro-social motivation).

During the last three decades, Labour and Conservative governments have favoured the term 'public *service* ethos' when referring to the concept in formal documents and debates. Here, the deployment of the term 'service' rather than 'sector' can be explained by reasons that go beyond disciplinary idiosyncrasies. First, the revised phraseology is representative of a widespread shift in the ideology and values that the government would like to see characterizing public service delivery. It marks a break with the tradition of bureaucracy towards one of 'customer-oriented service' where the public is no longer seen as users of these services, but as customers or purchasers (Brereton and Temple 1999; Le Grand 2006). Proponents of this approach perceive the set of values traditionally associated with 'ethos' to be characteristic of a tradition of professional paternalism which is to blame for the ailments and inefficiencies within the public sector. For them, the 'public sector ethos' embodies an anachronistic attribute of the public sector's culture and is therefore something in need of redefinition.

Second, the substitution of 'sector' for 'service' is indicative of the conviction held by recent governments that the values traditionally associated with public sector employment can also be upheld by those delivering a public service, but are employed by private organizations. The new 'public service ethos' therefore becomes an amalgam of principles associated with both the public and the private sector. The most recent example of the objective to associate 'ethos' with both sectors is the seventh Report of the Public Administration Select Committee (PASC) commissioned by the Labour government and published in 2002. The report asserts that a strong ethos is not a public sector monopoly and that many examples of successful private sector provision exist. In particular, it argues:

Public sector and public service are not identical. Nor is it possible to sustain the view that public sector workers always display a service ethos, or that private sector workers do not. (PASC 2002, para. 24)

The report goes on to suggest that due to the difficulty of differentiating between public and private provision in the United Kingdom, public service ethos can exist regardless of who is responsible for service delivery. Notably absent in the report is some further discussion of ways in which government agencies can ensure that private contractors abide by these principles, and the consequences if they fail to do so. Nevertheless, clear within these accounts is the desire to portray the private sector as capable of adhering to public service values. Within this context, the deployment of the term 'service' is a response to widespread criticisms regarding the impact of private sector involvement on the public sector ethos and an attempt to overcome scepticism and overt opposition towards market-based public sector reforms. Such endeavours have been pursued with more zeal by the government since the emergence of Public–Private Partnerships as the main plank of the public sector modernization agenda.

These assertions raise three interrelated questions. First, to what extent are the ingredients of the 'New Ethos' suitable for ensuring effectiveness in public services delivery? Second, to what extent can such values also be upheld by those delivering public services but who are employed by private organizations? Although it is recognized that certain values and motives are an essential ingredient of efficient service delivery, proponents of private sector involvement reject the conventional view that the public service ethos is a monopoly of public servants. Finally, does it matter if the defining characteristics of the public service ethos are changing or if such values cease to characterize public service employees? These themes will be the focus of the sections that follow.

14.2. **The implications of a 'New Ethos'**

From the beginning of its term in office, the Labour government acknowledged the existence of an 'ethos' amongst public servants and emphasized its significance in the context of public service delivery. But it was the government's conviction that the notion of the ethos was in need of modernization. The subsequent publication of the 'Modernising Government' White Paper in 1999 marked a clear shift in the ideology and culture that was to characterize public service delivery (Cabinet Office 1999). Prominent within it were notions of 'customer service' and 'responsiveness to customer needs'. The next step was to redefine 'ethos' and revise its constituent dimensions. To the traditional values of accountability, impartiality, and probity, the 2002 PASC report also included that of 'customer service'. Increasingly, notions of 'customer satisfaction' and models of 'customer service' traditionally associated with private sector management practices have gained prominence in the vocabulary of government officials and proponents of reform. According to John Reid (2004), the traditional ethos of public service needs to be supplemented by an additional element of 'customer care' or as Tony Blair put it 'in public services, customer satisfaction has to become a culture, a way of life, not an added extra' (Blair 2002). In his speech to the Social Market Foundation, the then pensions minister John Hutton called for 'making the goal of customer satisfaction fundamental to the ethos of public services' (Hutton 2005). The approach of the opposition has not been markedly different. While praising the ethos and professionalism of public servants, the Conservative leader David Cameron has called for more input by 'consumers' as a means of improving understanding of what constitutes good public service (Cameron 2006).

This has led many commentators to call for a new 'synthesized' ethos that draws on the core elements of bureaucratic principles of honesty and accountability as well as more market-based ones such as customer service, customer choice, and value for money (Brereton and Temple 1999; Aldridge and Stoker 2002). According to this thesis, the responsibility for determining the standards and patterns of service delivery ceases to rest exclusively with professionals. Instead, the exchange between provider and user is contractual in nature and it is the 'customer' that defines expectations and assesses outcomes. Admittedly, re-establishing the needs of the user as the central theme in service provision is a legitimate endeavour. However, this approach can be problematic in practice. According to Fountain (2001), the efficacy of a 'customer service' culture is based on the premise that customers can use 'exit' (meaning switching to other providers if the level of service falls below their expectations). The author, however, questions the extent to which this is feasible in a public service context. If one is not satisfied with the quality of treatment one receives from the local hospital, his or her ability to shop around for a better service is restricted. In addition to exit, it is vital for 'customers' to be able to exercise their 'voice'. However, this can also be difficult as the exercise of voice assumes knowledge. A key concern therefore is that voice will only benefit informed consumers (or those willing and able to invest in acquiring information) and can thus produce a stratified model of service provision. Because of their superior expertise and knowledge, traditionally public service users relied on professional groups to act on their behalf and safeguard their interests, admittedly sometimes with dubious outcomes. As Besley and Ghatak (2003) point out, although limiting user 'voice' may be paternalistic, it may stop certain groups from making incorrect decisions. Indeed, the public service ethos was born out of the very aspiration to overcome inequities in service provision and unevenly distributed outcomes.

Others see such consumerism as an unrealistic goal. As Needham (2007: 856) points out, treating users as customers in the same manner as the private sector does raises questions about 'the capacity of the government to keep responding to demands that are effectively limitless'. Such a capacity is further constrained by the current economic climate. In a context of mounting public debt that the United Kingdom has acquired as a result of the actions the Labour government took in response to the financial crisis in 2007, the ability to increase or even sustain existing levels of investment in the public service has been called into question (Chote et al. 2009). Beyond such pragmatic concerns, Needham warns of the potential trade-offs that the new synthesized ethos might entail. According to her, an ethos based on consumerist principles such as customer satisfaction runs the risk of prioritizing the attainment of individual wants to the detriment of collective objectives. A detailed analysis of the philosophical arguments for and against such a shift is beyond the scope of this chapter, but it is worth noting that under such conditions public interest is subordinated to personal desires and thus the concept of citizenship changes from being a 'contract' (involving certain rights and obligations) to a 'status' (only involving rights) (Borghi and van Berkel 2007).

The lack of consensus with regard to the exact attributes that should comprise the public service ethos has led some commentators to describe the concept as 'ambiguous' (Pratchett and Wingfield 1994) and 'nebulous' (Corby 2000), whereas others have altogether challenged its intrinsic value. According to the latter, the traditional attributes of the public service ethos are associated with inefficiencies, profligacy, and poor quality of services. Excessive fixation with the procedural aspects of service delivery has deprived public service users of the superior levels of customer service and flexibility that are characteristic of the private sector (Le Grand 2006). In some cases, evoking the public service ethos is described as a means to legitimize the behaviour of public servants, allow decisions to go unquestioned, assert their authority, and reinforce their status as 'gatekeepers' of the common good (Richards and Smith 1997). For the authors, the public service ethos can therefore be best understood as a Foucaultian concept entailing a system of power and knowledge designed to safeguard the interests of bureaucrats. As such, they make an elegant argument as to why defending the existence of a public service ethos becomes an issue of self-preservation rather than an attempt to ensure effectiveness of public service delivery. In light of such scepticism regarding the functions that the public service ethos serves, it is imperative to assess its intrinsic value. Such considerations are important in themselves, but they become more so when one wishes to engage in discourses about erosion or endurance and the role of the private sector in the process.

14.3. Private sector involvement and the public service ethos

Critics of the new model of service delivery argue that the established approach to public sector management with its emphasis on equity and accountability is being replaced by rationalistic and economic considerations. Such an environment places public servants in situations where transparency is threatened and ethical standards are being compromised (Du Gay 2000). Similar concerns have been raised by trade unions, with Unison, GMB, and RCN leading the debate. Indeed, the eroding public sector ethos and deteriorating standards of service delivery have been central to their campaigns against private sector involvement in the delivery of public services for more than a decade. On the other hand, proponents of public sector reform adopt a more sceptical view of the public service ethos and claim that arguments highlighting its importance are evoked by those who are against public sector modernization as a means to safeguard their interests. According to this camp, efficiency and 'value for money' should take precedence and so the values of public servants should be redefined to reflect such priorities. This debate has placed the public service ethos at the centre of research that seeks to evaluate the outcomes of public sector reform. In a context of intense private sector involvement in the delivery of public services and much speculation about the lack of altruistic values characterizing its workforce, it is essential to empirically evaluate whether the public sector is distinctive in this respect.

Few studies have compared the behaviour and motives of public sector employees with those of their private sector counterparts. Using unpaid overtime as a proxy for donated labour, Gregg et al. (2008) find a strong link between institutional structure and pro-social behaviour. In particular, employees in the non-profit sector are more likely than their profit sector counterparts to donate their labour and such propensity to donate labour affects self-selection into sectors. In a survey of public and PFI prisons, Koumenta (2010) compares the motives and values that characterize public and private sector employees working in the delivery of an identical public service. The findings demonstrate that private sector employees score significantly lower on public service ethos and that such an ethos increases with tenure more quickly for public sector workers than for their private sector counterparts. Overall, PFI employees score lower in the compassion and self-sacrifice dimensions of ethos and are less likely to adhere to the governance values that traditionally characterize public bureaucracies.

Drawing on the selection–attraction–attrition framework, this negative relationship between private sector employment and public service motivation can be seen as the outcome of either or all of the following three processes. First, it can be a selection effect meaning that the private sector fails altogether to attract employees who are predisposed towards public service values. Second, although the private sector might initially attract public service motivated individuals, it might fall short of retaining them due to lack of an environment conducive to such values. Therefore, the observed lower levels of public service motivation within the private sector sample could be suggesting that public service motivated individuals have exercised the 'exit' option and possibly migrated to the public sector. Third, the negative relationship between private sector employment and public service ethos could be an outcome of 'crowding out' of intrinsic motivation. Models put forward by economists are also particularly useful in explaining such observed differences. According to François (2000), pro-social behaviour is a stable individual tendency that determines willingness to commit one's costly labour towards high quality services because of concern about the level and quality of output produced. But whether such a predisposition translates into pro-social behaviour depends on the type of organization one works for. If one works for a profit-making organization the incentive to act pro-socially is absent, because employees know that their donated labour will be appropriated by the owners of the organization in the form of higher profits. Working for a not-for-profit organization on the other hand means that donated labour is directed towards promoting social welfare, a cause such individuals concur with. As such, the model predicts that public service motivation will be a characteristic predominantly of those working in non-profit organizations like the public sector or charities.

Clearly, the view that the public sector is exclusively populated by altruists or that somehow all public sector employees are inherently more caring than private sector ones is flawed. Well-known examples of unethical conduct by public servants include those of the Bilston College in Wolverhampton and Halton College in Cheshire, where the National Audit Office revealed cases of financial mismanagement and fraud. Similar cases have been reported in the NHS (see Wighton 1998) and local government with the most famous being that of T. Dan Smith, leader of the Newcastle Upon Tyne City Council, who in 1974 was imprisoned for accepting bribes from the private sector over the city's redevelopment scheme. For more recent examples, one needs to look no further than the MPs' expenses scandal that broke out in 2009. However, we also know that people's behaviour is often influenced by the environment in which they find themselves. Schick's research (1996) into the introduction of quasi-markets and targets in New Zealand finds higher levels of opportunism and self-interested behaviour amongst his sample of workers in privatized settings. Similarly, the capacity of control and reward systems to shape behaviour is well documented in the literature (see Frey 1997; Kreps 1997; Ryan and Deci 2000). In short, not all private sector employees are inherently self-interested utility maximizers but individuals adjust their behaviour as a response to contextual demands and codes of practice, in this case working within a market-based model.

Yet, one cannot help but question whether the debate about an eroding public service ethos is also a means to undermine the reform agenda by those who are ideologically opposed to it. In the face of rapid technological improvements, higher standards of living, and increased longevity, private sector involvement can be a vital means of financing new public services. As long as reforms improve access and efficiency, does it matter whether public service motivated behaviour is absent? Why romanticize bureaucratic models of service delivery if private sector involvement improves performance? Admittedly, a fundamental limitation within some of the existing literature on the public service ethos is that most of these studies take for granted that such orientations are a desirable characteristic of employees delivering public services. Implied in these accounts is the notion that a lack of an ethos is disadvantageous, but some examination as to why that is the case and who is to lose from the erosion of such values is missing. To this I now turn.

14.4. **The value of the public service ethos**

According to Le Grand (1997), individuals can either be altruists (knights) or self-interested utility maximizers (knaves), but due to a lack of a system that can group individuals into each category, control mechanisms should be based on the assumption that everyone is a knave. This will ensure that the behaviour of knaves is monitored while knights will be left to behave as altruists. Apart from the obvious question 'why staff public services with knaves in the first place if one can have knights instead', the logic behind his line of thinking is flawed as it overlooks the possibility of knights turning to knaves and the consequences of such knavish behaviour in the absence of effective monitoring systems. These points are elaborated below.

Specific features of the public sector make principal–agent relationships different to those in the private sector (Dixit 2002; Besley and Ghatak 2003). Due to information asymmetry, a common characteristic of public sector occupations is that of imperfect means by which effort can be monitored and output can be measured. In standard models of principal–agent relationships, when output is perfectly observable and outcomes are verifiable, the agent's effort is measured according to the value of the output and the agent is compensated accordingly. However, there is a great deal of complexity and multitasking involved in delivering public services and as a result performance measures can be noisy, expensive to monitor, and therefore costly to the taxpayer. Most importantly, there are aspects of the job that are important in delivering high-quality public services, yet such aspects are hard to include into formal contracts (Grout and Stevens 2003). For example, good health care provision involves low or no waiting lists and good education involves schools scoring high in exam results. Measurement according to these criteria is relatively straightforward. However, we also desire midwives to be compassionate and teachers to be caring. Naturally, if those aspects of the job for which we have good performance measures are included in contracts and those that do not are excluded, agents will focus their efforts on the former to the neglect of the latter. This would clearly be a socially inefficient outcome. However, what if the employee derives some sort of personal satisfaction from performing these tasks that are difficult to put into contracts because of his or her conviction that they will contribute to more socially beneficial outcomes? If, amongst other things, individuals are attracted to work in the delivery of public service by the desire to serve the public interest, then they will be more willing to commit their costly efforts towards attainment of such goals. Under such circumstances, public service ethos is itself an incentive for agents to act according to the principal's wishes as the self-interested choices of agents coincide with the principal's goals. If employees delivering public services are public service motivated, then the problems of moral hazard and incomplete contracts will diminish, leaving both organizations and society better off.

Second, as Burgess and Ratto (2003) point out, a key feature of public sector employment is that many public servants (such as benefits assessors, police officers, tax inspectors) are in such positions that enable them to make important decisions depending on factors which are not directly observable by their superiors. In such cases, the most efficient way to direct effort, reduce moral hazard, and ensure due process is by undertaking audits and formal enquiries of agent actions. Such ways of measuring performance, however, can be both noisy and costly to the public purse. However, if employees have internalized the objectives of the organization and they care about the level and quality of output, then monitoring becomes less problematic. As such, public service ethos can incentivize the agents to behave according to the principal's wishes and help ensure Pareto efficient outcomes for both the organization and society as a whole. Further to this, public organizations tend to be large labour-intensive bureaucracies characterized by many hierarchical levels and a high degree of departmentalization. Their size places constraints on managerial ability to monitor effort. As such, alternative control mechanisms have to be implemented. Amongst other things, cultivating and supporting a strong public service ethos can to some extent be a substitute for costly methods of monitoring and a means to ensure that employee effort is directed towards socially and organizationally beneficial outcomes.

Empirical studies confirm that employing pro-socially motivated individuals is associated with various positive outcomes. Naff and Crum (1999) find a strong positive relationship between public sector motivation and individual performance, as employees associate their work effort with better outcomes for the community. Similar conclusions are reached with regard to the contribution of public service motivation to organizational performance which includes a range of efficiency, administrative, and operational effectiveness measures (Kim 2005). Further, public service motivation has been linked to lower turnover and higher organizational commitment (Camilleri 2006; Castaing 2006) as well as other positive employee behaviours such as willingness to engage in whistle blowing as a means to protect the interests of the public (Brewer and Selden 1998).

14.5. Conclusion

The public sector ethos has been held to be a defining characteristic of the UK public sector for many decades, and in order to reflect on its future, one needs to glance at its past. In the 1920s, Sir Warren Fisher, the then head of the Civil Service, argued that the public sector ethos must characterize those working within the government and stressed the distinction between these values and those commonly found in the private sector. Other historical accounts highlight that the notion of ethos was born out of the aspiration to purify the political system by marking a critical break with the past practices of clientelism and self-interested behaviour (Greenaway 1995). Ironically, the concept of ethos emerged as a means of differentiating the culture of the private sector from the public. If one accepts the claim made by politicians and policymakers that the motives and values of private and public sector employees are identical, then the notion of a public sector ethos automatically ceases to be relevant. In other words, questioning the distinctiveness of public sector motives is no less than doubting the existence of a public sector ethos. But is this a desirable outcome? As service users and consumers should we not aspire for our public servants to be characterized by altruistic motives and a sense of commitment to serve the public interest? As the previous section has argued, the public service ethos serves as a corrective to information asymmetries inherent in the public service context. Buying into the mission of the public service produces what DiIulio (1994) refers to as 'principled agents' with subsequent benefits to public organizations and service users. This is not to say that certain groups of public sector employees are not also self-serving agents with an interest in upholding the privileged position of their profession (see Humphris et al., Chapter 7 in this volume). Indeed, neither of the two approaches can stand alone when trying to understand the behaviour of public servants. However, it is vital to have an appreciation of what could be sacrificed in the name of reform and adjust policymaking choices accordingly.

Although such considerations have rarely informed practice in the past, the evidence presented here makes a strong case for taking public service ethos more seriously at both a micro (i.e. organizational) and macro level. With regards to the former, a key conclusion that can be drawn is the significance of selection in ensuring that public sector organizations are largely populated by intrinsically motivated individuals. Given that public service motivation is partly an individual predisposition, then mechanisms to ensure that such individuals are selected to fill in public service jobs should be built into the recruitment process. Greater emphasis on such procedures should be afforded by HR managers when recruiting in jobs with a high public service ethos component such as front-line public services. But one should not stop here. Organizational policies can send powerful signals to employees regarding what behaviours are rewarded on one hand and how unethical conduct is punished on the other. As such, supporting and cultivating a strong public service ethos should become a key goal of HRM practice in the public sector. Public service providers should also consider the image they are projecting to potential applicants, for example, what role the ethos plays in job descriptions and subsequent organizational socialization practices.

Given the potential for public sector agencies to attract 'principled agents', should private sector involvement in the delivery of public services be abandoned? The answer is a qualified no. The private sector can in some circumstances deliver superior outcomes compared to the public. The conditions under which this is possible are well documented in the literature. According to Grout and Stevens (2003), the capacity to accurately regulate quality is one. Such a capacity would overcome the problem of incomplete contracts as it would enable the public sector to accurately specify the conditions of service delivery. Although this is not always a straightforward task, the private sector has produced better performance and higher levels of innovation when such involvement has been accompanied with a sound regulatory regime. Second, the private sector can improve performance when public service motivation is not important or else when there is little intrinsic motivation to crowd out (Moynihan 2008). For example, the evidence shows that PFI projects in the construction industry have been particularly successful in terms of quality and value for money (MacDonald 2002). Both these conditions relate to the nature of the services in question and in particular to how strong the public good component of a service is. Yet if we accept that the nature of some public goods and the preferences of those employed in their delivery are such that they distinguish them from private ones, then provision through the market model is inappropriate.

More recently, the Labour government has been keen to involve the not-for-profit sector in the delivery of public services. Politically, it is not a controversial idea and theoretically it makes good sense. Contrary to the private sector, mission alignment between public sector agencies and non-profit organizations is not problematic. According to François (2000), non-profit firms have a greater capacity to elicit public service motivated behaviour compared to for-profit ones. Similar to their public sector counterparts, non-profit employees are also motivated by altruistic considerations and therefore care about the level and quality of services produced (Perry and Wise 1990). Empirically, the evidence is limited but largely confirms such assumptions. Gregg et al. (2008) find higher levels of donated labour in not-for-profit firms compared to their profit-oriented counterparts. Whether not-for-profit employees also adhere to broader public service values such as accountability and due process is yet to be proved. If that is shown to be the case, there is no reason why provision of public services by the non-profit sector should not be encouraged by policymakers.

With regards to preserving a public service motivation culture, both Labour and Conservatives have been treading between rhetoric and reality. On one level, politicians from all parties acknowledge the existence of a common set of values that underpin public service institutions and the important purpose such ideologies have served throughout the years. They also appear keen to see these values preserved. But policy initiatives and manifestos send different signals. New Labour's public service reform programme was dominated by targets, key performance, and more recently user choice, whereas the latest manifesto titled 'The Choice for Britain' argued for the establishment of user rights and entitlements against which the performance of public agencies would be evaluated. The Conservatives have pledged to abolish the PFI but preserve private sector involvement in the delivery of public services, as well as to increase accountability of professionals to users. Implicit in such policy initiatives is the belief that public servants cannot be trusted and therefore the rules of the game need to be adjusted to ensure they deliver. Leaving aside the validity of such assumptions, policymakers should be reminded that policy initiatives have the capacity to distort organizational missions. This has implications not only with regard to who is attracted to work for the public sector but also with regard to their levels of public service motivation thereafter. If we wish pro-social behaviour to be an attribute of our public servants, then the existing policy paradigm needs to be revised to reflect such priorities.

☐ REFERENCES

Aldridge, R. and Stoker, G. (2002) *Advancing a New Public Service Ethos, New Local Government Network*, May, London: NLGN.

Bach, S. (2002) 'Public-sector Employment Relations Reform under Labour: Muddling Through on Modernization?', *British Journal of Industrial Relations*, 40(2), 319–49.

—— and Givan, R. (2004) 'Public Service Unionism in a Restructured Public Sector: Challenges and Prospects', in J. Kelly and H. Gospel (eds.) *Union Organising and Activity*, London: Routledge.

Besley, T. and Ghatak, M. (2003) 'Incentives, Choice and Accountability in the Provision of Public Services', *Oxford Review of Economic Policy*, 19(2), 235–49.

Blair, T. (2002) *The Courage of Our Convictions: Why Reform of the Public Services is the Route to Social Justice*, London: Fabian Society.

Borghi, V and van Berkel, R. (2007) 'New Modes of Governance in Italy and the Netherlands: The Case of Activation Policies', *Public Administration* 85(1), 83–101.

Brereton, M. and Temple, M. (1999) 'The New Public Service Ethos: An Ethical Environment for Governance', *Public Administration*, 77(3), 455–74.

Brewer, G.A., and Selden, S.C. (1998) 'Whistle Blowers in the Federal Civil Service: New Evidence of the Public Service Ethic', *Journal of Public Administration Research and Theory*, 8(3), 413–39.

Burgess, S. and Ratto, M. (2003) 'The Role of Incentives in the Public Sector: Issues and Evidence', *Oxford Review of Economic Policy*, 19(2), 235–49.

Cabinet Office (1999) *Modernising Government*, Cm. 4310. London: The Stationery Office.

Cameron, D. (2006) 'Public Service Ethos: Learning from the Frontline', *National Consumer Summit*, 6 June, http://www.guardian.co.uk/politics/2006/jun/06/publicservices.conservatives

Camilleri, E. (2006) 'Impact of Personal Characteristics and Public Service Motivation on the Performance of Public Sector Employees in Malta', *Paper prepared for presentation at the Annual Conference of the European Group of Public Administration* (EGPA), Public Personnel Policies Study Group, 6–9 September, Milan, Italy.

Castaing, S. (2006) 'The Effects of Psychological Contract Fulfilment and Public Service Motivation on Organizational Commitment in the French Civil Service', *Public Policy and Administration*, 21(1), 84–98.

Chote, R., Crawford, R., Emmerson, C., and Tetlow, G. (2009) *Britain's Fiscal Squeeze: The Choices Ahead*, IFS Briefing Notes, London: Institute for Fiscal Studies.

Corby, S. (2000) 'Employee Relations in the Public Services: A Paradigm Shift?', *Public Policy and Administration*, 15(3), 60–74.

DiIulio, J.D.Jr. (1994) 'Principled Agents: The Cultural Bases of Behavior in a Federal Government Bureaucracy', *Journal of Public Administration Research and Theory*, 4(3), 277–318.

Dixit, A. (2002) 'Incentives and Organisations in the Public Sector: An Interpretative Review', *Journal of Human Resources*, 37(4), 696–727.

Du Gay, P. (2000) *In Praise of Bureaucracy*, London: Sage.

Fountain, J.E. (2001) 'Paradoxes of Public Sector Customer Service', *Governance*, 14(1), 55–73.

François, P. (2000) 'Public Service Motivation as an Argument for Government Provision', *Journal of Public Economics*, 78, 275–99.

Frey, B.S. (1997) 'A Constitution for Knaves Crowds Out Civic Virtues', *Economic Journal*, 107, 1043–53.

Greenaway, J. (1995) 'Having the Bun and the Half-Penny: Can Old Public Service Ethics Survive in the New Whitehall?', *Public Administration*, 73(3), 357–74.

Gregg, P., Grout, P., Ratcliffe, A., Smith, S., and Windmeijer, F. (2008) 'How Important is Pro-Social Behaviour in the Delivery of Public Services?' *Working Paper* No. 08/197, Centre for Market and Public Organisation.

Grout, P.A. and Stevens, M. (2003) 'The Assessment: Financing and Managing Public Services', *Oxford Review of Economic Policy*, 19(2), 215–34.

Hutton, J. (2005) 'Public Service Reform: The Key to Social Justice', *Speech to the Social Market Foundation*, 24 August.

Kim, S. (2005) 'Individual-Level Predictors and Organisational Performance in Government Organisations', *Journal of Public Administration Research and Theory*, 15(2), 245–61.

Koumenta, M. (2010) 'The Role of Sectoral Status and Trade Union Membership in Upholding Public Service Motivation', *Paper presented at the International Research Society for Public Management*, University of Berne, Berne 7–9 April 2010.

Kreps, D. (1997) 'Intrinsic Motivation and Extrinsic Incentives', *American Economic Review*, 87 (2), 359–64.

Le Grand, J. (1997) 'Knights, Knaves or Pawns?', *Journal of Social Policy*, 26, 149–69.

—— (2006) 'The Blair Legacy? Choice and Competition in Public Services', Public Lecture, London School of Economics, 21 February.

MacDonald, M. (2002) Review of Large Public Procurement in the UK, Report prepared for HM Treasury, London: HMSO.

Moynihan, D.P. (2008) 'The Normative Model in Decline? Public Service Motivation in the Age of Governance', in J.L. Perry, and A. Hondeghem (eds.) *Public Service Motivation: State of Science and Art*, Oxford: Oxford University Press.

Naff, K.C. and Crum, J. (1999) 'Working for America: Does Public Service Motivation Make a Difference?', *Review of Public Personnel Administration* 19 (Fall), 5–16.

Needham, C. (2007) 'A Declining Public Service Ethos?', in P. Dibben et al. (eds.) *Modernising Work in the Public Services*, London: Palgrave Macmillian.

Perry, J.L. and Wise, L.R. (1990) 'The Motivational Bases of Public Service', *Public Administration Review*, 50(3), 267–373.

Pratchett, L. and Wingfield, M. (1994) *The Public Sector Ethos in Local Government: A Research Report*. London: Commission for Local Democracy.

Public Administration Select Committee (2002) *A Public Service Ethos*, Seventh Report, Session 2001-02m, www.publications.parliament,uk/pa/cm200102/cmselect/cmpubadm/263/26302htm

Reid, J. (2004) 'We can be Consumers and Citizens', *Guardian*, 13 November.

Richards, D. and Smith, M.J. (1997) 'The Gatekeepers of the Common Good: Power and the Public Service Ethos', *Paper presented at the Annual European Group of Public Administration Conference*, September, Leuven.

Ryan, R.M. and Deci, E.L. (2000) 'Intrinsic and Extrinsic Motivations: Classic Definitions and New Directions', *Contemporary Educational Psychology*, 25(1), 54–67.

Schick, A. (1996) *The Spirit of Reform*, Report prepared for the State Services Commission and the Treasury, New Zealand.

Wighton, D. (1998) 'NHS Chief to Face MPs' Grilling over Clinical Codes', *Financial Times*, 12 March, p. 9.

15 The Future of Public Sector Pay in the United Kingdom[1]

RICHARD DISNEY

15.1. The setting, and the key issues

The public sector pay bill currently constitutes around two-thirds of central government spending net of transfer payments in the United Kingdom. Public sector employment is over 20 per cent of total employment at just over 6 million people. With the tight squeeze on public spending for a sustained period from 2010–11 to 2015–16 (HM Treasury 2010), the appropriate size of the public sector pay bill and the viability of alternative methods for managing public sector pay and employment are assuming major importance in policy discussions. In particular, all the major political parties in the election envisaged tight controls on public sector pay levels in this period.

It is therefore an appropriate moment to consider the evidence of the issue of the appropriate public sector pay level. Specifically: is there evidence of significant pay 'premia' (or indeed penalties) to working in the public sector? And, if there is such evidence, what is the implication of such pay differences for public policy? These issues are considered in the first part of this chapter. That discussion yields several broad conclusions:

- First, looking at the long-run trend in relative pay, there is *not* a substantial difference between public and private sector pay, once we control for both 'measured' characteristics of workers as recorded in statistical surveys and for their underlying heterogeneity (in which category should be included differences in ability and in aptitude for particular jobs, which are rarely recorded in surveys). Comparisons of public and private pay over particular time periods are highly sensitive to the start date at which comparisons are made. In part this reflects the fact that pay differentials between public and private sector pay tend to move *counter-cyclically*— that is, private pay rises faster than public pay in a boom, with the reverse in a recession.
- On balance, women do slightly better in the public sector than they do in the private sector, but this may be due to differences in the nature of jobs in female-dominated occupations between the two sectors. Over the life cycle,

'career jobs' in the public sector (such as the education and health professions) tend to allow interruptions to work such as periods of child-rearing rather better than private sector jobs (e.g. by more generous holiday and parental leave arrangements). This difference is reflected in the contrasting evolution of pay for women over the life cycle in the public and private sectors. For men, there is little evidence of significant disparities in pay across the public and private sectors although, again, life-cycle profiles differ between the sectors, especially for graduate men.

- *Total* remuneration differs across the public and private sectors. In general, public sector workers are more likely to be covered by defined benefit pensions and to obtain higher average pensions even than those covered by pension plans in the private sector due to longer job tenures and earlier retirement dates (Disney et al. 2009, 2010). On the other hand, other fringe benefits are more prevalent in the private sector. Bonuses and performance-related pay exist in both sectors, but take the form of relatively small 'merit awards' in the public sector rather than the potentially large rewards related to individual economic performance in private sector organizations.
- There is evidence that pay differentials affect the relative type and quality of entrants and leavers from sectors. There is therefore a potential trade-off between public sector pay and the quality of public sector workers. In a tight labour market, limiting public sector pay increases relative to the private sector will inevitably tend to depress the quality of applicants to, and boost that of leavers from, public sector employment, but that policy will have much less impact in a recession.

Having considered the evidence, it is appropriate to consider explanations for these findings concerning public–private pay differentials—in particular, what 'stories' can be adduced to explain any residual differences in pay profiles in the public sector relative to the private sector once we control for worker characteristics. This forms the content of the second part of the chapter.

Ultimately, as just suggested, the scope for pay differentials for equivalent-quality workers between the public and private sectors is limited by the scope for worker exit and entry. Nevertheless, there are real differences both between and within public and private sector labour markets, some of which impede the operation of 'competitive forces' across sectors. Among the key points made in this second part of the chapter are:

- Pay-setting mechanisms in the public sector are *heterogeneous.* They range from centralized collective bargaining, through independent national pay recommendations (the system of pay review bodies) and arbitration, to local pay-setting. There is more scope for decentralized pay-setting in the public sector than is often acknowledged (both by permitting local organizations, such as Foundation Trusts in health care, to set their own pay arrangements and also because of the scope for recruitment and retention premia even within the centralized pay-setting machinery).[2] However, it appears that this facility for implementing local differences in pay is underutilized in practice, except perhaps among the highest paid public sector employees. It is not clear why this is so. It may stem from fear of union action, or from the threat of equal pay claims. But, equally plausibly, pay rigidities arise from quasi-monopsonistic activities by employers such as National Health Service (NHS) Trusts that are anxious to avoid 'leapfrogging' of pay, and also from direct interference by central government.

- Equally important, public sector occupations are heterogeneous and this diversity is changing over time. For example, few people would have predicted prior to 2008 that the public sector workforce would be increased between the third quarters of 2008 and 2009 by the inclusion of over 200,000 additional workers in banking and finance (having already incorporated Northern Rock into public sector employment in 2007) (Office for National Statistics 2009). The composition of the public sector workforce now looks very different from ten, let alone twenty-five, years ago.
- Differential incentives between sectors arise because of the relative difficulty of measuring output in the public sector, and indeed parts of the private sector (see Chapter 13 by Roberts). Consequently, there may be not just different pay levels but also different pay *structures* between the two sectors—in particular, public sector workers are less likely to have 'spot market' equilibrium wages at each point in the life cycle reflecting age-specific productivity. Deferred remuneration—and not just pensions—will play a greater role in the public sector as an incentive device (Ippolito 1997).
- Market structure is a key issue. Econometric studies of public sector pay effects have often been motivated by the methodology used for the statistical measurement of the premium to belonging to a trade union or being covered by a collective agreement, and indeed monopolistic trades unions are often an important actor in public sector pay determination. But whereas the model of market power that underpins the trade union 'pay effect' is relatively straightforward to model, the potential monopsonistic power of public sector employers complicates the issue of public pay-setting.
- The idea of 'vocation' or 'public service' is very hard to model empirically but is pertinent to standard economic models of incentives in the labour market (see Chapter 14 by Koumenta). Such norms and concepts may explain why recruitment to the public sector is relatively insensitive to fluctuations in the public–private sector pay differential, although of

course such fluctuations are ultimately likely to impact on labour quality (as in Nickell and Quintini 2002). In addition, for some parts of the public sector labour market, where access is governed by training places and/or where the public sector is the main employer in a given occupation, a model in which workers 'queue' for jobs rather than a simple market clearing model may be the most appropriate underlying description of the labour market. The scope for using in-migration to the United Kingdom as an alternative to training or an increase in overall pay in order to attract recruits then comes under consideration.

15.2. Public–private sector pay differentials

Many studies have found evidence of pay premia or penalties in the public sector relative to private sector workers. In particular, many studies find large pay premia for women working in the public sector. Such studies in general use econometric methods that are not dissimilar to those utilized in measurement of the wage differential associated with trade union status.[3] Ideally, a comparison of public and private sector pay should be based on the pay of identical workers who differ only with respect to the sector in which they are employed. Finding comparable workers has been a challenge for those, such as Review Bodies, charged with making public sector pay recommendations, and it is a major difficulty facing economists when using statistical methods. Consequently, it has been difficult for economists to agree on the size and nature of the public–private sector pay differential. This section sets out to explain these difficulties, and to show how attempts to resolve them have progressively helped economists reach their current assessment.

Modelling the public sector 'premium' or 'penalty' has relied on a limited range of tried and tested specifications.[4] These are based on a very general model (e.g. written down formally in Disney and Gosling 2003) in which the pay of an individual in each sector depends on a set of measured individual attributes (such as age, education, and training), and a set of unmeasured attributes which may be sector-specific (such as aptitude, affinity for a particular job, drive, loyalty, and other unmeasured factors). Typically, those variables that can be measured, including indeed whether the individual himself or herself is a public sector worker, are measured with error.[5] And in a very general model the returns not only to measured attributes such as investment in education but also to unmeasured factors such as aptitude and ability could potentially differ for each individual across sectors.

A very general model which allows for unmeasured attributes and for sector-specific returns to measured and unmeasured factors is impossible to estimate without further assumptions (what are termed 'parameter restrictions'— e.g. that returns to some worker characteristics are identical across sectors). Moreover, data availability may limit our capability to estimate particular parameters. Consequently, various studies of public pay have generated different estimates of the public sector pay effect not least because they have imposed different restrictions on this general model.

15.2.1. TIME SERIES MODELS

Time series models have sought to measure the pay gap between the two sectors holding the industrial and employment compositions constant. Data on individual workers are unavailable. Since individual worker affiliation is not observed, any average public sector pay 'effect' must be 'identified' off a weighted average of series on public and private sector wages with the weight given by the (time varying) proportion ρ of workers in the public sector. However, it is questionable whether the implied coefficient on ρ tells us anything about the coefficient of interest, which is the average public sector pay effect for an otherwise-identical worker. This issue has been extensively discussed in the closely related context of time series estimates of the union–non-union wage differential (e.g. Layard et al. 1978; Lewis 1986).

A more promising avenue in time series analysis is to utilize data for, say, particular subgroups of public workers in order to examine the *time variation* in relative wages between this group and other workers (preferably in occupations which require similar qualifications)—see, for example, Elliott and Duffus (1996). This approach is potentially interesting since, although such time series methods cannot estimate an average public sector 'effect' as such, they can tell us whether events such as macroeconomic shocks or public pay policies lead to variations in wage relativities over time—evidence much favoured in pay negotiations.

Unfortunately, without data on the composition of these groups, caution must be exercised in inferences from such findings. Changing pay relativities, as already noted, have implications for the quality (composition) of public sector workers (as in Nickell and Quintini 2002). In addition, changing composition driven by employment growth may have major effects. To take a very specific local example, the Health Departments in the United Kingdom have argued that recent periods of rapid employment growth in the NHS are associated with the hiring of workers at the lower end of pay bands. Over time, such changes in composition of the workforce would affect both the *level* of pay (in this case, lower than trend) and the *growth* of pay (in this case, faster than trend).[6]

15.2.2. CROSS-SECTION-BASED ESTIMATES

In a regression of public–private sector pay using cross-sectional differences, a number of restrictions are also generally implemented—it is often assumed, for example, that the value of worker attributes such as qualifications and age are the same across the two sectors—an assumption which is unlikely to hold for age, to take an example of such a characteristic. Whilst this problem can be solved statistically by adding suitable interactions or by undertaking appropriate decompositions, there are other, more fundamental, problems with these methods. When the regression is estimated by Ordinary Least Squares (OLS), since many worker characteristics such as ability are not observed in the data, the restriction is typically imposed that they are the same in both sectors. This restriction is implausible because individuals are unlikely to be randomly allocated across sectors in relation to these unobservable characteristics—such as individual-specific abilities in particular occupations. Instead, individuals are likely to be selected, or self-select, into the sector where their relative productivity (and pay) is likely to be the higher. This selection is likely to bias the coefficients on both individual measured characteristics and the measured sector average pay effect.

A large literature has therefore attempted to 'correct' the estimates of the pay gap by some form of Instrumental Variable (IV) procedure that requires the researcher to find observed variables that are uncorrelated with wages but that are a significant determinant of public sector status. Suitable instruments are rarely available and interpretation is made harder by the 'double hurdle' nature of the model (individuals must choose a sector and then be selected into employment by an employer in that sector).

Studies for a variety of countries which control for selection include those that identify off functional form (e.g. years of schooling versus highest qualification achieved), such as Belman and Heywood (1989) for the United States and Van Ophem (1993) for the Netherlands, or off background family characteristics, as in Borland et al. (1998) for Australia and Dustmann and Van Soest (1998) for Germany. From a reading of their paper, the identification strategy of Rees and Shah (1995) for the United Kingdom is not clear.

A popular extension to the cross-section method (which does not, however, focus on identification issues) is the use of quantile regression methods to examine whether public sector pay 'premia' or 'penalties' differ across the public and private sector earnings distributions (as in, e.g. Poterba and Rueben 1994; Disney and Gosling 1998; Melly 2002). It is often noted that the public sector pay distribution is more compressed than the private sector pay distribution, and this should lead naturally to quantile regression methods finding different 'penalties' or 'premia' across the distribution.

Caution should again be exercised, however, before inferring from these measured pay differences that, for example, more educated workers in the public sector 'do worse' than those in the private sector while less educated workers 'do better'. Whilst it is probably true that the private sector allows higher rewards to the most productive workers (not least because individual productivity—such as achievement of sales targets—is easier to measure in that sector), it may also be the case that higher qualified public sector workers are simply of lower quality/ability in the public sector. At the lower end of the distribution, it is probably true that public sector trades unions have been more successful in raising wages for lower paid workers than in the private sector, whilst legislative measures to limit exploitation, low wages, and discrimination are also easier to enforce in the public than in the private sector. There is some tentative evidence in Disney and Gosling (2003) to suggest that the process of contracting-out and compulsory competitive tendering of public sector occupations (many of them manual) has eroded this difference in wages of manual workers between sectors in recent years in the United Kingdom.

15.2.3. PANEL-DATA-BASED ESTIMATES

Panel data—that is, tracking the same individuals over a period of time—are a more attractive means of identifying public sector pay 'effects', since such data permit a richer set of hypotheses and potential estimation strategies. In particular, by tracking the same workers, it is possible to control for worker characteristics that are not measured in conventional pay surveys such as individual ability and other attributes that do not change much over time, and thus give a more reliable measurement of the pay gap for the occupations concerned. There are, however, several pitfalls inherent in the restrictions that may be implemented to utilize panel-data-based methods.

A common specification with panel data restricts the basic econometric model so that the effect of unobservable characteristics of the worker on the wage does not vary over time or vary between the public and private sectors. Often, it is also assumed that the public sector pay effect is time-invariant for the whole period or sub-periods of the data. Such methods, commonly termed a 'fixed effect' regression, net out the effect of fixed, unobservable individual-specific characteristics without recourse to an explicit IV procedure and to whatever exclusion restrictions are thereby implied. Perhaps because of data limitations, relatively few studies of the public sector premium of this type exist. However, studies which explicitly compare coefficients derived from cross sections and panel data methods (as in Disney and Gosling, 1998) often suggest quite sharp differences in estimated coefficients between the two methods. For example, that study, using British Household

Panel Survey data for 1991–5, found a 'penalty' of 9 per cent for male graduates working in the public sector when using OLS methods, whereas 'fixed effect' methods gave male graduates in the public sector a 'premium' of over 13 per cent relative to private sector graduates.

Such a disparity in findings has been extensively discussed in the closely related area of attempts to measure the trade union markup (Card 1996). A well-established argument, as in Freeman (1984) and Swaffield (2001), is that estimates of the public sector premium using a standard differences or mean deviations method will be biased downwards by measurement error, especially when sectoral changes are self-reported. The possibility of measurement error in such circumstances is particularly high when, as in the recent UK experience, contracting-out of public services often leaves employees of private companies working in public sector establishments. However, Disney and Gosling (2003) note that the bias may go either way when job changes are endogenous—indeed as we saw in the example for male graduates, both the sign changes and the coefficient are larger in the mean deviations method than in the OLS case. Disney and Gosling exploit the introduction of contracting-out and compulsory competitive tendering (CCT) in the 1980s and 1990s to utilize changes in the *sectoral* composition of the workforce as instruments. Nevertheless, their parameter estimates of the public sector pay effects for various subgroups (delineated by gender and educational group) are not particularly robust and, moreover, the estimator only generates an average value of the effect for each subgroup over the whole time period.

As Jakubson (1991) points out, the fixed effects specification is unnecessarily restrictive when panel data are available. First, it is possible to test for asymmetries (e.g. if workers move between two sectors, we can test whether the measured changes in pay associated with the transitions are symmetric). Second, and more generally, we can use alternative specifications to the fixed-effects model to test whether the public sector pay effect *is* time-invariant. Many of the policy issues that revolve around public sector pay concern the *trajectory* of public sector pay relative to private sector pay over time. For example, the 2007 report of the Nurses and Other Health Professionals Review Body (NOHPRB), which recommends pay increases for this remit group, states:

We would observe that our role is to take a longer-term view about the appropriate pay relativities to deliver the level and standard of labour force that the NHS wants.... [If] the NHS pay structure [is] falling behind the market.... The result would be that at some point problems would need to be addressed through a 'catch-up' award, introducing unnecessary volatility into NHS pay. (NOHPRB 2007: para#7.74)

In such a policy context, as mentioned previously, it seems strange to utilize data with temporal dimensionality to establish a single, constant, public sector pay 'effect', particularly where there are reasons for thinking in the long run that this net effect may not be large. Better, surely, to utilize methods appropriate to examine the *time variation* of measured public sector 'penalties' and 'premia' even if the average absolute measure of the pay 'effect' may thereby be open to question. Disney and Gosling (2008) use more general panel data methods, as suggested indirectly by Jakubson (1991), to test whether there are systematic (and significant) differences in the time path of public and private sector wages, and to establish whether significant, time-varying, public sector pay effects can be identified. Their method can be summarized by saying that, in essence, if we know in which sector the individual is located and his or her observed pay, and we assume fixed individual characteristics, then with panel data we can use all the observations of the individuals' sector status and wage level to solve for the predicted average public sector pay effect.

Figure 15.1 illustrates time-varying estimates of the average public sector 'effect' on pay for women estimated in Disney and Gosling (2008) using panel data methods which control for both differences in observable characteristics and unobservables (via the panel data estimator). It therefore handles the issue of changing composition of the public sector workforce over time described previously. The coefficients can be interpreted as average public

Figure 15.1. Estimates of Average Public Sector Pay Effect, 1975–2006
Source: New Earnings Survey/ASHE, Disney and Gosling (2008).

sector 'premia' or 'penalties' for each year for men and women, netting out all differences in characteristics; so, for example, on average, public sector men in 2005 were paid 3 per cent more than their private sector counterparts (a difference which is barely statistically significant), whereas women were paid 7 per cent more (which is statistically different).

Figure 15.1 suggests that the average public sector worker incurred a 'penalty' relative to the private sector until the early 1990s and women, at least, a 'premium' thereafter. For women, over the whole period, there is probably a slight premium on average; for men the reverse. Note that the recessions in the early 1980s and 1990s were associated with a reduction in the penalty/ jump in the premium, that is, any public sector wage effect is *counter-cyclical*. However, attempts by the government in the late stages of the recessions to curb public spending, and the recovery of the private sector, both led to a reduction in the premium/increase in the penalty during the upturn in the economy.

15.2.4. PAY OVER THE LIFE CYCLE

An important aspect of pay is how individual pay varies over the life cycle. As argued in the next section, it is easier to measure 'productivity' for workers in the private than the public sector, given the nature of government services. This implies that private sector labour markets are more likely to exhibit 'spot market' rates of pay. Moreover, as noted by Postel-Vinay and Turon (2007), the life cycle gives scope for job mobility that tends to smooth out transitory pay differences. Consequently, pay differentials at a point in time may be compressed over the life cycle, even though the age–pay relationship varies across sectors.

Figure 15.2 illustrates both these points, using representative median age earnings profiles constructed from Labour Force Survey data. For men, the profiles illustrate the sharper peak in earnings in the private sector in the late-middle working lifetime, whereas public sector profiles grow more slowly but peak later. This (as well as relative access to employer-provided pensions) illustrates the greater 'backloading' of pay among white-collar workers in the public sector. Although there is a significant 'pay penalty' to public sector graduate men around age 40, there is little difference in earnings over the whole life cycle.

For women, the profiles peak earlier and then level out in the public sector, whereas hourly pay declines in the private sector. This largely arises from the fraction of women who switch to part-time work after child-bearing— although this is hourly pay, part-time pay rates are lower. However, the nature of female-dominated occupations in the public sector and greater 'family-friendly' arrangements in that sector mitigate the effect.

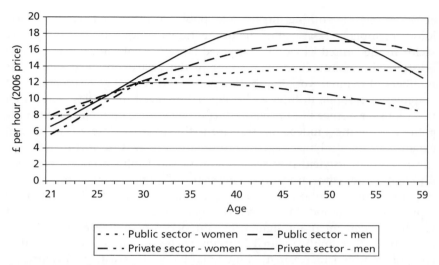

Figure 15.2. Median Age Earnings Profiles, Public and Private Sector Graduates

15.3. **What is 'special' about working in the public sector?**

Standard economic models predict that pay differences in competitive markets across individuals arise from differences in measured and unmeasured ability—the former typically measured by experience and qualifications whilst the latter may be netted out by appropriate techniques. Driving a wedge between pay and productivity may be various factors such as market power (whether of workers or producers/employers) and more systematic social inequalities such as discrimination. In the short run, the relative scarcities or surplus of particular skills may drive occupational differentials, although with competitive access to training, long-run occupational differences in pay should be driven by non-pecuniary advantages rather than relative supply, with relative demand affecting the employment mix. All this is standard textbook labour economics. Why should public sector workers be systematically differently rewarded in such a world? I consider some explanations.

15.3.1. OCCUPATIONAL COMPOSITION OF THE PUBLIC SECTOR

One possibility is that the workers in the public sector do systematically different jobs from those in the private sector, and this is why rates of pay differ. Some jobs are often seen as intrinsically 'public sector jobs': public administration, nursing, teaching, or security (police, armed forces, intelligence services, etc.). Yet there is nothing intrinsically 'public sector' about many of these jobs—a simple comparison of the occupational composition of the public sector in the United Kingdom compared to, say, twenty-five years ago, will illustrate this point. The public sector in the 1980s contained significant numbers of manual workers—both in local and central government—and employees of public utilities and other nationalized industries. Almost all these jobs have since been privatized, contracted-out, or subjected to competitive tendering—indeed this transformation forms an interesting 'natural experiment' in studying wage determination which is, unfortunately, not 'clean' enough to yield precise estimates of the public–private sector pay differential.[7] At the same time, the share of public sector employment in some white-collar professions (e.g. managers, auditors) has expanded rapidly in that period. Most recently (2008–9), public sector employment has been augmented by significant numbers of employees in banking institutions. The public sector in Britain has become more non-manual in composition, and increasingly dominated by workers with higher professional qualifications (Disney et al. 1998).

Even in specific sectors, the market context of different jobs varies. For example, in the NHS, some jobs are located in private-sector-dominated occupations (such as managerial positions), whereas some (such as specialist nursing and radiography) are public-sector-dominated jobs. Other occupations, such as nursing care assistants or physiotherapy, are more evenly divided between the public and private sector. A simple generalization as to what is a 'public sector job', even in a public-sector-dominated activity—the provision of primary and hospital-based health care—is not straightforward.

Further back in history, jobs which we might now regard as wholly 'public sector' have not been exclusively so in the past. Tax collection was often contracted-out to private agents who could retain a share of the revenues that they raised. Armies and militia were often raised as mercenaries or by conscription. The development of a 'public sector' seems often to have been brought about by historic events or geographical circumstances. One of the earliest examples of a systematic attempt to develop a large-scale public sector in England was the expansion of publicly managed naval storehouses and dockyards in the first part of the sixteenth century—by the mid-1560s, public dockyards constituted the largest single employer of workers on regular salaries in England (Rodger 1997). English dockyards also became one of the first 'test beds' for a large-scale privatization—with mixed results at best. Other countries for which a navy was not the primary line of defence had different contractual arrangements for naval forces. In contrast, the English army continued to rely on conscription from militias and payment of mercenary troops for a considerable period thereafter.

15.3.2. USE OF INCENTIVES

A pertinent distinction between the public and private sectors lies in the differential use of incentive-based pay in the two sectors. This in part arises from the difficulty of measuring 'output' or 'productivity' in the public sector described previously. Typically, public sector outputs are not marketed and have been measured until recently in accounting terms by input values since 'prices' cannot be attached to production. Contrast this with the private sector where, in the economics textbook if nowhere else, the term 'marginal revenue product' has some meaning.

Even in the absence of plausible means of tying pay to measurable output, there are however other techniques, familiar to personnel economics, for motivating workers to work harder such as deferring pay (by back-loading remuneration across the life cycle or by employer-provided pensions).[8] Deferred pay, whether by minimizing shirking and thereby reducing the relative value of jobs with other employers (the outside option), or through explicit incentive procedures such as promotion, is an alternative strategy for employers to 'spot market' equilibrium pay-setting in which pay is broadly linked at each point in the lifetime to productivity and which should generate the standard 'inverted U' age-earnings profile. Figure 15.2 for graduate men provided some evidence that deferred pay is a more prevalent strategy in the public sector than the private sector. Differences in pay between the public and private sectors at any given age will therefore reflect different pay-setting strategies as well as differences in underlying worker productivity.

Nevertheless, deferred pay may be a somewhat blunt instrument for raising individual productivity. Recent attempts to 'incentivize' public sector pay by making pay progression (not just through promotion) conditional on performance have been a response to this difficulty: evidence for this can be seen in the development of 'bonus pots' for senior civil servants and other high echelon public sector management in the United Kingdom, although satisfactory measurement of 'above-average' performance remains a difficulty. However, arguably throughout history such a solution to the problems of public sector management has been sought: for example, Allen (2002) has (perhaps somewhat fancifully) argued that the British navy was successful against that of the French in the Napoleonic wars because of the greater use by the former of piece rates (prize money), harsh penalties for shirking (capital punishment), and incentive-based promotions.[9]

15.3.3. MARKET POWER

An intrinsic difference between the public sector and large parts of the private sector is that the public sector is a unitary employer (this despite frequent attempts to 'decentralize' public sector management, and the important distinction between federal and centralized governments). Much of public sector pay bargaining—whether 'face to face' or conducted by specialized agencies such as 'Review Bodies'—is conducted at the national level. This scope for national bargaining in turn generates a 'countervailing power' to the public employer insofar as public sector workers are typically more heavily unionized than private sector workers. The existence of unions is typically given as one rationale for a measured public sector pay premium but of course unionization is in part a response to the potential monopsonistic power of the public employer and the effect on pay of bilateral market power can go either way.

Much of the evidence adduced for what Manning (2003) terms the 'static' theory of monopsony has emanated from United States' evidence on local school boards, health agencies, etc., which have market power in the local labour market relative to the local supply of teachers, nurses, etc. (for a survey, see Boal and Ransom 1997). Unsurprisingly, perhaps, economists differ on whether this is strong evidence for monopsony power (for a sceptical view, see Hirsch and Schumacher 1995). The older literature, written from an industrial relations viewpoint, tends to suggest that certain groups, notably female-dominated public sector professions, are more likely to face adverse effects arising from monopsonistic power, whereas strongly unionized and often male-dominated public sector groups earn a positive differential (see e.g. Fogel and Lewin 1974 on local bargaining in a large US metropolitan area).

Although monopsony has largely fallen out of fashion in analysing public sector pay, it is arguable that centralized pay structures in the public sector lend themselves to such an analysis. Pay in the NHS in the United Kingdom has since 2004–6 been governed by the Agenda for Change (AfC) framework (see National Audit Office 2009). AfC is a national job-evaluated pay agreement, but with the scope for national recruitment and retention premia, for local area cost supplements, and for local recruitment premia. In principle, there is enough flexibility in the AfC pay structure to permit variations in pay to reflect not just job content but also market shortages and local labour market conditions. However, the NHS Pay Review Body (NHSPRB) has often questioned whether the AfC pay structure is used flexibly enough. For example, in its 2009 report, the NHSPRB argued (2009: paras 3.70, 3.71):

The Health Departments and NHS Employers (NHSE) told us that they did not support a national RRP [Recruitment and Retention Premium]for pharmacists [or indeed any other new group], stating that local solutions are more appropriate. *However, NHSE also told us that it did not support local RRPs, as in its view they would destabilise the internal NHS market and possibly lead to pay spirals.* [author's italics]

In our view, the combination of these two positions undermines the use of the provisions within AfC that were designed specifically to address shortages of particular groups . . . Failure to use the scope for pay flexibility offered by AfC through RRPs may lead employers to consider strategies to recruit to hard-to-fill vacancies which have long-term undesirable consequences. These include 'grade drift' and other de facto revisions to the agreed AfC job structures that could ultimately lead the NHS labour market back to the pre-AfC era of local pay differentiation. Such strategies are incompatible with a key object of AfC which is to meet equal pay for work of equal value.

The views of the Review Body can be interpreted as saying that employers and the Health Departments are anxious to avoid any 'leapfrogging' of local pay rates that would arise were particular groups of workers to be in local short supply. But this is precisely how competitive labour markets work!

Attempts to 'incentivize' pay and to decentralize bargaining to reflect local labour market conditions can be seen as a relatively recent response to the problem of market power in public sector pay bargaining. Disney and Gosling (2003) provide tentative evidence that among low-paid public sector manual (and traditionally unionized) workers in the United Kingdom, any evidence of a positive wage premium has been eliminated by the introduction of compulsory competitive tendering and contracting-out in a range of services such as refuse collection and ancillary service provision from the mid-1980s onwards. On the other hand, moves to decentralize power to individual employers (e.g. in the NHS where trusts have been given a degree of autonomous status and, in the case of Foundation Trusts, the freedom to vary considerably pay and employment conditions) have so far, as suggested above, provided little evidence of independent pay-setting or decentralized bargaining. The whole tension between public centralized bargaining leading to better quality management but restrictive practices and labour inefficiency *versus* decentralization and contracting-out leading to cheaper delivery and lower quality service provision again has its antecedents in history.[10]

15.3.4. WORKER SELECTION

A key issue in examining pay determination is worker preferences. In a narrow sense, we might be interested in why a worker chooses to work in a particular job or sector. Background characteristics, notably occupational and sectoral choices of parents, are often used as a method of identifying sectoral choices made by workers (see, in this context, e.g. Dustmann and Van Soest 1998) so that pay premia or penalties to working in a particular sector can be conditioned on the (potentially self-selected) characteristics of the workers.

In a broader and more intangible sense, however, it is often argued (not least by public sector unions) that employees in the public sector are motivated by particular notions of 'public service' or 'loyalty' to a job which motivate them in addition to pay considerations (see chapter 14 by

Koumenta). If people are motivated by such considerations, rather than simply by remuneration levels, we might expect an impact on the pay of particular groups (such as nurses, teachers, etc.) where personal preferences might be paramount. Such an idea has some parallel with what Alan Manning (2003) terms 'dynamic monopsony'—the observation that employers retain market power insofar as the observed wage dispersion for broadly identical workers illustrates that workers do not necessarily immediately quit when their own wage is inferior to an outside option—presumably either because they like their existing job or have very limited information on outside wages.

Extend this argument to a particular occupation, or sector, and we are closer to what Heyes (2005) terms the 'economics of vocation': some workers receive a non-pecuniary benefit from providing a higher quality of service in their job so that their total pecuniary and non-pecuniary remuneration exceeds the wage and they remain in the job even in the face of a higher outside pecuniary option. Unlike pure incentive 'stories' (such as 'efficiency wages'), higher wages (whether or not coupled with greater monitoring) in such circumstances do not necessarily generate greater average productivity. In Heyes's analysis, higher wages attract workers who are *not* motivated by vocational considerations, so that average productivity may fall. This is a worker composition effect. In Frey (1993), in contrast, 'intrinsic motivation' of individual workers declines where there is increased monitoring coupled with greater emphasis on pecuniary rewards as this combination 'crowds out' the intrinsic motivation of particular workers. This is a change in behaviour of an existing workforce. Either way, the 'economics of vocation' or 'intrinsic motivation' suggests that attempts to 'incentivize' public sector pay may turn out to have perverse results and the public sector might produce better results in terms of productivity with lower pay levels but less emphasis on 'performance targets', etc.[11]

15.4. **Conclusion**

This chapter has surveyed broad explanations for differences in pay between public and private sector workers, and the econometric methods used to measure these effects. There are other important issues in public sector pay determination, such as the effect of specific bargaining arrangements (e.g. of the use of review bodies to make pay recommendations in some sectors of UK public employment, see Chapter 16), and the role of workplace characteristics, but I have not considered these here. This omission is partly for reasons of length but also because such issues tend to be considered *in the public sector context* rather more by industrial relations specialists than by economists and econometricians. This may well be a significant deficiency in the analysis of the topic by economists.

The standard tool in the analysis of public sector pay effects in most of the studies described here is a wage equation augmented by an indicator of public sector affiliation, with the coefficient on the latter interpreted as 'the' public sector pay effect. The methodology behind such studies and, presumably, the expected inferences to be drawn from the estimates are heavily influenced by the literature on union wage effects, which also has as its basic building block a wage equation augmented by an indicator of union status (whether union membership or affiliation).

But there are three reasons for thinking that simply hijacking this methodology to examine public sector pay 'effects' is flawed. First, while the rationale for finding union wage premia is simple—the existence of market power—any theoretical rationalization for differences in public and private sector wages is far less transparent, as the discussion in Section 3 demonstrated. Second, most methods generate a measured 'public sector pay effect' which is time invariant and often constant across large groups of heterogeneous public sector workers. This may be appropriate for measuring the average effect of unions (although there is also evidence of time-varying union premia) but seems less appropriate for policy questions concerning relative *trends* (or time variation) in public sector pay relative to the private sector for which attempts to measure a time invariant pay effect are not useful. Finally, while the public sector wage literature has picked up on some of the statistical issues that have motivated econometric studies of the union wage effect—notably endogeneity and self-selection—some of the other issues that have motivated union wage studies (such as the use of more sophisticated panel data methods, and seeking 'treatments' in labour markets that might generate testable hypotheses) are less well developed in the literature on public sector pay.

At the time of writing, public sector workers may face a pay freeze for two years. The imposition of such a pay policy follows previous episodes, depicted in Figure 15.1, whereby public sector workers fare relatively better in recessions only for public sector pay increases to be 'reined in' by subsequent governments as part of a general package of budget retrenchment measures. As the economy and private sector earnings recover, public pay then starts to lag behind private sector pay growth and there is inevitable pressure for 'catch-up' awards to restore relativities between public and private sector pay. In the interim and as the economy recovers, recruitment difficulties and union dissatisfaction tend to increase in the public sector and the quality of the public sector workforce declines, until some pay adjustments are made. This cycle, which was observed in, for example, the mid- to late 1970s and the late 1980s to early 1990s, seems likely to recur in the next few years. Future econometric measures of public sector pay effects will likely reflect these trends.

In conclusion, there are a large and expanding number of studies internationally on the public sector wage effect (the bibliography here is not comprehensive). However, the deficiencies in the literature are also notable: a lack of careful theoretical models to underpin empirical estimates; a lack of analysis—at least in the economics literature—of the implications of different pay-setting arrangements in the public sector; relatively unsophisticated panel data models which do not allow for the type of wage dynamics described here; and a lack of evidence based on 'treatments'—of which the wholesale attempts to privatize and contract-out public sector activities around the world would seem to be an obviously appropriate set of case studies.[12] None of these analyses are easy to do but may prove to be the directions that future research will take.

☐ NOTES

1. Presented at the CEP Seminar in honour of Professor David Metcalf, 14 December 2009, Centre for Economic Performance, London School of Economics. The author was a member of the NHS Pay Review Body (and its antecedent) from 2003 to 2009; no views presented here should be attributed to that body except when they are cited as such. Since 2009, the author has been a member of the Senior Salaries Review Body, with David Metcalf. The same disclaimer applies. The author thanks participants at a seminar organized by the Office of Manpower Economics and the CMPO, University of Bristol, for comments on an earlier version of this chapter.
2. On this subject, see Wolf (2010) for an alternative opinion. HM Treasury has also tended to pay lip service to the idea of greater decentralization of public sector wage determination (with consequent greater variability in local pay) but tends to be reluctant in practice to dispense with its own capacity to intervene in public pay-setting via the national level.
3. An area in which David Metcalf has been active for many years; see, for example, Metcalf and Stewart (1992).
4. For general surveys, see also Bender (1998) and Gregory and Borland (1999).
5. For example, a cook in a local authority school who is employed by a private sector company which has obtained the catering contract by competitive tendering may misclassify himself or herself as a public sector worker. The employer, it is presumed, *does* know whether each worker is a public or private sector worker, and this is in fact at the basis of the econometric identification strategy utilized by Disney and Gosling (2003).
6. The same point has been made more generally in the context of changing composition and hours of workers over the business cycle, and how this affects measured earnings growth (Blundell et al. 2003).
7. On which, see Disney and Gosling (2003) and also, *inter alia*, Card (1986) and Haskel and Szymanski (1993).
8. Standard references include Lazear (1979, 1981). See also Ippolito (1997).
9. Somewhat fancifully, because better quality of cannon and better rates of fire of cannon seem to have been the primary factors for British success: see Rodger (2004).
10. Following our earlier historical theme, the history of British naval dockyards and warship construction, which were alternately centrally managed interspersed with periods of

contracting-out, illustrates the trade-off between high quality and high labour cost on the one hand (publicly managed) and productive efficiency, lower cost, and lower quality on the other (when dockyard services and construction were contracted-out): see Baugh (1965) and Morriss (1983).

11. Anecdotal evidence, but certainly confirmed by visits to individual public sector employers by public pay Review Body members in Britain, suggests that excessive targeting, reorganizations, performance criteria, 'excess paperwork', and other by-products of the desire to 'incentivize' the public sector often draw more adverse criticism from workers than a perceived problem of low pay relative to comparable private sector jobs. Public sector workers do, however, find the implications of the arguments adduced by Frey as intrinsically more appealing than that of Heyes, although both draw on the identical idea of incomplete contracts.

12. In addition to the studies mentioned in note 2, I have only been able to find Monteiro (2004) and Grosfeld and Nivet (1999) that examine the consequences for pay of privatizations.

☐ REFERENCES

Allen, D. (2002) 'The British Navy Rules: Monitoring and Incompatible Incentives in the Age of Fighting Sail', *Explorations in Economic History*, 39, 204–31.

Baugh, D. (1965) *British Naval Administration in the Age of Walpole*, Princeton, NJ: Princeton University Press.

Belman, D. and Heywood, J. (1989) 'Government Wage Differentials: A Sample Selection Approach', *Applied Economics*, 21, 427–38.

Bender, K. (1998) 'The Central Government–Private Sector Wage Differential', *Journal of Economic Surveys*, 12(2), 427–38.

Blundell, R., Reed, H., and Stoker, M. (2003) 'Interpreting Aggregate Wage Growth: The Role of Labour Market Participation', *American Economic Review*, 93(4), 1114–31.

Boal, W. and Ransom, M. (1997) 'Monopsony in the Labor Market', *Journal of Economic Literature*, XXXV(March), 86–112.

Borland, J., Hirschberg, J., and Lye, J. (1998) 'Earnings of Public and Private Sector Employees in Australia: Is there a Difference?' *Economic Record*, 74(March), 36–53.

Card, D. (1986) 'The Impact of Deregulation on the Employment and Wages of Airline Mechanics', *Industrial and Labor Relations Review*, 39(July), 527–38.

—— (1996) 'The Effects of Unions on the Structure of Wages: A Longitudinal Analysis', *Econometrica*, 64(July), 957–77.

Disney, R. and Gosling, A. (1998) 'Does it Pay to Work in the Public Sector?' *Fiscal Studies*, 19(4), 347–74.

—— —— (2003) 'A New Method for Estimating Public Sector Pay Premia: Evidence from Britain in the 1990s', *CEPR Discussion Paper* 3787, London.

—— —— (2008) 'Changing Public Sector Wage Differentials in the UK', Institute for Fiscal Studies *Working Paper* W08/02, London.

—— Goodman, A., Gosling, A., and Trinder, C. (1998) *Public Pay in the 1990s*, Commentary No. 72, London: Institute for Fiscal Studies.

—— Emmerson, C., and Tetlow, G. (2009) 'What is a Public Sector Pension Worth?' *Economic Journal*, 119(November), F517–35.

—— —— —— (2010) 'The Value of Teachers' Pensions in England and Wales', *Fiscal Studies*, 31(March) 121–50.

Dustmann, C. and Van Soest, A. (1998) 'Public and Private Sector Wages of Male Workers in Germany', *European Economic Review*, 42, 1417–41.

Elliott, R. and Duffus, K. (1996) 'What has been Happening to Pay in the Public Service Sector of the British Economy? Developments over the Period 1970–1992', *British Journal of Industrial Relations*, 34(1), 51–86.

Fogel, W. and Lewin, D. (1974) 'Wage Determination in the Public Sector', *Industrial and Labor Relations Review*, 27(April), 410–31.

Freeman, R. (1984) 'Longitudinal Analysis of the Effects of Trade Unions', *Journal of Labor Economics*, 2(1), 1–26.

Frey, B. (1993) 'Shirking or Work Morale? The Impact of Regulating', *European Economic Review*, 37(8), 123–32.

Gregory, R. and Borland, J. (1999) 'Recent Developments in Public Sector Labour Markets', in O. Ashenfelter and D. Card (eds.) *Handbook of Labor Economics*, Volume 3C, pp. 3573–630, Amsterdam: North-Holland.

Grosfeld, I. and Nivet, J.F. (1999) 'Insider Power and Wage Setting in Transition: Evidence from a Panel of Large Polish Firms 1988–1994', *European Economic Review*, 43(4–6), 1137–47.

Haskel, J. and Szymanski, S. (1993) 'Privatisation, Liberalisation, Wages and Employment: Theory and Evidence', *Economica*, 60, 161–81.

Heyes, A. (2005) 'The Economics of Vocation or "Why is a Badly Paid Nurse a Good Nurse"?', *Journal of Health Economics*, 24, 561–9.

Hirsch, B. and Schumacher, E. (1995) 'Monopsony Power and Relative Wages in the Labor Market for Nurses', *Journal of Health Economics*, 14(October), 443–76.

HM Treasury (2010) *The Budget 2010*, HC61, June, House of Commons. The Stationery Office.

Ippolito, R. (1997) *Pensions Plans and Employee Performance: Evidence, Analysis and Policy*, Chicago: Chicago University Press.

Jakubson, G. (1991) 'Estimation and Testing of the Union Wage Effect Using Panel Data', *Review of Economic Studies*, 58, 971–91.

Layard, R., Metcalf, D., and Nickell, S. (1978) 'The Effect of Collective Bargaining on Relative and Absolute Wages', *British Journal of Industrial Relations*, XVI(November) 287–302.

Lazear, E. (1979) 'Why is there Mandatory Retirement?' *Journal of Political Economy*, 87(December), 1261–84.

—— (1981) 'Agency, Earnings Profiles, Productivity and Hours Restrictions', *American Economic Review*, 71, 606–20.

Lewis, H.G. (1986) *Union Relative Wage Effects: A Survey*, Chicago: Chicago University Press.

Manning, A. (2003) *Monopsony in Motion: Imperfect Competition in Labor Markets*, London: Princeton University Press.

Melly, B. (2002) 'Public–Private Sector Wage Differentials in Germany: Evidence from Quantile Regressions', *mimeo*, SIAW, University of St Gallen, Switzerland.

Metcalf, D. and Stewart, M. (1992) 'Closed Shops and Relative Paper: Institutional Arrangements or High Density?' *Oxford Bulletin of Economics and Statistics*, 54(November), 503–16.

Monteiro, P. (2004) 'Using Propensity Matching Estimators to Evaluate the Impact of Privatisation on Wages', *NIPE Working Paper* 1/2004, Universidado do Minho.

Morriss, R. (1983) *The Royal Dockyards during the Revolutionary and Napoleonic Wars*. Leicester: Leicester University Press.

Mueller, R. (1998) 'Public–Private Sector Wage Differentials in Canada: Evidence from Quantile Regressions', *Economics Letters*, 60, 229–35.

National Audit Office (2009) *Department of Health: NHS Pay Modernisation in England Agenda for Change*, Report by the Comptroller and Auditor General HC125 Session 2008–2009, 29 January 2009, London: The Stationery Office.

NHSPRB (2009) NHS Pay Review Body: *Twenty-Fourth Report*, Cm 7646, London: The Stationery Office.

Nickell, S. and Quintini, C. (2002) 'The Consequences of the Decline in Public Sector Pay in Britain: A Little Bit of Evidence', *Economic Journal*, 112(February), F107–18.

NOHPRB (2007) Review Body for Nurses and Other Health Professionals: *Twenty-Second Report*, Cm 7029, London: The Stationery Office.

Office for National Statistics (2009) *Statistical Bulletin: Public Sector Employment Q3 2009*, http://www.statistics.gov.uk/pdfdir/pse1209.pdf

Postel-Vinay, F. and Turon, H. (2007) 'The Public Pay Gap in Britain: Small Differences that (don't) Matter?' *Economic Journal*, 117(October), 1460–503.

Poterba, J. and Rueben, K. (1994) 'The Distribution of Public Sector Wage Premia: New Evidence Using Quantile Regressions', *NBER Working Paper #4734*.

Rees, H. and Shah, A. (1995) 'Public–Private Sector Wage Differentials in the UK', *Manchester School*, LXIII(March), 52–68.

Rodger, N. (1997) *The Safeguard of the Sea: A Naval History of Britain, 660–1649*, London: Penguin Books.

—— (2004) *The Command of the Ocean: A Naval History of Britain, 1649–1815*, London: Penguin.

Swaffield, J. (2001) 'Does Measurement Error Bias Fixed-Effects Estimators of the Union Wage Effect?' *Oxford Bulletin of Economics and Statistics*, 63(4), 437–58.

Van Ophem, H. (1993) 'A Modified Switching Regression Model for Earnings Differentials between the Public and Private Sectors in the Netherlands', *Review of Economics and Statistics*, 75, 215–24.

Wolf, A. (2010) *More than we Bargained for: The Social and Economic Costs of National Wage Bargaining*, London: CentreForum Publications.

16 At the Public Convenience? How should we Set Public Sector Pay and How should we Change it?

A.N. OTHER[1]

16.1. Introduction

At a time of public expenditure cuts, the issue of how we should remunerate our public sector workers is of central importance. In the run-up to the election, there were calls for freezing of public sector pay and even of significant public sector pay cuts,[2] and in June 2010, the new Conservative Liberal Democrat coalition government announced a two-year freeze of public sector pay as part of its plan to restore public finances. Such measures are likely to give rise to falling public sector real wages. The policy analysts who are pushing these proposals are suggesting that: public sector pay has been allowed to rise too high relative to private sector pay; public sector workers are 'feather bedded' with secure pensions which are increasingly not available to private sector workers; the public sector has been allowed to expand under New Labour in a way which has led to inefficiency; and that the quickest way to reduce the burden of public sector borrowing is to have public expenditure cuts and since a large fraction of public sector spending is on wages (of teachers, doctors, nurses, civil servants, police, armed forces, and the like), then a clear policy imperative is to reduce the public sector pay bill.

To assess these claims it is clear that we need to take a detailed look at what has happened to public sector pay in the United Kingdom in recent years, how public sector pay is determined, whether the present institutional arrangements work, and what decisions the government should take.

This chapter will briefly review trends in public and private sector pay in the United Kingdom over the last ten years and outline how public sector pay has been set and uprated in the United Kingdom. In Section 3, we analyse the workings of the Pay Review Bodies (PRBs) over the last twenty-eight years in the United Kingdom in terms of what determines the size of a PRB recommended uplift and the size of the pay award actually made. Section 4 then turns to examine the impact of the PRBs on wage rises. In conclusion, the chapter will attempt to provide an answer to the question of how we should set public sector pay and how we should change it.

16.2. **The evolution of public sector pay determination and the PRB system**

In the United Kingdom over the last thirty years, there has been a slow decline in the earnings of individuals working in the public sector relative to private sector earnings (see Dolton and McIntosh 2003, and Chapter 15 by Disney). In 1976, female earnings in the public sector were 42 per cent higher than those in the private sector. In the same year, male earnings were 13 per cent higher in the public sector on average than in the private sector. By 2006, female public sector earnings were only 13 per cent higher than those in the private sector. In the same year, male public sector earnings were lower than their private sector counterparts.

What explains these basic trends in public and private sector labour markets? The decline in relative public sector pay is partly due to the public expenditure constraints of successive governments over the 1979–2008 period and partly the increasing private sector demand for professional, technological, and highly skilled labour which has forced up relative wages in that sector. This declining relative wage has caused real recruitment problems for occupations like teachers and nurses.

The analysis of public/private sector pay in recent times must begin with a careful examination of what the actual position on pay rises in the two sectors is. This is provided in Figure 16.1, which shows increases over the last ten years. Here we see that periods of public sector pay growing faster than private sector pay roughly match the amount of time private sector pay has outstripped

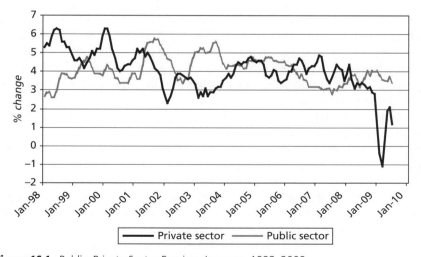

Figure 16.1. Public–Private Sector Earnings Increase, 1998–2009

public sector pay. Indeed, the per-period difference in the two series is only 0.02 per cent—negligible indeed. Perhaps the most striking thing about this graph—and clearly what has caused all the recent consternation—are the dramatic events since March 2008 when private sector pay increases turned negative, whilst the government was left to honour existing contracts and multi-year deals on public sector pay rises.[3] However, this does not take into account the swings and roundabouts which have taken place over the previous ten years. Taken over the whole 1998–2009 period, there is no difference between public sector and private sector pay rises. By the end of 2009, there was already an indication that private sector pay had bounced back and so it is not clear that a major government correction in the form of a public sector pay freeze is necessary.

It should be stressed that the analysis of Figure 16.1 takes the existing wage structure as given and only looks at the earnings increase year on year or month on month. It—of course—does not pose the more difficult question of whether there is a justified pay differential between the two sectors. Much of the recent literature on public/private sector differences has focused on modelling this differential in pay in the two sectors (see Chapter 15 by Disney).[4] A good proportion of this literature has been devoted to trying to account for the different composition of public and private sectors. This involves the use of various decomposition techniques to attempt to account for the difference in the mix of occupations, observable characteristics, and other sources of differences in the two sectors. More recent papers have attempted to model the choice of entering one of these two sectors at the same time as modelling the determination of earnings in these two sectors. It is suggested that there is some form of self-selection in terms of the kind of person who chooses to enter one sector rather than another. Even after using these techniques there is a wide range on estimates of the public/private wage differential after conditioning for all the differences in the two sectors. Gregory and Borland (1999) present a summary of the estimates for the United Kingdom which vary from 9 to 38 per cent for women and 5 to 33 per cent for men depending on the year of the data and on whether we consider manual or non-manual workers.

There are a variety of systems to determine public sector pay which operate in different countries. In many European countries, like France, Germany, and Italy, the whole public sector has wages uprated by a cost-of-living adjustment on an annual basis with local bilateral bargaining between unions and employers to work out exceptions and minor adjustments to working conditions. In such countries it is rare for any specific group of workers to be given a pay rise which varies much across the country. In many other countries, trade unions and employers negotiate bilaterally each year without a steer from the central government on what is a 'baseline cost-of-living' rise for the year and the 'going rate' for pay rises. A few countries, such as the United States, have an autonomous state structure in which each state has its own budget and negotiates with each occupation separately about pay rises. The PRB system is a phenomenon unique to Britain in terms of its widespread coverage of non-managerial public sector employees. Some countries such as Canada, Japan, and the Netherlands have similar independent review systems governing the pay of senior civil servants, but they do not have such systems for other public sector workers.

Since the establishment of the Doctors and Dentists Review Body (DDRB), Top Salaries Review Body (TSRB), and the Armed Forces Pay Review Body (AFPRB) in 1971 by the Heath government, the pay review system has evolved over the past decades to cover nearly 1.8 million people or around 25 per cent of public sector workers (Horsman 2004). Given the significant size of its remit group, it is important that the pay determination process within the PRB system, and its impact on public sector pay, is well understood.

There are now six PRBs:[5] the Doctors and Dentists Review Body (DDRB), Senior Salaries Review Body (SSRB), the Armed Forces Pay Review Body (AFPRB), National Health Service Review Body (NHSRB), Prison Service Pay Review Body (PSPRB), and School Teachers Review Body (STRB). These review bodies are charged with making recommendations on pay for their remit groups with regard to: the need to recruit, retain, and motivate staff; regional and local variation in labour markets; government departments' output targets and expenditure limits; and the overall government inflation target. We seek to understand the process by which the PRBs fulfil this remit.

The main function of these independent review bodies is to advise the government about appropriate pay awards. This leads to an examination of exactly how public sector pay gets determined and how does it change. Prior to 1971, there were a variety of mechanisms in place for different occupations. A major constraint in public sector pay determination has been government expenditure allocated to separate government departments.[6] These limits may at least partially constrain the decisions of the PRBs.

Most public sector employees in the United Kingdom are represented by national unions or professional associations. In the non-PRB public sector in recent years, there has been a tendency to move away from centralized wage setting towards individual government departments being responsible for wage setting. There have also been occasional instances in the PRB occupations where individualized pay settlements have been introduced based on changing contracts, performance-related elements, or the movement towards more flexible working arrangements. For example, hospital consultants and GPs have both had new contracts in the last five years. Also a form of performance-related pay was introduced for teachers in 2000 and there are now negotiations taking place about the use of more classroom assistants to cover elements of work done by teachers.

While each of the six PRBs currently in existence has its own defining characteristics, the PRBs are linked by several common features. All are established with a chair and a committee of members appointed by either the Prime Minister or the relevant government department minister, and are serviced by an independent civil service secretariat, the Office of Manpower Economics (White 2000). Barring the statutory underpinnings of the teachers' pay arrangements, PRB recommendations are non-binding, although the government rarely rejects them outright. The deliberation process, involving consultation with both trade unions and employers' bodies, starts at different times in the year for different PRBs. However, most of the pay increases are usually implemented from April of each year.

Some of the PRBs cover groups which had been previously covered under Whitley-style negotiating processes which had broken down. In some PRB occupations, such as the medical and teaching professions, the state acts as a near-monopsonist. In fact, some PRB occupations are also those denied the opportunity to bargain independently over remuneration, or in need of protection from arbitrary policy changes. These factors have led the system to be portrayed as 'a surrogate for the operation of the forces of either the market or collective bargaining' (Thomason 2003). Indeed, the system is traditionally viewed as a form of pay determination distinct from conventional collective bargaining. White (2000) appropriately describes the PRBs as institutions 'halfway between fully-fledged collective bargaining and unilateral imposition by government'.

White (2000) documents the chronological development of the PRB system and its role in public sector pay determination through the changing political and macroeconomic climate of the past three decades. In particular, he highlights a distinction in the rationale behind the establishment of the first three PRBs in 1971, and the creation of the following PRBs for nursing groups and teachers. While the creation of the former PRBs was a pragmatic response to fill the gap left by the collapse of the previous Kindersley Committee and provide some form of independent pay review for the groups involved, the latter are viewed as arrangements to contain conflict over pay determination following a period of increasing militancy and industrial action. It has been further suggested that the PRB system has remained politically attractive over the past decades as an 'arms length' mechanism for the government in dealing with public sector groups deemed to be politically sensitive, while avoiding open conflict. In a study of the PRBs' behaviour under the Labour government, Horsman (2003) suggested that the PRBs have an independent 'policy personality' that is generally consistent over the long term whilst politically expedient in the short run.

16.3. **How do PRBs make their recommendations?**

Since the first PRBs were introduced in 1971, we now have thirty-eight years worth of data on their recommendations and what pay awards were subsequently implemented. Figure 16.2 presents an historical perspective on the role of PRBs in public sector pay settlements. It shows the trends in recommended pay awards by the different PRBs over the period 1971–2008. We can see from this that, in the first twenty-two years until 1993, public sector pay awards were rather large and sometimes apparently erratic due to changing inflationary pressures. After this we entered a period of unprecedented stability in terms of wage settlements. It is only over this period from 1993 that the Labour Force Survey (LFS) data on wages exists, which permits an analysis of the impact of the PRBs on wages. In each year over this period, all the recommended pay awards (and all the settlements) were broadly in line with inflation and very stable. This means we could continue to argue that the PRBs have actually done their job and brought most pay settlements into line with government expenditure targets. The corollary of this argument is that they are no longer necessary. However, a converse argument is that our analysis does not allow us to observe the counterfactual—that is, a world where PRBs do not exist. It could be argued that in such a world we may well return to erratic inflationary pay settlements. This analysis is not able to judge this—we are merely able to quantify the impact of the PRBs relative to the pay awards in the non-PRB public sector.

In this section, we use this data to analyse how the PRBs made their decisions and examine the evidence of whether the recommendations were statistically

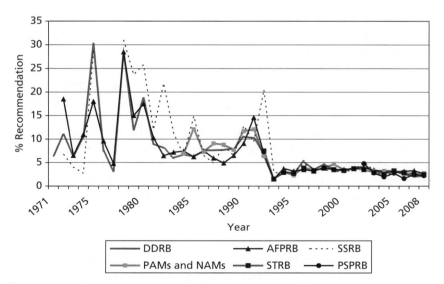

Figure 16.2. PRB Percentage Pay Uplift Recommendations, 1971–2008

different to the awards. Since not all the PRBs existed in 1971, the data set is an unbalanced panel. We use as our explanatory variables as many of the influences which could be found in data terms to condition their deliberations.

16.3.1. DATA

For the nursing occupations, recommendations for professions allied to medicine (PAMs) and that for nurses and midwives (NAMs) were made separately until 2004, when the two remit groups were combined under the Review Body for Nursing and Other Health Professions (NOHPRB). Hence, these recommendations have been separated to form two distinct series.

16.3.2. EXPLANATORY VARIABLES

As set out in each PRB report, the role of the PRBs is to make pay recommendations using evidence obtained on the state of the economy, motivation, recruitment, and retention concerns, as well as economy-wide pay comparisons. Thus, the following categories of regressors were considered as potential explanatory variables for pay review recommendations (PRR) and actual pay increases (ACT).

For each PRB, the level of price inflation—as an indicator of the extent of the change in the cost of living—and average earnings—as evidence of what pay settlements are being agreed in the rest of the economy—are potential key influences in public sector pay determination, given the above emphases on the prevalent economic conditions and broad pay comparability. Consequently, three inflation indicators were considered: these include the percentage change in the retail price index in the year preceding the pay review (RPILAG), the rate of change of RPILAG over the months immediately preceding the review (RPIFD), and a forecast variable for inflation in the year of the review (FORECAST). Cost-of-living indicators and inflation indicators derived from survey data were also explored but were excluded, as these data series were incomplete for a significant part of the time frame. Similarly, two average earnings indicators were considered: the percentage change in the average earnings index for the whole economy in the year prior to the review (AEILAG) and the rate of change of AEILAG over six months immediately preceding the review (AEIFD). The use of AEIFD and RPIFD captures the effect of recent trends in average earnings and inflation on pay determination.

In addition, general labour market variables are likely to play a significant role. In particular, the unemployment rate for the whole economy in the year preceding the review (UNRLAG) is a possible indicator of the need for pay rises to facilitate recruitment and retention—a tighter labour market may create pay pressures resulting from unfilled vacancies in key occupations of geographical locations. Equally, the number of working days lost in the year preceding the review (WDLLAG) gives an indication of overall worker discontent, which may affect the outcomes of the pay review process if the PRBs are indeed an important mechanism in averting employer–employee conflict, as White (2000) suggested.

Government Comprehensive Spending Reviews are a fairly new innovation, but governmental expenditure constraints have always been relevant to potential earning uplift recommendations. Budget considerations are also potentially relevant, given the presence of governmental representatives in the administration of the review process and especially since the implementation decision is undertaken by the government. Therefore, we consider two possible indicators of budget constraints that may limit pay increases—the public sector net cash requirement in the preceding year (PSNCRLAG), which is an indicator of government borrowing, and total public sector real current expenditure in the preceding year (PSGROWLAG).

In addition, a set of controls was included for which political party was in power, if it was an election year, and the level of government popularity at the time.

16.3.3. MODEL SPECIFICATION

Preliminary estimation suggested that variables RPILAG, RPIFD, FORECAST, AEILAG, and AEIFD were closely related. To avoid statistical problems of multicollinearity, a more parsimonious specification of inflation and average earnings was sought. To this end, the correlation structure of the above set of variables was first investigated. The results are shown in Table 16.1. The strong correlation between RPILAG and AEILAG indicated that it would be very difficult to distinguish between the effects of the two indicators. Furthermore, these variables are also highly correlated with the FORECAST variable. Preliminary estimation also suggested that the variable PSNCRLAG had an insignificant effect on any of the dependent variables considered.[7] The following fixed-effects panel specification was used which is appropriate for looking at changes over time in PRB recommendations and outcomes:

$$\text{DEPVAR}_{it} = \beta_1 \text{RPIFD}_t + \beta_2 \text{FORECAST}_t + \beta_3 \text{AEIFD}_t$$
$$+ \beta_4 \text{UNRLAG}_t + \beta_5 \text{PSGROWLAG}_t + \beta_6 \text{WDLLAG}_t$$
$$+ \text{Political Controls} + \text{CONSTANT} + \text{FIXED}_i + \varepsilon_{it}$$

where the dependent variable (DEPVAR_{it}) may be pay review recommendations (PRR_{it}) or actual pay increases ACT_{it}:

Table 16.1. Fixed-Effects Panel Estimation of the Determinants of Pay Review
Recommendations and Actual Pay Awards, 1971–2006

Dependent variable	Recommendations (PRR)	Actual pay awards (ACT)
Variable	Parameter estimate	
Rate of change of inflation (RPIFD)	−3.758*** (0.890)	−2.247** (1.105)
Forecast of inflation (FORECAST)	0.320** (0.165)	0.791*** (0.252)
Ave earnings index first derivative (AEIFD)	4.100*** (0.882)	2.506*** (0.522)
Unemployment rate $(t-1)$ (UNRLAG)	−0.633*** (0.253)	−0.427*** (0.171)
Public sector borrowing growth $(t-1)$ (PSGROWLAG)	−0.571*** (0.094)	−0.619*** (0.225)
Working days lost $(t-1)$ (WDLLAG)	0.172*** (0.044)	0.051 (0.043)
No. of groups	7	7
No. of observations	169	170
R^2 [within]	0.7189	0.6512
Wald statistic $[X^2_{(11)}]$	41,181.61	122,374.87
BIC	913.9	900.0
AIC	876.3	862.4

Notes: Non-parametric bootstrap standard errors in parentheses.

***: Denotes statistical significance at the 1 per cent level; **: denotes statistical significance at the 5 per cent level; *: denotes statistical significance at the 10 per cent level. These equations include an indicator if the Labour party is in power (LAB), an indicator of whether the review year was an election year (ELECT), and political survey indicators to measure the popularity of the ruling government (POGAVE) and the variance of the popularity of the government (POGV); and an additional dummy was used for the time periods of the Blair Labour government (BLAIR).

$$\sum_i \text{FIXED}_i = 0,^8$$
$$\varepsilon_{it} \sim \text{i.i.d.} N(0, \sigma_\varepsilon^2),^9 \tag{1}$$

This was chosen over a random-effects specification for simplicity and due to the low cost in terms of degrees of freedom resulting from the small number of PRB groups relative to the time dimension.

16.3.4. ESTIMATION RESULTS

Estimation results for dependent variables PRR and ACT are reported in panels 1 and 2 of Table 16.1, respectively. Because of the relatively small sample sizes in our analysis, bootstrap standard errors are given for all parameter estimates.

In the estimation of the determinants of PRR above, strongly significant coefficients were obtained on the slope indicators, RPIFD and AEIFD. In particular, if inflation in the six months preceding the review is rising at the rate of 1 percentage point per month, the PRR is reduced by about 3.8 percentage points. This suggests that the magnitude of pay recommendations is dampened by the need to contain inflationary pressures on the economy. On the other hand, an increase in the AEI measure at the same rate appears to be accommodated by pay recommendations that are 4.1 percentage points higher. This suggests that rising average earnings in the economy is an opposing force to rising price inflation in determining pay recommendations during periods where earnings and inflation move in tandem due to a need to maintain broad pay comparability. Given the low correlation found between RPIFD and AEIFD in the previous section, this result is robust and not a consequence of collinearity between regressors. A significant positive coefficient on FORECAST at the 5 per cent level also implies that the forecast level of inflation for the review year influences pay decisions positively. Hence, while rising inflation trends exert a negative pressure on pay recommendations, a forecasted inflation level which is 1 percentage point higher leads to a 0.3 percentage points increase in pay recommendations, possibly due to pressure from the union side to match pay to predicted cost-of-living increases.

Other significant parameter estimates exhibited the expected signs. In particular, a rise in real public sector current expenditure of £1b (2005 prices) in the preceding fiscal year is associated with a 0.6 percentage point decrease in pay recommendations. This implies that government budget constraints are factored into the pay deliberation process and thus affect not only the actual pay rise implemented but also recommendations made. Thus, Treasury concerns have a clear impact even at the recommendation stage.

A possible sign of the influence of recruitment and retention concerns on the pay review process is the negative relationship obtained between UNRLAG and the PRR. A 1 percentage point increase in the unemployment rate in the preceding year is associated with a −0.6 percentage points lower pay recommendation for the current year, *ceteris paribus*. Taking into account the specialized skill requirements of some PRB occupations such as the medical and nursing professions, the economy-wide unemployment rate in the preceding year cannot be an accurate measure of current supply conditions in these labour markets given the time required to acquire the relevant skills, and especially if the education decision takes into account long-term expected returns. Nevertheless, a high general unemployment rate might be an indication of reduced competition from other sectors for labour of the equivalent skill level, and thus of some labour market slack. Under such circumstances, one might expect a less critical role for immediate pay increases in retaining workers and attracting entrants into PRB occupations.

The small but significant positive relationship found between the number of working days lost in the preceding year, which is indicative of trade union militancy, and the PRR confirms that the PRB deliberation process has characteristics similar to wage-bargaining models. In many models of union wage determination, for example, increased militancy due to greater trade union power leads to greater bargaining power and thus a larger bargained wage increase. In the case of PRB occupations, while specific remit groups are denied the right to industrial action *per se*, we posit the existence of an indirect relationship. Increased trade union militancy in the general economy can result in a greater willingness to recommend larger pay increases, in an attempt to forestall potential conflict.

With actual pay rises implemented (ACT) as the dependent variable in Table 16.1, Panel 2, coefficients of the same signs are obtained for most explanatory variables in this model compared to the previous one shown in panel 1 of Table 16.1. However, estimated magnitudes of the effects of RPIFD and AEIFD are almost halved while that of FORECAST has more than doubled. Compared to the PRBs, the government appears to be more willing to make pay concessions for higher forecasted inflation levels and associated cost-of-living changes, but less so for the purpose of bringing public sector pay in line with average earnings trends. Also, the estimated magnitude on the UNRLAG parameter is reduced by a third compared to that in the PRR case, indicating that actual pay awards are less responsive to signs of rising unemployment, perhaps to ensure that recruitment and retention needs are sufficiently met.

On the other hand, the effect of working days lost in the previous year (WDLLAG) is now insignificant at the 20 per cent level. This highlights a key difference between traditional forms of pay bargaining and the PRB structure of pay determination—while pay concessions to avoid conflict are present at the recommendation stage, these are not followed through at the implementation stage since recommendations are non-binding and the final implementation decision rests with the government.

16.3.5. THE IMPACT OF THE PRBS ON WAGE RISES

Using data from the LFS, Dolton, Makepeace, and Marcenaro (2007) (DMM) compare the earnings of these workers in order to assess the impact of the PRBs on the relative earnings of their remit groups. DMM consider how real weekly earnings evolved over time within specific occupations of interest and examine how the differences between comparable workers in PRB occupations, in the remainder of the public sector and in the private sector, changed in each year from 1993 to 2006. In this section, we review their findings on whether any gains in real earnings for the PRB occupations have been translated into improvements in relative pay.

The evidence we presented suggests that the pattern of relative pay varied with some PRB occupations doing substantially better than comparable workers in the private sector and some worse. In several public sector occupations, men incur a much larger earnings penalty than women. Real earnings are often significantly different in occupations covered by PRBs compared with the remainder of the public sector although this depends on year and occupation.

Many papers have looked at either specific occupations such as nurses or teachers in isolation or the broad aggregate such as the public sector as a whole. The DMM paper examines a range of public sector occupations associated with the PRBs providing some insight into the effects of the PRBs. It deals with more occupations than most previous work, although it does report results for more broad aggregates. It also provides an update of some previous analysis.

The approach adopted by DMM (2007) to identify the impact of the PRBs is to use a difference-in-difference (diff-in-diff) estimation method. This method relies on comparison of the difference between any specific PRB group and other (non-PRB) public sector workers relative to the private sector. Specifically, they compared the change in the estimates for different occupational groups in two consecutive years using the non-PRB public sector as the control group. They then did this for every pair of years for each occupational group. They also suggested an estimation method which allows inference for each diff-in-diff point estimate. This means they were able to examine the complete trend in occupational impacts of the PRBs over the whole period from 1993 to 2008. The crucial identification assumption in this methodology is that the unobservable factors in occupational choices will remain largely the same in two consecutive years. In large samples this is not an unreasonable assumption. Using this identification strategy, they found (for the most part) that the PRBs have little or no impact over and above comparable public sector pay not covered by the PRBs.

Turning to the estimation of the measured impact of the PRBs, Figure 16.3 illustrates what is happening. This figure graphs the diff-in-diff estimates for each occupation for each pair of years. The zero X-axis is the public sector non-PRB reference group against which all the difference estimates are calibrated. The collective line for the private sector is represented by the bold line of estimates—which, for both men and women, never strays far from the horizontal axis. The rest of the lines represent the diff-in-diff estimates for each occupation separately. Most of the changes for men, in Figure 16.3, lie in the interval $[-0.05, 0.05]$ and are not statistically significant. The significant changes appear as outliers such as Medical Practitioners and Nurses and Midwives in 1999–2000. The women's chart (not reported) also shows that most of the changes are bunched in a relatively small interval and are insignificant.

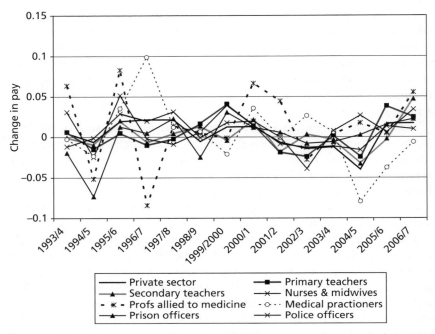

Figure 16.3. Male Year-on-Year Difference-in-Difference Impact Estimates of the PRBs Relative to the Non-PRB Public Sector, 1993–2007

The conclusion of this analysis is that pay increases in the PRB public sector, the non-PRB public sector, and the private sector are not significantly different over most of the time period for nearly all occupations. This finding might appear to cast doubt on whether the PRBs still have an effective role to play since their awards reflect what is happening elsewhere in the public sector. However, this result is more or less exactly what the government might have wanted, that is, to have consistent, meaningful pay rises for all the relevant occupations without there being any evidence that any one of these pay rises was significantly higher than a comparable set of workers in the rest of the public sector or the private sector.

16.4. **Conclusion**

Using an empirical approach, we have attempted to shed light on the pay determination process which has been used for a large fraction of public sector employees over the last thirty-five years. Panel analysis of data collected on the pay recommendations and actual pay awards yielded quantitative evidence of the influence of PRB remit concerns, such as inflation, earnings comparability, and recruitment, on pay recommendations and awards. We also reported on an attempt to address the question of the actual impact of the PRB on relative wages of workers in the public sector as compared to the private sector.

Looking first at how PRBs make decisions, our results suggest that they are mindful of the level of current earnings inflation and the forecasted level of price inflation—but inclined to recommend lower awards when inflation is rising. This is rational as they are charged with both being fair and also to being aware of what is in the tax payers' best interest—so they may wish to be seen not to be inflationary. At the same time, the PRBs are aware of the aggregate labour market position in the sense that sensibly their recommendations are lower when unemployment is higher. In addition, their recommendations are also in the best interest of the tax payers as their recommendations are lower when the Public Sector Borrowing Requirement rises. What is abundantly clear, from even the most cursory examination of Figure 16.1, is that from 1993 onwards we have been in a new era of public sector wage increases compared with the previous two decades. Arguably, this pattern has been secured by the presence of the PRBs and may not have happened otherwise. Specifically, we are now in an era where all recommendations and all PRB remit group wage rises are *de facto* very close to the level of inflation. This then poses the question of whether we really need the PRBs to make recommendations at all—could not we just use the inflation rate to fix all public sector earnings. It is very unlikely that such a mechanism, administered by the government, would be seen as objective. In addition, it would not make unions feel as if they had been consulted and had their individual concerns listened to.

On the question of what effect the PRBs have on public sector pay when we compare it to private sector pay and pay in the non-PRB public sector, it is overwhelmingly clear that the answer is that their decisions are virtually neutral—in the sense that the PRBs confer no earnings advantage on the groups under their remit as compared to public sector workers who are not under the remit of a PRB or compared to private sector workers. This conclusion was reached using a difference-in-difference model which compares these groups across consecutive time periods. This result is really rather dramatic as it suggests that the PRBs are being fair in the sense that they do not disproportionately favour their remit group—nor to they 'do them down'.

In conclusion, how should the government set public sector pay? Well, the evidence presented suggests that, for key occupations in the public sector, having an objective arbitration body which actively manages the pay rises of their group on a year-to-year basis taking evidence on all sides about the state of the labour market recruitment, retention, and inflation provides a solution to the problem of setting public sector pay. This structure avoids strikes and lengthy industrial disputes and unrest. It is neutral in the sense of there being long run equality of pay rises in the public and private sector, and in that of being able to take account demonstrably of all the factors in their remit. And it is fair in the sense that it does not award public sector employees pay which is above their private sector counterparts. This suggests that the government should not be tempted to get rid of the PRBs—indeed there may even be good grounds for extending them to cover the major groups of public sector workers not presently covered.

This said—how should the government reduce public spending? The only option would appear to be the time-honoured method of not cutting public sector pay—but letting it fall behind in real terms over time. Even suggesting centrally induced, capped limits like 1 per cent could indeed be counterproductive. This would wrest responsibility for pay issues from the PRBs and make government seem directly responsible, and could in fact induce trade unions to seek no less that 1 per cent when it is quite possible that some PRBs may have even recommended less than this! Finally, the government should not confuse the scandal of MPs' expenses and the high pay of senior BBC personnel with the remuneration of the mass of ordinary public sector workers like teachers and nurses. Specifically, it should not seek to redress the sins of the former with pay cuts to the latter.

☐ NOTES

1. The author wishes to stress that the views expressed in this chapter are his own and cannot be attributed to the Office of Manpower Economics, any government official, any Pay Review Body, or any Pay Review Body member. Thanks are due to Adeline Aw, Gerry Makepeace, and Oscar Marcenaro-Gutierrez for access to their work and to Steve Palmer for helping out with the data.
2. For example, the *Telegraph* of the 5 July 2009—Steve Bundred claimed that NHS and education workers 'could tolerate a pay freeze as they had done well over the last 10 years'.
3. For example, the teachers, police, and nurses were all in the middle of multi-year PRB 'deals' which would have been difficult to renege on.
4. See Gregory and Borland (1999) for a summary.
5. Note also that the position of the Police is unusual as officially the Police Review Board is not a PRB as its terms of reference are quite distinct. However, this body is still serviced by the Office of Manpower Economics.
6. This has variously been modelled by Zabalza et al. (1979) as an 'expenditure constraint', Leslie (1985) as 'cash limits', and by Borjas (1980) as 'Federal budget limits'.
7. To resolve these issues, the search for a sensible and relatively parsimonious specification was carried out by comparing the Akaike Information Criterion (AIC) and Bayesian Information Criterion (BIC) across models with different regressors but at least one variable from each regressor category.

8. FIXED$_i$ are the fixed effects associated with each PRB group. The given constraint is needed to avoid multicollinearity in the specification.
9. Where i.i.d. $N(\cdot)$ indicates that the ϵ_{it} are independently drawn from an identical normal distribution.

☐ REFERENCES

Borjas, G. (1980) Wage Policy is the federal Bureaucracy, American Enterprise Institute for Public Policy Record, Washington, DC.

Dolton, P. and Aw, A. (2007) 'What Determines Public Sector Pay Review Body Decisions in the UK', LSE, *mimeo*.

—— and McIntosh, S. (2003) 'Public and Private Sector Labour Markets', in R. Dickens, P. Gregg and J. Wadsworth (eds.) *The Labour Market under New Labour: The State of Working Britain*, Chap. 14, Basingstoke: Palgrave Macmillan.

—— Makepeace, G., and Marcenaro-Gutierrez, O. (2007) 'The Earnings of Workers Covered by Pay Review Bodies: Evidence from the Labour Force Survey', Paper delivered at the Royal Economic Society, Warwick University.

Gregory, B. and Borland, J. (1999) 'Recent Developments in Public Sector Labor Markets', in O. Ashenfelter and D. Card (eds.) *Handbook of Labor Economics*, Vol. 3, Chap 53, Amsterdam: North-Holland.

Horsman, M. (2003) 'Continuity and Change: Public Sector Pay Review Bodies, 1992–2003', *Public Money & Management*, 23(4), 229–36.

—— (2004) 'The Pay Review Bodies Revisited', *Public Money & Management*, 24(5), 317–20.

Leslie, D. (1985) 'The Economics of Cash Limits as a Method of Pay Determination', *Economic Journal*, 95, 662–78.

Thomason, G.F. (1985) 'The Pay Review Bodies', *Health Services Manpower Review*, 11(3), 1–6.

—— (2003) 'Adjusting the Role of the Pay Review Bodies', *Croner's Human Resources and Employment Review*, 1(2), 81–6.

White, G. (2000) 'The Pay Review Body System: Its Development and Impact', *Historical Studies in Industrial Relations*, 9 (Spring 2000), 71–100.

Zabalza, A., Turnbill, P., and Williams, G. (1979) 'The Economics of Teacher Supply', Cambridge: Cambridge University Press.

☐ INDEX